· THE · ILLUSTRATED ·
ESCOFFIER

Filet de Boeuf Saint-Germain

· THE · ILLUSTRATED ·
ESCOFFIER

RECIPES FROM THE CLASSIC FRENCH TRADITION

Selected and Edited by Anne Johnson

CONSULTANT EDITORS
H. L. CRACKNELL AND R. J. KAUFMANN

OCTOPUS BOOKS LIMITED

First published in 1987 by
Octopus Books Limited
59 Grosvenor Street
London W1X 9DA

Adapted from:
The Complete Guide to the Art of Modern Cookery
by A. Escoffier
translated by H. L. Cracknell and R. J. Kaufmann
(London: Heinemann, 1979)

ISBN 0 7064 2822 6

Printed in Hong Kong

Acknowledgements
Editor   Andrew Jefford
Art Editor   Alyson Kyles
Designer   Bob Gordon
Production   Sara Hunt, Maryann Rogers

Photography by Martin Brigdale
Martin Brigdale was assisted by Philomena O'Neill

Food prepared for photography by Nichola Palmer (all
photographs excluding those listed below)
Anne Hildyard (pages 11, 15, 27, 35, 51 and 67)
Nichola Palmer was assisted by Juliet Brigstocke and
Angela Drake

Stylist   Andrea Lambton

The publishers would like to thank the following companies
for their kindness in providing materials and equipment used
in the photography for this book:

Harrods
Knightsbridge
London SW1X 7XL

Josiah Wedgwood and Sons Limited
Barlaston
Stoke-on-Trent ST12 9EF
and at
Wedgwood House
32–34 Wigmore Street
London W1H 0HV

Gallery of Antique Costume and Textiles
2 Church Street
London NW8 8ED

NOTES
1. Metric and imperial measurements have been calculated
separately, and are approximate rather than exact equivalents.
Therefore use only one set of measurements, either metric or
imperial, when preparing the recipes.

2. Words printed in *italics* in the recipe methods indicate that
the word is included in the short Glossary on pages 188–189.

CONTENTS

AUGUSTE ESCOFFIER

INTRODUCTION

One may wonder as to the motive in producing a selected and illustrated version of Escoffier's *Guide to Modern Cookery*, when the book in its original form is still selling well worldwide.

The reason, I believe, is revealed in the foreword and introductions that Auguste Escoffier himself wrote to the first and subsequent editions of the *Guide*.

"My intention is to offer my colleagues a tool rather than merely a recipe book . . . something to be placed on a nearby shelf for easy reference . . . [but that would] leave them free to develop their own methods and follow their own inspiration. . . . The art of cooking, which in many ways is similar to that of fashion design, will evolve as society evolves. . . . Only basic rules remain unalterable. . . . It may be feared that in order to satisfy the requirements of an ever-more hurried clientele, cooking would be simplified to such a degree that our art would become merely a trade. This will not take place because simplicity does not exclude beauty. I am convinced that the ability to give the supreme touch to a modest dish, presenting it in an elegant yet appropriate manner, will always be the indispensable compliment to technical expertise."

This is all well and good, but it should not be forgotten that Escoffier was addressing himself to professional chefs. Today, when interest in refined cooking is spreading rapidly through society, new presentation of the *Guide* seemed called for. Of the 5,000 or so recipes in the *Guide*, a number are seldom prepared today as their ingredients have disappeared or become outmoded or outpriced. In *The Illustrated Escoffier*, a careful selection of recipes has been made, ingredients or methods have been adapted where necessary, and beautiful colour photographs have been painstakingly taken of many of the dishes.

However, this new version should be used exactly as the *Guide* itself was intended to be, with readers free to adapt according to their own inspiration, in order to present the results to their guests in an elegant, genuine manner.

It is the hope of all those who have contributed to *The Illustrated Escoffier* that it will be welcomed and appreciated by those for whom the adaptation has been made: enthusiastic home cooks wishing to take part in the best tradition of French classic cooking.

PIERRE P. ESCOFFIER

STOCKS & SAUCES

Fonds Brun

1.5 kg (3 lb 6 oz) shin of beef, on the bone
1.5 kg (3 lb 6 oz) knuckle of veal or lean veal trimmings
150 g (5 oz) carrot, peeled and roughly chopped
150 g (5 oz) onion, peeled and roughly chopped
6 tablespoons clean fat, such as strained dripping
1 knuckle raw ham, blanched
150 g (5 oz) fresh pork rind, blanched
1 bouquet garni
4.5 litres (8 pints) water

*B*one the beef and veal, break the bones up small and lightly brown them in the oven. Fry the carrot and onion in half the fat until nicely browned.

Place the bones, vegetables, ham, pork rind and bouquet garni in a stockpot, then add the cold water. Bring to the boil, skim and simmer gently for at least 12 hours, adding water as required to keep the liquid at the same level throughout.

Cut the beef and veal meat into large dice, heat the remaining fat and fry until brown. Place in a pan, cover with some of the prepared stock and boil until reduced to a glaze. Repeat this process 2 or 3 times.

Add the rest of the prepared stock, bring to the boil, skim to remove all fat, and allow to simmer gently until all the flavour has been extracted from the meat; maintain the level of the liquid with water as required.

Strain and reserve for use.

Makes approximately 2.5 litres ($4\frac{1}{2}$ pints)

Fonds de Gibier

1 kg (2 lb) game, to include a variety selected from rabbit,
pheasant, venison or hare, preferably older animals and
birds, but fresh
75 g (3 oz) carrot, peeled and sliced
75 g (3 oz) green of leek, sliced
75 g (3 oz) onion, peeled and sliced
40 g ($1\frac{1}{2}$ oz) celery, sliced
65 g ($2\frac{1}{2}$ oz) mushroom, sliced, or mushroom trimmings
25 g (1 oz) butter
1 clove garlic
15 g ($\frac{1}{2}$ oz) parsley stalks
1 pinch chopped fresh thyme
1 bay leaf
good pinch salt
15 juniper berries and 1 clove, tied together in muslin

*C*ut the game into pieces and brown in a hot oven (220°C, 425°F, Gas Mark 7). Place the vegetables in the bottom of a heavy pan and fry until brown in the butter with all the flavouring ingredients except the juniper and clove. Add the browned pieces of game.

Deglaze the roasting pan with a little water and add to the other ingredients. Cover all with water, add the juniper and clove and bring to the boil. Skim carefully. Allow to simmer very gently, skimming as and when necessary, for 3 hours, maintaining the level of the liquid with water as required.

Strain and reserve for use.

Makes approximately 1.5 litres ($2\frac{1}{2}$ pints)

Fonds Blanc

1.5 kg (3 lb 6 oz) shin of veal, veal trimmings and veal bones
4 raw chicken carcasses, with giblets
1 teaspoon salt
125 g (4½ oz) carrot, peeled and roughly chopped
65 g (2½ oz) onion, peeled and roughly chopped
50 g (2 oz) leek, chopped
15 g (½ oz) celery, chopped
1 bouquet garni

B one the shin and chop the bones very small. Place all the bones and meat in a stockpot, cover well with cold water and add the salt. Bring to the boil, skim carefully and add the vegetables and bouquet garni. Allow to simmer gently, uncovered, for 3 hours, removing scum and fat and adding boiling water as required to keep the liquid to the same level for half the cooking time. Add no more liquid thereafter. Strain and reserve for use.

Fonds Blanc de Volaille
White chicken stock is made exactly the same way, but with more chicken in proportion to veal. This can be achieved by using more giblets or carcass, or by using a whole, quartered boiling fowl in place of an equal weight of veal.
MAKES APPROXIMATELY 1.5 LITRES (2½ PINTS)

Fumet de Poisson

1.5 kg (3 lb 6 oz) bones and trimmings of sole, whiting or brill
65 g (2½ oz) onion, peeled and sliced
40 g (1½ oz) white of mushroom, chopped
1 pinch salt
a few parsley stalks
1.5 litres (2½ pints) water
½ bottle good dry white wine
a few drops lemon juice
5 peppercorns

P ut the fish bones and trimmings, onion, mushroom, salt and parsley stalks into a pan and cover with the water. Add the wine and lemon juice. Bring to the boil quickly, skim and allow to simmer very gently for 20 minutes. Add the peppercorns and continue cooking for 10 more minutes.
Strain and use as required.
MAKES APPROXIMATELY 1.5 LITRES (2½ PINTS)

Glace de Viande

A meat glaze is used to impart a brilliant shine and an unctuous coating to finished dishes, to reinforce the quality of a sauce, or to strengthen a preparation of which stock is too weak. It is usually made using a Fonds Brun, page 8, though a lighter-coloured glaze can be made using a Fonds Blanc, left. Chicken and game glazes can be prepared by the same method using Fonds Blanc de Volaille, left, or Fonds de Gibier, page 8.

Place 500 ml (18 fl oz) of stock in a large pan and allow it to reduce. Skim carefully as the reduction takes place. When an appreciable degree of reduction has taken place, strain the stock into a smaller pan and repeat this process from time to time, skimming and straining carefully and reducing the heat each time. The final reduction should take place over a very moderate heat. The glaze is ready when it adheres to the back of a spoon in the form of a glossy coating.

Jus de Veau Lié

4 litres (7 pints) Fonds Brun, page 8
25 g (1 oz) arrowroot

R eserve 100 ml (3½ fl oz) of the cold stock for use later. Bring the rest of the stock to the boil, then allow it to reduce to a quarter of its original volume.

Dilute the arrowroot in the reserved cold stock, stir into the boiling stock and allow to cook gently for 1 minute. Pass through a fine strainer. The resultant gravy should be transparent and light brown in colour, and have a fresh, clean taste.

MAKES APPROXIMATELY 1 LITRE (1¾ PINTS)

Sauce Velouté

50 g (2 oz) butter
65 g (2½ oz) flour, sifted
1 litre (1¾ pints) Fonds Blanc or Fumet de Poisson, left, depending on the flavour of the dish in preparation

F irst prepare a *white roux* by mixing the butter and flour together in a heavy pan and placing over a moderate heat for just a few minutes, stirring frequently, to eliminate the raw flavour of the flour. Allow to cool.

Gradually stir the stock into the roux, making sure that you obtain a smooth consistency. Bring to the boil, stirring continuously, and allow to simmer very gently for $1\frac{1}{2}$ hours, skimming carefully from time to time. Strain and use as required.

MAKES APPROXIMATELY 1.2 LITRES (2 PINTS)

Sauce Espagnole

50 g (2 oz) clarified butter
65 g (2½ oz) flour, sifted
2.5 litres (4½ pints) Fonds Brun, page 8
25 g (1 oz) streaky bacon, rinded and chopped
50 g (2 oz) carrot, peeled and roughly chopped
25 g (1 oz) onion, peeled and roughly chopped
1 sprig thyme
1 small bay leaf
50 ml (2 fl oz) dry white wine
100 g (4 oz) tomato purée or 200 g (7 oz) fresh
tomatoes, roughly chopped

Start making this sauce at least one day before you need it. First make a *brown roux* by mixing the *clarified butter* and flour together in a heavy pan and place over a moderate heat to cook, stirring frequently, until an even light brown colour is obtained. When cooked, the roux should be smooth and smell of hazelnuts or baked flour.

Place 1.5 litres (2½ pints) of the Fonds Brun in a heavy pan and bring to the boil. Add the roux, mix well with a wooden spoon or whisk, and bring to the boil, stirring continuously. Turn down the heat and allow to simmer gently.

Meanwhile, place the bacon in a dry pan and fry to extract the fat. Add the vegetables and herbs and fry until golden brown. Carefully drain off the fat and add these ingredients to the sauce. Deglaze the pan with the white wine, reduce by half and add to the sauce. Allow to simmer gently for 1 hour.

Pass the sauce through a conical strainer into another pan, pressing lightly. Add a further 500 ml (18 fl oz) of the Fonds Brun, bring back to the boil and allow to simmer gently for a further 2 hours. Then strain and stir occasionally until cold.

The following day, add the remaining Fonds Brun and the tomato purée or fresh tomatoes. Bring the sauce to the boil stirring continuously with a wooden spoon or whisk. Allow to simmer gently for 1 hour, skimming carefully.

Pass through a fine strainer and stir occasionally until the sauce is quite cold.

MAKES APPROXIMATELY 1 LITRE (1¾ PINTS)

Sauce Demi-glace

300 ml (½ pint) Sauce Espagnole, left
150 ml (5 fl oz) Fonds Brun, page 8
100 ml (3½ fl oz) Glace de Viande, page 9
1 tablespoon sherry, port or Madeira (optional)

This sauce is made by bringing Sauce Espagnole to a final stage of perfection by carefully adding the Fonds Brun, mixing, simmering and skimming until reduced to about 200 ml (7 fl oz). It is then finished at the last moment with a small quantity of meat glaze.

Demi-glace can be flavoured with various fortified wines, such as sherry, port or Madeira. This addition should be made at the very end and the sauce should not be allowed to boil again after this addition. For a tomato-flavoured Demi-glace, either increase the proportion of tomato or tomato purée in the Sauce Espagnole used, or add 1 tablespoon of tomato purée with the Fonds Brun, before making the final reduction.

MAKES APPROXIMATELY 300 ML (½ PINT)

Sauce Poivrade

25 ml (1 fl oz) oil
50 g (2 oz) carrot, peeled and diced
40 g (1½ oz) onion, peeled and diced
a few parsley stalks
1 small pinch chopped fresh thyme
½ bay leaf, crushed
50 ml (2 fl oz) wine vinegar
200 ml (7 fl oz) reserved marinade from dish in preparation
500 ml (18 fl oz) Sauce Espagnole, left
4 peppercorns, crushed
25 g (1 oz) butter

Heat the oil in a pan, add the vegetables and herbs, and fry gently until lightly coloured. Add the wine vinegar and 100 ml (3½ fl oz) of the reserved marinade and reduce by two-thirds. Add the Sauce Espagnole and simmer gently for 45 minutes, adding the crushed peppercorns after 35 minutes.

Strain, pressing firmly to extract all the flavour, then add another 100 ml (3½ fl oz) of the reserved marinade. Bring to the boil, skim and simmer gently for 35 minutes to reduce. Pass again through a fine strainer, this time without pressing, and finish with the butter.

MAKES APPROXIMATELY 500 ML (18 FL OZ)

Consommé Carmen

Sauce Chasseur

150 g (5 oz) butter
150 g (5 oz) button mushrooms, sliced
25 g (1 oz) shallot, peeled and finely chopped
150 ml ($\frac{1}{4}$ pint) dry white wine
1 tablespoon tomato purée
200 ml (7 fl oz) Sauce Demi-glace, page 10
1 tablespoon chopped fresh tarragon and chervil, mixed

M elt 30 g (1$\frac{1}{4}$ oz) butter in a small pan, add the mushrooms and fry gently. Add the shallot and cook together for a few more minutes.

Add the white wine. Reduce by half and add the tomato purée and the Sauce Demi-glace. Bring to the boil, allow to simmer gently for a few minutes and finish by whisking in the remaining quantity of butter and the chopped fresh tarragon and chervil. Do not re-boil.

MAKES APPROXIMATELY 500 ML (18 FL OZ)

Sauce Duxelles

100 ml (3$\frac{1}{2}$ fl oz) dry white wine
100 ml (3$\frac{1}{2}$ fl oz) mushroom cooking liquor
20 g ($\frac{3}{4}$ oz) shallot, peeled and chopped
275 ml (9 fl oz) Sauce Demi-glace, page 10
1 tablespoon tomato purée
1 pinch chopped fresh parsley

Dry duxelles
15 g ($\frac{1}{2}$ oz) knob butter
1 tablespoon chopped onion
100 g (4 oz) mushrooms, finely chopped

P lace the wine and *mushroom cooking liquor* in a pan with the chopped shallot and reduce to one third of its original quantity.

Meanwhile, prepare the dry duxelles by heating the butter and frying the onion gently for a few minutes. Add the mushrooms and cook gently until all the moisture has evaporated.

Add the Sauce Demi-glace to the reduced white wine and mushroom liquor, then add the tomato purée and dry duxelles. Allow to simmer gently for 5 minutes and finish the sauce with the chopped parsley.

MAKES APPROXIMATELY 500 ML (18 FL OZ)

Sauce Béchamel

65 g (2$\frac{1}{2}$ oz) butter
65 g (2$\frac{1}{2}$ oz) flour, sifted
1 litre (1$\frac{3}{4}$ pints) boiling milk
1 onion, peeled and finely sliced
1 sprig thyme
salt
pepper
1 pinch grated nutmeg

F irst prepare a *white roux* by mixing together 50 g (2 oz) of the butter and the flour in a heavy pan and placing over moderate heat for just a few minutes, stirring frequently, to eliminate the raw flavour of the flour. Allow to cool.

Gradually stir the milk into the roux so as to obtain a smooth sauce and bring to boiling point. Fry the onion gently in the remaining butter but do not allow to brown, then add the thyme, salt, pepper and grated nutmeg. Add this mixture to the sauce and simmer for 1 hour. Pass through a fine strainer.

If you are not going to use the sauce immediately, coat the surface with a little butter to prevent a skin forming. For the thick or very thick Sauce Béchamel required for certain recipes, allow to simmer and reduce considerably before straining and using. For a light Sauce Béchamel, thin with a little boiling milk before straining and using.

MAKES APPROXIMATELY 1.2 LITRES (2 PINTS)

Sauce Suprême

1 litre (1$\frac{3}{4}$ pints) Sauce Velouté made with Fonds Blanc de Volaille, pages 9–10
1 litre (1$\frac{3}{4}$ pints) Fonds Blanc de Volaille, page 9
100 ml (3$\frac{1}{2}$ fl oz) mushroom cooking liquor
350 ml (12 fl oz) double cream
65 g (2$\frac{1}{2}$ oz) butter

P lace the Sauce Velouté, Fonds Blanc de Volaille and *mushroom cooking liquor* in a heavy pan. Bring to the boil and reduce quickly, while simultaneously adding two-thirds of the cream, a little at a time, and stirring the sauce continuously with a straight-edged wooden spatula.

When the sauce has been reduced by one-third, pass it through a fine strainer. Finish the sauce with the remaining cream and the butter.

MAKES APPROXIMATELY 1.5 LITRES (2$\frac{1}{2}$ PINTS)

Sauce Mornay

100 ml (3½ fl oz) Fumet de Poisson, page 9, or cooking liquor
1 litre (1¾ pints) Sauce Béchamel, page 12
25 g (1 oz) Gruyère, grated
25 g (1 oz) Parmesan, grated
50 g (2 oz) butter

Add the fish stock, or the cooking liquor from the fish with which the sauce is to be served, to the Sauce Béchamel. (If the sauce is required for a dish other than fish, the fish stock or cooking liquor should be replaced by the cooking liquor from the dish under preparation, or by milk.) Reduce by a third and add all the grated cheese.

Reheat for a few seconds, mix well to ensure that the cheese is melted, and finish with the butter.

MAKES APPROXIMATELY 1 LITRE (1¾ PINTS)

Sauce Hollandaise

2 tablespoons vinegar
5 tablespoons water
salt
coarsely ground pepper
5 egg yolks
450 g (1 lb) unsalted butter, softened or melted
a few drops lemon juice

Place the vinegar with 4 tablespoons water in a pan with a pinch each of salt and pepper. Reduce by two-thirds and transfer to a *bain-marie*.

Add another tablespoon water and the egg yolks to the reduction and whisk continuously over a gentle heat, while very gradually adding the butter. The sauce will thicken as the temperature rises and the yolks are cooked, but great care should be taken that the mixture does not overheat or it will separate. Add a few drops of water from time to time so as to ensure the sauce remains light.

Check the seasoning and add a few drops of lemon juice. Pass through a fine strainer and keep at a lukewarm temperature until the sauce is required, to prevent it from separating.
Note: It is best to avoid the use of an aluminium pan in the preparation of this sauce because of the risk of discoloration.

MAKES APPROXIMATELY 500 ML (18 FL OZ)

Sauce Mayonnaise

2 egg yolks
salt
white pepper
½ tablespoon wine vinegar or lemon juice
300 ml (½ pint) olive oil
2 tablespoons boiling water

Whisk the egg yolks in a basin with the seasonings and a little of the vinegar or lemon juice.

Add and whisk in the oil, drop by drop to begin with, then faster in a stream, as the sauce begins to thicken. Adjust the consistency occasionally by adding a few more drops of vinegar or lemon juice.

Lastly, add the water, which ensures that the emulsification holds, even if the sauce is not used immediately.

MAKES APPROXIMATELY 400 ML (14 FL OZ)

Sauce Béarnaise

100 ml (3½ fl oz) dry white wine
100 ml (3½ fl oz) tarragon vinegar
2 tablespoons chopped shallot
6 peppercorns, crushed
2 tablespoons chopped fresh tarragon
1 tablespoon chopped fresh chervil
4 egg yolks
300 g (11 oz) butter, softened
salt
cayenne pepper

Place the wine and the vinegar in a small pan with the shallot, peppercorns and half of the herbs. Bring to the boil and reduce to a quarter of its original volume. Allow to cool.

Whisk the egg yolks into the wine and vinegar reduction and, over a gentle heat, gradually whisk in the butter.

When all the butter has been incorporated and the sauce is very thick, pass through a fine strainer, correct the seasoning and add a little cayenne pepper. Finish by stirring in the remaining tarragon and chervil. Do not allow the sauce, at any time, to reach a temperature much higher than blood heat, or it will curdle.
Note: It is best to avoid the use of an aluminium pan in the preparation of this sauce because of the risk of discoloration.

MAKES APPROXIMATELY 400 ML (14 FL OZ)

Sauce au Beurre

25 g (1 oz) flour
25 g (1 oz) melted butter
500 ml (18 fl oz) boiling water
salt
3 eggs yolks
50 ml (2 fl oz) double cream
a few drops lemon juice
200 g (7 oz) butter

Mix the flour and melted butter together in a pan. Add the boiling water gradually, whisking thoroughly after each addition, and season. Make a *liaison* of the egg yolks, cream and lemon juice, and add this to the sauce.

Reheat to thicken, pass through a fine strainer and finish away from the heat, just before serving, with the butter.

MAKES APPROXIMATELY 800 ML (1 PINT 8 FL OZ)

Sauce Tomate

15 g (½ oz) butter
25 g (1 oz) streaky bacon, diced and blanched
25 g (1 oz) onion, peeled and roughly diced
40 g (1½ oz) carrot, peeled and roughly diced
1 bay leaf
1 sprig thyme
25 g (1 oz) flour
1.25 kg (2¾ lb) ripe tomatoes, squashed
400 ml (14 fl oz) Fonds Blanc, page 9
1 clove garlic, peeled and crushed
salt
pepper
1 pinch caster sugar

Melt the butter in a flameproof casserole, then add the bacon and fry gently. Add the vegetables and herbs and fry until golden brown. Sprinkle with the flour and stir. Cook until golden brown and allow to cool. Add the rest of the ingredients, then bring to the boil, stirring continuously.

Cover with a lid and place in a moderate oven (180°C, 350°F, Gas Mark 4) for 1½–2 hours, then strain into a clean pan. Stir and return to the boil for a few minutes. If you are not using this sauce immediately, coat the surface with butter in order to prevent a skin from forming on the top.

MAKES APPROXIMATELY 1 LITRE (1¾ PINTS)

Fondue de Tomate

125 g (4½ oz) onion, peeled and finely chopped
25 g (1 oz) butter or 1 tablespoon olive oil
750 g (1 lb 10 oz) tomatoes, peeled, depipped and chopped
1 clove garlic, peeled and crushed
salt
pepper
1 pinch caster sugar (optional)

Fry the chopped onion gently in the butter or oil and add the tomato flesh, crushed garlic, seasoning and optional sugar. Allow to simmer gently until all the liquid has evaporated.

MAKES APPROXIMATELY 500 ML (18 FL OZ)

Sauce Provençale

100 ml (3½ fl oz) olive oil
800 g (1¾ lb) tomatoes, peeled, depipped and roughly chopped
salt
pepper
1 pinch caster sugar
1 clove garlic, peeled and crushed
1 tablespoon chopped fresh parsley

Heat the oil in a pan until almost smoking hot. Add the chopped tomato flesh and season with salt, pepper and sugar. Add the crushed garlic and parsley. Cover with a lid and allow to simmer gently for 30 minutes.

MAKES APPROXIMATELY 500 ML (18 FL OZ)

Sauce aux Pommes

450 g (1 lb) apples, peeled, cored and sliced
15 g (½ oz) sugar
1 pinch cinnamon
50 ml (2 fl oz) water

Place the apples in a pan with the sugar, cinnamon and water. Cover with a lid and cook gently until soft, then make into a smooth sauce by beating with a whisk.

This sauce should always be served lukewarm.

MAKES APPROXIMATELY 300 ML (½ PINT)

Bisque de Crevettes

CONSOMMES & SOUPS

Consommé Carmen

450 g (1 lb) very lean beef, trimmed and chopped
1 carrot, roughly chopped
2 leeks, roughly chopped
½ large red pepper
5 tablespoons tomato purée
1 egg white
1.5 litres (2½ pints) Fonds Blanc, page 9

To garnish
1 tomato
½ red pepper
1 tablespoon boiled long-grain rice
6 sprigs chervil

*P*lace the meat, vegetables, tomato purée and egg white in a small stockpot, mix well and add 1.25 litres (2¼ pints) of the Fonds Blanc. Bring to the boil, keeping the bottom of the pan clean using a flat-ended spatula and taking great care that the consommé is disturbed as little as possible. After boiling point has been reached, simmer very gently for 1½ hours without disturbing the consommé in any way.

Meanwhile, prepare the garnish. Peel the tomato by placing it in boiling water for a few seconds so that the skin can be removed easily. Remove the pips, cut the flesh in dice, and poach for 7–8 minutes in the rest of the Fonds Blanc along with the red pepper, cut into *julienne*. Remove and cool.

When the consommé is cooked, ladle it out gently without disturbing the crust of ingredients on the top, and pass it through a clean muslin cloth. Place the poached tomato and pepper and the boiled rice directly into the hot consommé just before serving and garnish each bowl with a sprig of chervil. *See photograph on page 11.*

SERVES 6

Consommé au Chasseur

450 g (1 lb) lean mixed game flesh, chopped
600 g (1 lb 6 oz) fresh game bones, roasted
65 g (2½ oz) leek, roughly chopped
25 g (1 oz) dried boletus mushrooms
1 sprig sage
1 pinch dried rosemary
2 crushed juniper berries
pepper
1 egg white
1.5 litres (2½ pints) Fonds de Gibier, page 8

To garnish
1 tablespoon julienne of mushrooms, stewed in a little butter and lemon juice
65 ml (2½ fl oz) port
6 sprigs chervil

*P*lace the chopped meat and roasted bones, vegetables, herbs, flavourings and egg white in a small stockpot, mix well together and add the game stock. Bring to the boil, keeping the bottom of the pan clean using a flat-ended spatula and taking great care that the consommé is disturbed as little as possible. After boiling point has been reached, simmer very gently for 1½ hours without disturbing the consommé in any way.

Meanwhile prepare the garnish. When the consommé is cooked, ladle it out gently without disturbing the crust of ingredients on the top, and pass it through clean muslin. Stir the mushrooms and port into the hot consommé just before serving and garnish each bowl with a sprig of chervil.

SERVES 6

Bisque de Crevettes

40 g (1½ oz) carrot, peeled and diced
40 g (1½ oz) onion, skinned and diced
2 parsley stalks, chopped
1 sprig thyme
½ bay leaf
150 g (5 oz) butter
450 g (1 lb) whole raw prawns, washed
salt
pepper
15 ml (1 small tablespoon) brandy
200 ml (7 fl oz) dry white wine
900 ml (1½ pints) Fonds Blanc, page 9, or Fonds Blanc
de Volaille, page 9
100 g (4 oz) long-grain rice
65 ml (2½ fl oz) double cream
cayenne pepper

*F*ry the vegetables and herbs in 25 g (1 oz) of the butter until golden brown, then add the washed prawns and cook together for a few minutes. Season with salt and pepper, sprinkle with the brandy and wine and allow to cook gently to reduce. Add 150 ml (¼ pint) of the Fonds Blanc and allow to cook gently for 10 minutes. Cook the rice in another 450 ml (¾ pint) of the Fonds Blanc.

Shell some of the prawns and reserve for garnishing. Finely pound the remainder of the prawns and add the rice and its cooking liquid together with the cooking liquid from the prawns. Pass through a fine sieve and dilute with the remaining 300 ml (½ pint) of Fonds Blanc. Bring to the boil, pass through a fine strainer and keep warm in a *bain-marie*.

Finish the bisque before serving with the rest of the butter and the double cream. Correct the seasoning and add a little cayenne pepper.

Garnish with the reserved shelled prawns. *See photograph on page 15.*

SERVES 6

Velouté d'Eperlans

90 g (3½ oz) white breadcrumbs
600 ml (1 pint) boiling milk
100 g (4 oz) fillet of smelt
200 g (7 oz) flesh of whiting, John Dory or sole
75 g (3 oz) onion, peeled and finely chopped
2 tablespoons lemon juice
175 g (6 oz) butter
150 ml (¼ pint) Fumet de Poisson, page 9
4 egg yolks
120 ml (4 fl oz) double cream
cayenne pepper

*M*ake a light *panada* by simmering the breadcrumbs in the boiling milk for about 10 minutes. Meanwhile, stew together the fish and the onion with the lemon juice and 75 g (3 oz) of the butter for a few minutes, then add the milk panada.

When all the ingredients are cooked, pass them through a fine sieve or process in a blender and then sieve. Adjust the consistency with the fish stock, strain and reheat without boiling.

Finish with a *liaison* of egg yolks and cream, and blend in the remaining butter. Season lightly with cayenne pepper.

SERVES 6

Soupe à l'Ardennaise

150 g (5 oz) butter
350 g (12 oz) chicory (Belgian endive), shredded
75 g (3 oz) white of leek, shredded
100 g (4 oz) potato, peeled and cut into small square slices
1 litre (1¾ pints) boiling milk
salt
pepper

*M*elt half the butter in a pan, add all the vegetables and cook gently for a few minutes. Then add the boiling milk, season and simmer gently until the vegetables are cooked.

Finish at the last minute by adding the remaining butter. Serve with thin slices of French bread.

SERVES 6

Soupe à la Dauphinoise

100 g (4 oz) turnip, peeled
100g (4 oz) vegetable marrow flesh
100 g (4 oz) potato, peeled
40 g (1½ oz) butter
500 ml (18 fl oz) water
500 ml (18 fl oz) milk
salt
pepper
4 leaves of chard or white beet, shredded
25 g (1 oz) vermicelli
6 sprigs chervil

Put the vegetables into small square or round slices and cook them gently with the butter. Add the water and milk, season and, when the vegetables are half-cooked, add the shredded leaves of chard or white beet.

About 15 minutes before the soup is cooked, sprinkle in the vermicelli. Garnish each bowl with a sprig of chervil.

SERVES 6

Soupe à la Nevers

250 g (9 oz) very small Brussels sprouts, trimmed
100 g (4 oz) butter
200 g (7 oz) carrot, peeled and sliced
1.2 litres (2 pints) Fonds Blanc, page 9
salt
pepper
25 g (1 oz) vermicelli

To garnish
6 small sprigs chervil

Blanch the Brussels sprouts and stew them in half the butter for about 20 minutes or until almost cooked. Meanwhile stew the carrots in the remaining butter for about 20 minutes. Add a little of the stock to the carrots, season and finish cooking them in the stock.

About 20 minutes before serving, add the sprouts to the carrots, along with the remaining stock. Sprinkle in the vermicelli and finish cooking everything together.

Check and adjust the seasoning. Garnish each bowl of soup with a small sprig of chervil.

SERVES 6

Soupe à l'Ail

1.5 litres (2½ pints) water
125 g (4½ oz) small cloves garlic, peeled and crushed
2 small sprigs sage
2 cloves
salt
pepper
1 loaf French bread
75 g (3 oz) grated cheese
olive oil

Bring the water to the boil with the garlic, sage, cloves and seasoning, and allow to simmer gently for 15 minutes. Meanwhile, cut 12 small slices of French bread, sprinkle with grated cheese and place them in a moderate oven (180°C, 350°F, Gas Mark 4) for a few minutes, to melt the cheese. Place these melted cheese croûtons in a warmed soup tureen, sprinkle with a little olive oil and pour the soup over them through a fine strainer, lightly pressing the ingredients as you do so. Allow the bread to soak for 2 minutes before serving.

SERVES 6

Crème d'Artichauts à la Noisette

6 medium artichoke bottoms
40 g (1½ oz) butter
600 ml (1 pint) light Sauce Béchamel, page 12
4 hazelnuts, inner skin removed, lightly roasted
and crushed
salt
pepper
150 ml (¼ pint) Fonds Blanc, page 9
200 ml (7 fl oz) single cream

Blanch the artichoke bottoms, and stew them in the butter until they are soft, taking care not to allow them to colour. Slice 5 of them.

Reserve the whole artichoke bottom for the garnish and add the others to the béchamel, together with the hazelnuts and seasoning. Allow to cook gently for 10 minutes, then pass through a fine sieve or process in a blender. Adjust the consistency with the stock, strain and reheat.

Finish just before serving by stirring in the cream. Garnish with the reserved artichoke bottom cut into small dice.

SERVES 6

Soupe à la Dauphinoise

Crème Agnès Sorel

450 g (1 lb) fresh white mushrooms
450 ml (¾ pint) thin Sauce Béchamel, page 12
600 ml (1 pint) hot Fonds Blanc de Volaille page 9
300 ml (½ pint) single cream

To garnish
50 g (2 oz) mushroom, cut into julienne and stewed in butter
25 g (1 oz) cooked white of chicken, cut into julienne
50 g (2 oz) salt ox tongue, cut into julienne

Wash the mushrooms and pass through a fine sieve or work finely in a food processor. Add the mushroom to the Sauce Béchamel and simmer very gently for 7–8 minutes. Pass through a fine sieve. Dilute to the required consistency with the hot stock. Strain again, reheat without allowing to boil and finish at the last moment with the cream.

Garnish each bowl of soup with a little of the cooked *julienne* of mushroom and the julienne of chicken and ox tongue.

SERVES 6

Crème Choisy

750 g (1½ lb) lettuce
75 g (3 oz) butter
1 pinch sugar
600 ml (1 pint) thin Sauce Béchamel, page 12
85 ml (3 fl oz) hot Fonds Blanc, page 9
300 ml (½ pint) single cream

To garnish
6 small sprigs chervil
100 g (4 oz) small croûtons
50 g (2 oz) butter

Blanch the lettuce and refresh under cold running water. Drain and squeeze out all the moisture. Roughly shred the lettuce and stew with the butter, sugar and a little salt. Add the Sauce Béchamel and simmer gently for about 30 minutes. Pass through a fine sieve and adjust the consistency of the soup with the hot stock. Strain. Reheat the soup without allowing it to boil and finish at the last moment with the cream.

Garnish each bowl with a small sprig of chervil and the croûtons of bread fried in the butter.

SERVES 6

Potage Palestine

500 g (1¼ lb) Jerusalem artichokes, peeled, sliced and placed
in acidulated water until ready to use
150 g (5 oz) butter
15 g (½ oz) hazelnuts, inner skin removed, lightly roasted
and crushed
600 ml (1 pint) Fonds Blanc, page 9
25 g (1 oz) arrowroot
150 ml (¼ pint) cold milk

Cook the artichokes gently in 50 g (2 oz) of the butter for 5–10 minutes without browning, then add the hazelnuts, stock and a little seasoning. Heat to boiling point, reduce the heat and simmer gently until the artichokes are soft.

Purée the vegetables either by rubbing through a fine sieve or by processing in a blender. Adjust the consistency by thickening the soup with the arrowroot, previously mixed with the cold milk. Bring back to the boil and strain finely.

Reheat and finish with the remaining butter.

SERVES 6

Potage Okra

40 g (1½ oz) onion, peeled and finely chopped
40 g (1½ oz) butter
75 g (3 oz) lean bacon, rinded and diced
300 g (11 oz) raw chicken flesh, diced
1.25 litres (2¼ pints) Fonds Blanc de Volaille, page 9
125 g (4½ oz) okra, sliced
150 g (5 oz) tomato flesh, roughly chopped
salt
pepper
Worcestershire sauce
2 tablespoons boiled long-grain rice

Fry the chopped onion gently in the butter without colouring it and add the bacon. Fry for a few more minutes until golden in colour. Add the diced raw chicken flesh and fry this also until golden, stirring frequently.

Add the Fonds Blanc de Volaille, bring to the boil and allow to simmer gently for 25 minutes without a lid. Then add the okra and tomato flesh and continue cooking gently for another 25 minutes. Skim, then season to taste with salt, pepper and a little Worcestershire sauce. Add the boiled rice and serve.

SERVES 6

Potage Pastorelle

350 g (12 oz) white of leek, sliced
50 g (2 oz) onion, peeled and sliced
75 g (3 oz) mushrooms, sliced
150 g (5 oz) butter
600 ml (1 pint) Fonds Blanc, page 9
salt
pepper
450 g (1 lb) potatoes, peeled and sliced
300 ml (½ pint) boiling milk

To garnish
50 g (2 oz) small white mushrooms, sliced
75 g (3 oz) butter
50 g (2 oz) potato, peeled and diced

Stew the leek, onion and mushrooms in 50 g (2 oz) of the butter. Add the stock, season, add the sliced potato and simmer gently until soft. Pass through a fine sieve. Use the milk to adjust the consistency of the soup. Finish at the last moment with the rest of the butter.

To garnish, stew the mushrooms in half the butter and sauté the diced potato in the remaining butter until soft and golden brown. Garnish the soup with the mushrooms and potato.

Serves 6

Potage Dubarry

450 g (1 lb) cauliflower, blanched
250 g (9 oz) potatoes, peeled and sliced
900 ml (1½ pints) milk
salt
125 g (4½ oz) butter

To garnish
6–8 sprigs fresh chervil
100 g (4 oz) small croûtons
50 g (2 oz) butter

Cook the blanched cauliflower and the sliced potatoes in 750 ml (1¼ pints) of the milk. Season, then sieve finely.

Bring the remaining milk to the boil and use it to adjust the consistency of the soup. Finish with the butter. Garnish with sprigs of chervil and croûtons fried in butter.

Serves 6–8

Potage Cormeilles

500 g (1¼ lb) French beans
185 g (6½ oz) butter
350 g (12 oz) potatoes, peeled and sliced
600 ml (1 pint) Fonds Blanc, page 9
salt
pepper
250 ml (8 fl oz) boiling milk

Reserve about 50 g (2 oz) of the beans to cook later, for the garnish, and blanch the rest of them in boiling water for 5 minutes. Drain then stew them together with 65 g (2½ oz) of the butter and the potatoes. Add the stock, season and allow to simmer gently for about 30 minutes or until cooked. Pass through a fine sieve, or process in a blender and then sieve, and adjust the consistency with the boiling milk.

Finish with the remaining butter, then check the seasoning, adjusting if necessary. Garnish with the reserved French beans, freshly cooked and cut into diamond shapes.

Serves 6

Potage Bressane

750 g (1½ lb) pumpkin flesh
750 ml (1¼ pints) milk
salt
1 pinch sugar
300 g (11 oz) croûtons, cut from white bread, uncooked
225 g (8 oz) butter
100 ml (3½ fl oz) cream

To garnish
50 g (2 oz) small Italian pasta shapes
milk

Cut the pumpkin into large pieces and put in a pan with the milk, salt and sugar. Bring to the boil.

Meanwhile fry the croûtons in half the butter. Add these to the pan containing the pumpkin flesh and the milk and simmer all together gently for about 20 minutes. Pass through a fine sieve or process in a blender and then sieve.

Finish with the remaining butter and the cream, then check the seasoning, adjusting if necessary. Garnish with the small Italian pasta shapes cooked in milk.

Serves 6–8

Potage Saint-Germain

750 g (1 lb 10 oz) shelled fresh peas
150 g (5 oz) butter
75 g (3 oz) green of leek, sliced
40 g (1½ oz) lettuce leaves, shredded
1 pinch salt
1 pinch sugar
1 pinch chopped fresh chervil
75 ml (3 fl oz) water
600 ml (1 pint) Fonds Blanc, page 9
6 sprigs chervil

*R*eserve some of the smallest peas for a garnish, then stew the rest of the peas gently together with 60 g (2¼ oz) of the butter, the leek, lettuce leaves, seasonings and water until they are cooked.

Pound them well or process in a blender, then pass through a fine sieve. Adjust consistency with the stock, reheat to boiling point and strain.

Reheat before serving. Cook the reserved peas in 15 g (½ oz) of the butter. Finish the soup at the last moment with the remaining butter. Garnish each bowl with a few of the reserved peas and a sprig of chervil.

SERVES 6

Potage Garbure-Cooper

350 g (12 oz) onions, peeled and finely sliced
100 g (4 oz) butter
1 litre (1¾ pints) Fonds Blanc, page 9
French bread, thinly sliced
100 g (4 oz) grated Cheddar

*F*ry the onion gently in half the butter until soft and golden brown. Add the stock and allow to simmer gently for 10 minutes.

Rub through a fine sieve or process in a blender and then sieve, then pour into a shallow ovenproof tureen or flat, individual ovenproof soup bowls. Cover the surface with thin slices of French bread and sprinkle the bread with the grated cheese. Melt the remaining butter and pour this over the top of the cheese.

Gratinate quickly in a very hot oven (240°C, 475°F, Gas Mark 9) and serve immediately.

SERVES 6

Potage Portugaise

150 g (5 oz) butter
40 g (1½ oz) lean bacon, rinded and diced
40 g (1½ oz) onion, peeled and chopped
40 g (1½ oz) carrot, peeled and chopped
1 sprig thyme
1 small bay leaf
500 g (1¼ lb) fresh ripe tomatoes, peeled, depipped and roughly chopped
1 clove garlic, crushed
1 pinch sugar
75 g (3 oz) long-grain rice
750 ml (1¼ pints) Fonds Blanc, page 9

To garnish
2 tablespoons diced tomato flesh lightly cooked in butter
2 tablespoons boiled long-grain rice

*H*eat 50 g (2 oz) of the butter in a pan and add the bacon, vegetables and herbs. Fry gently until golden brown. Add the roughly chopped tomato flesh, the crushed clove of garlic, the sugar, rice and 600 ml (1 pint) of the stock.

Simmer gently until tender, then pass through a fine sieve or process in a blender. Adjust the consistency with the remaining stock, strain and reheat.

Finish at the last minute with the remaining butter. Garnish each bowl with a small quantity of cooked diced tomato flesh and boiled rice.

SERVES 6

Potage Réjane

75 g (3 oz) white of leek, cut into julienne
25 g (1 oz) butter
100 g (4 oz) cooked white chicken meat, cut into julienne
600 ml (1 pint) boiling Fonds Blanc, page 9
75 g (3 oz) potato, peeled and cut into julienne

*C*ook the leek gently in the butter until soft but not coloured. Add the *julienne* of chicken and leek to the stock and simmer gently for 10 minutes, taking care that the soup does not become cloudy.

Then add the potato and simmer all together gently until cooked. Serve immediately.

SERVES 6

Potage Saint-Germain

HORS D'OEUVRE

Salade de Moules et Céleri

1.75 litres (3 pints) mussels, cleaned
125 g (4½ oz) onion, sliced
15 g (½ oz) parsley stalks
pinch crushed peppercorns
200 ml (7 fl oz) water
1 small head crisp white celery, very finely sliced

Mustard Sauce
10 g (⅓ oz) dry mustard
juice of ½ small lemon
175 ml (6 fl oz) double cream
salt
freshly ground black pepper

Place the mussels in a deep pan with the onion, parsley stalks, crushed peppercorns and water, then cover and cook at high heat for 5–7 minutes until the shells have opened. Remove the mussels from the shells and remove the beards. Use only the mussels which have opened during cooking.

Meanwhile make the Mustard Sauce. Mix the mustard and lemon juice in a basin then add the cream, blending thoroughly together. Season with salt and flavour well with freshly ground black pepper.

Place the cooked mussels in a bowl with the finely sliced celery and toss lightly with the prepared sauce. The salad can either be served as it is in an hors d'oeuvre dish, or the mussels can be replaced in the half shells before arranging with the salad in the dish.

SERVES 6

Salade Dorzia

1 cucumber
1 teaspoon salt
200 g (7 oz) cooked white of chicken
250 g (9 oz) cooked long-grain rice

Vinaigrette
100 ml (3½ fl oz) olive oil
25 ml (1 fl oz) wine vinegar
1 teaspoon made mustard
1 teaspoon chopped capers
½ tablespoon chopped fresh parsley
½ tablespoon chopped fresh tarragon, chervil and chives, mixed
15 g (½ oz) onion, peeled and finely chopped
salt
pepper

Peel the cucumber, cut in half lengthways, remove the seeds then cut into short *bâtons*. Place these in a colander, lightly salt and leave for 10–15 minutes to drain. Rinse and remove from the colander, pat dry with a clean teatowel or paper towels and put the bâtons in a salad bowl.

Cut the chicken into short *julienne* and add these to the cucumber along with the cooked rice.

Make the vinaigrette by whisking all the ingredients together thoroughly. Pour over the salad and mix lightly.

SERVES 6

Salade de Céleri-rave

500 g (1¼ lb) celeriac, peeled
10 g (⅓ oz) dry mustard
a few drops lemon juice
150 ml (¼ pint) double cream
1 pinch salt
freshly ground black pepper

Cut the raw celeriac into thick *julienne*. Make a Mustard Sauce according to the instructions given in the recipe for Salade de Moules et Céleri, page 24, but using the ingredients listed above. Mix the celeriac well with the sauce.

SERVES 4–6

Croquettes de Morue à l'Américaine

750 g (1 lb 10 oz) dried salt cod
750 g (1 lb 10 oz) potatoes, peeled and cut into pieces
salt
75 g (3 oz) butter
pepper
grated nutmeg
2 egg yolks
2 tablespoons very thick Sauce Béchamel, page 12
flour
1 beaten egg
white breadcrumbs
oil for deep frying

Soak the fish in cold water for 24 hours, changing the water 2–3 times. Poach it gently in water for 10–15 minutes and flake it, removing any skin and bones.

Cook the potatoes quickly in salted water until they are just cooked. Drain, dry out in the oven, and pass them through a sieve. Replace in the pan, add the butter, salt, pepper and grated nutmeg to taste, and beat well over heat. Then remove from the heat and mix in the egg yolks.

Mix the flaked fish with the mashed potato and add the thick Sauce Béchamel. Mould the mixture into balls weighing approximately 75 g (3 oz) each on a well-floured surface, then roll each one in the beaten egg and breadcrumbs and fry them in hot or very hot oil (180°–190°C, 350°–375°F) until golden brown. These croquettes are best served with Sauce Tomate, page 14.

SERVES 6

Harengs à la Dieppoise

6 fresh herrings, cleaned
25 g (1 oz) butter

Marinade
600 ml (1 pint) dry white wine
300 ml (½ pint) wine vinegar
2 carrots, peeled, fluted and thinly sliced
4 small onions, peeled and cut into rings
2 shallots, peeled and sliced
1 sprig thyme
2 bay leaves
4 parsley stalks
10 peppercorns
salt

To garnish
1 lemon, fluted and sliced

Prepare the marinade in advance by mixing all the ingredients together, seasoning with salt, bringing the marinade to the boil and simmering gently for 10 minutes. Arrange the herrings in a shallow, buttered pan and cover with the boiling marinade.

Poach the herrings gently for 12 minutes and allow them to cool in the liquid. When cool, chill them further in the refrigerator.

Serve the herrings very cold with a spoonful or two of the cooking liquid. Garnish with some of the carrot slices and onion rings and slices of *fluted lemon*.

SERVES 6

Canapés aux Crevettes

Canapés, or toasts, are made from white bread cut into various shapes and no more than 5 mm (¼ inch) thick. These are then either fried in *clarified butter* or, more usually, toasted.

To make these Canapés aux Crevettes, coat round toasts with a pink shrimp butter, made by pounding cooked shrimps or prawns to a fine paste, then mixing this paste with an equal quantity of well-softened butter and passing the mixture through a fine sieve.

Then pipe a border around each round toast using the pink shrimp butter in a piping bag with fancy tubes. Fill the centres with a rose pattern of shrimps and finish each canapé with a caper in the middle. *See photograph on page 27.*

25

Beignets à la Niçoise

A beignet is any food or mixture of foods which has been dipped in frying batter and then deep fried.

Beignets à la Niçoise are made using round slices of raw fresh tuna fish, about 2.5–4 cm (1–1½ inches) in diameter and 2 cm (¾ inch) thick. Wrap each slice with some thin strips of anchovy fillet marinaded in oil.

Dip in light Pâte à Frire (see below) and deep fry immediately in very hot oil (190°C, 375°F). Arrange on a serviette in neat piles and garnish with a contrasting border of deep-fried parsley.

Pâte à Frire

125 g (4½ oz) flour, sifted
1 pinch salt
25 ml (1 fl oz) olive oil or melted butter
200 ml (7 fl oz) lukewarm water
2 egg whites

I f the batter is required for immediate use, place all the ingredients except for the egg whites in a basin and mix by turning them over gently with a wooden spoon. This prevents the batter from becoming elastic (an elastic batter will not stick to the items dipped into it). If the batter is prepared in advance, all the ingredients except for the egg whites can be mixed well and then allowed to rest for a while, during which time the batter will lose its elasticity.

Whisk the egg whites stiffly and fold these into the batter immediately before use.

MAKES APPROXIMATELY 450 ML (¾ PINT)

Barquettes de Laitances à la Florentine

B arquettes differ from tartlets only in their shape, which is a sort of pointed oval as opposed to round. Barquette tins are generally lined with either Pâte à Foncer (opposite) or Feuilletage, page 28, and baked blind to a light golden colour.

These particular barquettes are filled with roughly chopped spinach, which has been gently cooked with a little butter. Poach some soft herring roe lightly in dry white wine, and place a slice of roe on top of each filled barquette. Coat with well-seasoned Sauce Mornay, page 13, sprinkle with Parmesan and gratinate lightly under a hot grill.

Médaillons d'Anchois

W rap fillets of anchovy, marinaded in oil, round the edges of thick slices of cooked potato or baked beetroot. Then fill the centres, according to taste, with chopped hard-boiled egg, caviare or a purée of cooked soft herring roes.

Concombres à la Danoise

2 large cucumbers
225 g (8 oz) smoked salmon
225 g (8 oz) smoked herring
3 hard-boiled eggs

To garnish
a little grated horseradish

C ut the cucumbers into halves, and then into sections; scoop out the seeds from the middle of each section, then trim each section into rounded boat-shaped barquettes. Purée the smoked salmon, dice the herring and finely chop the hard-boiled eggs; mix together carefully. Then fill the centres of the cucumber cases with this mixture and sprinkle the surface of the stuffed cucumbers with a little grated horseradish.

SERVES 6

Pâte à Foncer

250 g (9 oz) flour, sifted
1 pinch salt
125 g (4½ oz) butter, softened
50 ml (2 fl oz) water

M ake a well in the flour and place the salt, butter and water in the centre. Mix the flour gradually into the butter and water until it is incorporated and forms a paste. Mix the pastry dough together for a moment, then press it firmly between the palm of the hand and the worktop, pushing small pieces away from the main ball of dough with the heel of the hand, thus assuring the complete blending of all the ingredients. Do this twice.

Form into a ball then wrap in a cloth and place in the refrigerator, preferably for a few hours, before use.

MAKES APPROXIMATELY 400 G (14 OZ)

(from left to right)
Bouchées à la Reine, Concombres à la Danoise, Canapés aux Crevettes

Bouchées à la Reine

Bouchées (or vol-au-vent) which are being served as an hors d'oeuvre are normally slightly smaller than usual and are sometimes called bouchées mignonnes. Their shape often varies according to the type of filling so that guests can easily differentiate between them.

To make Bouchées à la Reine, prepare some fancy, round vol-au-vent cases using Feuilletage (see below). The classic filling for these is a creamed chicken purée but modern practice is to use a *salpicon* of diced white, cooked chicken meat, mushrooms and truffles. This is then mixed with a Sauce Velouté, pages 9–10, enriched with *mushroom cooking liquor* and egg yolks, flavoured with lemon juice and black pepper, and finished with a little extra butter. (This variation on velouté is known as Sauce Allemande or Sauce Parisienne.) Use the pastry tops as lids. *See photograph on page 27.*

Feuilletage

250 g (9 oz) strong flour
1 pinch salt
150 ml (5 fl oz) cold water
250 g (9 oz) butter

Sift the flour and salt together and make a well in the centre. Add the cold water and mix to a paste. Roll into a ball without working it too much and leave to rest for 20 minutes. Meanwhile, work the butter until it has the same texture as the dough. Roll the paste out evenly to form a 15-cm (6-inch) square of even thickness. Place the well-kneaded butter in the centre and fold over the edges of the paste to enclose it completely, thus forming a square block. Allow to rest for 20 minutes.

Roll out the paste and give it two turns, as follows. First of all, roll it out to form an oblong 40 cm (16 inches) long by 15 cm (6 inches) wide, then fold it in three. Turn this package through 90° and roll out and fold as before. Turn the package through 90° again.

Allow the paste to rest for 10 minutes in the refrigerator, then roll the dough out twice more, turning the package through 90° after each folding. Allow to rest for another 10 minutes in the refrigerator and repeat the procedure.

After six turns, and 30 minutes' rest in the refrigerator, the puff pastry is ready for use. Trimmings left over after use should be reassembled into a ball and kept in the refrigerator. They can then be used to make small tartlet and barquette cases.

MAKES APPROXIMATELY 650G (1 LB 7 OZ)

Rougets au Safran

6 small red mullets, cleaned
olive oil
6 tomatoes
600 ml (1 pint) dry white wine
1 pinch salt
6 peppercorns
4 parsley stalks
1 tablespoon chopped fresh fennel
1 sprig thyme
1 bay leaf
1 clove garlic, crushed
10 coriander seeds
1 large pinch saffron threads

To garnish
1 lemon, fluted and sliced
sprigs of fennel

Put the fish in a well-oiled flameproof dish. Peel and core the tomatoes, remove the pips and chop the tomato flesh roughly. Place this around the mullets. Cover with white wine and add all the flavourings.

Bring to the boil, cover and place in a moderate oven (180°C, 350°F, Gas Mark 4). Monitor the oven temperature so as to ensure that the fish simmers very gently for 10–12 minutes, then remove from the oven and allow the fish to cool fully in the cooking liquid.

Serve with a little of the cooking liquid, vegetables and flavourings and garnish with slices of carefully *fluted lemon* and sprigs of fennel.

SERVES 6

Rougets au Safran

EGG DISHES

Oeufs Brouillés d'Aumale

50 g (2 oz) butter
225 g (8 oz) ripe, red tomatoes, peeled, depipped and chopped
250 g (9 oz) calf's kidney
salt
pepper

Sauce Madère
100 ml (3½ fl oz) Sauce Espagnole, page 10
75 ml (2½ fl oz) Fonds Brun, page 8
½ tablespoon Glace de Viande, page 9
1 tablespoon Sercial Madeira

Oeufs Brouillés
8 eggs
100 g (4 oz) butter
2 tablespoons double cream
1 pinch chopped fresh parsley

Heat 25 g (1 oz) of the butter in a pan, add the tomato flesh and cook gently and carefully to a smooth, almost dry purée. Keep warm.

Meanwhile, skin, core and cut the kidney into small dice, season and sauté quickly in the remaining 25 g (1 oz) of butter, then drain and place in a clean saucepan. Place the Sauce Espagnole and Fonds Brun in another saucepan and reduce by approximately one-third. Add the meat glaze, season well and pass through a fine strainer over the diced and sautéed kidney. Reheat but do not re-boil, then add and shake in the Madeira and keep warm.

To make the scrambled eggs, first beat the eggs carefully with a whisk without making them frothy, then season lightly. Gently heat 50 g (2 oz) of the butter in a small heavy pan (not aluminium) and add the beaten eggs. Place over a moderate heat. Stir continuously with a wooden spoon, taking care that the heat remains even; cooking the eggs too rapidly will cause lumps to form which impare the essential quality of the dish.

When the eggs have obtained a light, smooth texture, and before they become over-set and hard, remove the pan from the heat. Now quickly mix in the remaining butter, then the prepared tomatoes and the double cream and place in a deep, warmed serving dish. Make a hollow in the centre of the eggs and fill this with the mixture of kidney and Sauce Madère. Sprinkle the kidney with a pinch of chopped parsley and serve.

SERVES 4–6

Oeufs à la Bretonne

6 eggs
50 g (2 oz) mushrooms, sliced
75 g (3 oz) butter
50 g (2 oz) onion, peeled and finely sliced
50 g (2 oz) white of leek, finely sliced
100 ml (3½ fl oz) Fonds Blanc, page 9
300 ml (½ pint) Sauce Béchamel, page 12

Hard-boil the eggs. Meanwhile, sauté the mushrooms in 25 g (1 oz) of the butter and put to one side.

Stew the onion and leek gently for a few minutes in the remaining butter and finish cooking them by adding the stock and simmering gently until quite soft. Then add the cooked mushrooms and the Sauce Béchamel.

Cut the hard-boiled eggs in half lengthways. Pour a third of the vegetable and béchamel mixture into the bottom of a serving dish and arrange the eggs on top. Cover with the remaining vegetables and sauce.

SERVES 6

Oeufs sur le Plat Montmorency

4 tablespoons creamed asparagus tips
4 eggs

To garnish
4 artichoke bottoms
25 g (1 oz) butter
16 asparagus tips

*P*lace a tablespoon of creamed asparagus tips in four individual ovenproof dishes, break in the eggs and bake in a moderate oven (190°C, 375°F, Gas Mark 5) for about 8–10 minutes. Meanwhile, blanch the artichoke bottoms, slice them and fry gently in the butter.

When the eggs are cooked, garnish each one with 4 green asparagus tips and the fried slices of artichoke bottom.

SERVES 4

Oeufs Pochés en Berceau

4 medium potatoes
225 g (8 oz) cooked white of chicken
3 tablespoons double cream
4 eggs

Sauce Aurore
300 ml ($\frac{1}{2}$ pint) Sauce Velouté, pages 9–10, warmed
2 tablespoons Fondue de Tomate, page 14, warmed
25 g (1 oz) butter

*B*ake the potatoes and keep warm. Meanwhile, finely chop the cooked white of chicken and warm through in the cream.

To make the Sauce Aurore, add the Fondue de Tomate to the Sauce Velouté and finish with the butter. Poach the eggs.

Cut off a third from the tops of the cooked potatoes and scoop out some of the insides, leaving the potatoes in the shape of a crib or cradle. Put the chicken and cream mixture inside the potatoes. Coat the eggs with the Sauce Aurore and place an egg on top of each potato.

SERVES 4

Oeufs à la Portugaise

4 eggs
4 large firm tomatoes
salt
pepper
2 tablespoons olive oil
1 tablespoon coarsely chopped fresh parsley

Sauce Portugaise
2 tablespoons olive oil
1 small onion, peeled and very finely chopped
350 g (12 oz) tomatoes, peeled, depipped and roughly chopped
1 clove garlic, peeled and crushed
salt
pepper
1 pinch sugar
$\frac{1}{2}$ tablespoon tomato purée

*F*irst make the Sauce Portugaise. Heat the oil in a pan, add the onion and fry quickly until golden. Add the roughly chopped tomato flesh along with the garlic, seasoning and tomato purée. Cover the pan with a lid and allow to simmer gently until well flavoured and fairly thick.

Hard-boil the eggs. Meanwhile, cut the 4 large firm tomatoes in half and hollow out their centres. Season lightly and fry them very gently in the oil until slightly softened.

Place half a hot hard-boiled egg on each half tomato. Coat with the hot, thick sauce. Place a pinch of the chopped parsley on each and serve in egg dishes.

SERVES 4

Oeufs sur le Plat à la Savoyarde

350 g (12 oz) potatoes, peeled and thinly sliced
50 g (2 oz) butter
75 g (3 oz) grated Gruyère
4 eggs
8 tablespoons double cream

*F*ry the thin slices of potato gently in the butter until just soft. Then divide them between four individual ovenproof dishes and sprinkle with the grated cheese. Break in the eggs, coat each one with 2 tablespoons of cream, and bake in a hot oven (220°C, 425°F, Gas Mark 7) for about 5 minutes.

SERVES 4

Oeufs sur le Plat Mirabeau

15 g (½ oz) anchovy fillets
50 g (2 oz) butter, softened
4 eggs

To garnish
4 large black olives, stoned and halved
2 tablespoons fresh tarragon leaves, blanched
8–10 thin strips of anchovy fillet

*P*ound the anchovy fillets to a fine paste, then add and mix in three quarters of the softened butter and pass through a fine sieve. Coat four ovenproof dishes with this anchovy butter, break an egg into each dish and bake in a moderate oven (190°C, 375°F, Gas Mark 5) for about 8–10 minutes.

When the eggs are ready, garnish each one with two large halves of black olives filled with the rest of the butter mixed with some finely chopped tarragon leaves. Surround each yolk with thin strips of anchovy fillet, and decorate with the remaining blanched tarragon leaves.

SERVES 4

Oeufs à la Bruxelloise

250 g (9 oz) chicory (Belgian endive), washed
75 g (3 oz) butter
100 ml (3½ fl oz) Fonds Blanc de Volaille, page 9
100 ml (3½ fl oz) Sauce Béchamel, page 12
4 eggs
2 biscottes, finely crushed

*B*raise the whole chicory heads in a single layer in a covered dish with half of the butter and all of the Fonds Blanc de Volaille in a moderate oven (160°C, 325°F, Gas Mark 3) for about an hour. Then slice the chicory and reheat it in the remaining butter mixed with the Sauce Béchamel.

Cover the bottom of four ovenproof egg dishes with the chicory, make an indentation with the back of a spoon in each and break one egg into each indentation. Sprinkle lightly with the finely crushed *biscottes* and bake in a hot oven (220°C, 425°F, Gas Mark 7) for about 5 minutes or until the eggs are lightly set. Serve immediately.

SERVES 4

Oeufs Maximilienne

2 large tomatoes
1 tablespoon olive oil
2 tablespoons chopped fresh parsley
1 clove garlic, peeled and crushed
4 eggs
75 g (3 oz) Parmesan, grated
1 tablespoon fried breadcrumbs

*C*ut the tomatoes in half, discard the pips and fry the halves gently in the oil. Sprinkle the insides with 1 tablespoon of the chopped parsley mixed with the crushed garlic.

Break an egg on to each half tomato. Sprinkle with the grated cheese, mixed with the rest of the chopped parsley and the fried breadcrumbs.

Place them in a moderately hot oven (200°C, 400°F, Gas Mark 6) for about 8–10 minutes to cook and gratinate at the same time. Serve immediately.

SERVES 4

Oeufs en Cocotte à la Florentine

250 g (9 oz) spinach leaves, lightly cooked and roughly chopped
40 g (1½ oz) butter
2 tablespoons double cream, heated to boiling point
4 eggs
30 g (1 oz) Parmesan, grated

*S*tew the lightly cooked and roughly chopped spinach leaves in most of the butter, reserving a little to grease four small individual, ovenproof egg *cocotte* dishes. Line these dishes with the stewed spinach and add ½ tablespoon of boiling cream to each one.

Break in the eggs and sprinkle with the grated Parmesan. Cook in a *bain-marie* in the oven, without a lid, so that the eggs cook and the tops become glazed at one and the same time. This will take about 8–10 minutes in a moderate oven (190°C, 375°F, Gas Mark 5). Serve immediately.

SERVES 4

Oeufs sur le Plat Mirabeau

Oeufs à la d'Orléans

200 g (7 oz) cooked breast of chicken
50 ml (2 fl oz) fresh Sauce Tomate, page 14
4 cooked tartlet cases
30 g (1¼ oz) pistachios, freshly skinned
25 g (1 oz) butter, softened
100 ml (3½ fl oz) hot Sauce Béchamel, page 12
4 eggs

Cut the cooked chicken meat into small dice and bind it with the tomato sauce. Fill the tartlet cases (made using Pâte à Foncer, page 26) with this *salpicon* of chicken. Keep warm.

Pound the pistachios until fine or grind them in a food processor, moistening with a few drops of water to form a paste. Add the softened butter, mix together and pass through a fine sieve. Add this to the béchamel before using as below.

Meanwhile, poach or soft-boil the eggs. Coat them with the pistachio-flavoured béchamel and place one on each prepared tartlet. Serve in egg dishes.

SERVES 4

Oeufs à la Serbe

1 medium aubergine, diced
4 tablespoons olive oil
4 rashers lean bacon
4 eggs

Riz Pilaff
50 g (2 oz) onion, peeled and chopped
75 g (3 oz) butter
150 g (5 oz) unwashed Patna rice, dry weight
350 ml (12 fl oz) Fonds Blanc, page 9

To prepare the rice, fry the onion gently in half the butter until golden brown. Add the rice and continue to fry. Add the stock, cover with a lid and cook in a moderate oven (180°C, 350°F, Gas Mark 4) for 18 minutes.

Meanwhile, fry the diced aubergine gently in half the olive oil. As soon as the rice is cooked, turn it on to a serving dish. Fork in the remaining butter and add the fried aubergine.

Grill the bacon rashers. Heat the remaining oil and quickly fry the eggs on both sides until the whites are crisp. Arrange the eggs and bacon on top of the prepared rice.

SERVES 4

Oeufs Froids à la Niçoise

4 cooked tartlet cases
150 g (5 oz) tomatoes, peeled, depipped and diced
100 g (4 oz) cold cooked French beans, diced
100 g (4 oz) cold boiled potatoes, diced
4 eggs
100 ml (3½ fl oz) Sauce Mayonnaise, page 13
2 tablespoons puréed tomato flesh

Fill the tartlet cases (made using Pâte à Foncer, page 26) with a mixture of tomato, beans and potato. Poach the eggs, then cool, drain and dry them. Place one on top of each prepared tartlet. Mix the mayonnaise with the fresh tomato purée and use this to coat the eggs.

SERVES 4

Oeufs Mollets Chivry

100 g (4 oz) spinach leaves
50 g (2 oz) sorrel leaves
25 g (1 oz) watercress leaves
150 ml (¼ pint) Sauce Béchamel, page 12
25 g (1 oz) butter
6 eggs
6 cooked tartlet cases

Sauce Chivry
65 ml (2½ fl oz) white wine
2 large sprigs chervil and parsley, chopped
2 pinches chopped fresh tarragon, chives and shallot
300 ml (½ pint) Sauce Velouté, pages 9–10, heated to boiling
25 g (1 oz) butter, softened

Blanch the spinach, sorrel and watercress leaves. Refresh, drain and squeeze out all the moisture. Pound with the béchamel, then sieve and reheat with the butter.

To make the Sauce Chivry, bring the wine to the boil in a pan, add half quantities of each of the herbs and all of the shallot and allow to infuse for 10 minutes. Strain. Add to the velouté and finish, away from the heat, with the butter, flavoured and coloured with the remaining herbs.

Soft-boil the eggs. Place a little of the green vegetable purée in each tartlet case (made using Pâte à Foncer, page 26) and set an egg coated with Sauce Chivry on top.

SERVES 6

Oeufs à la d'Orléans

OMELETTES

The theory of the preparation of an omelette is both straightforward and, at the same time, complicated, for the simple reason that people's tastes for this dish are very different – some like their omelettes firm and well done, while others prefer them runny and underdone. The important thing is to know – and respect – the preferences of your guests.

The actual method of preparation of the omelette – which is, after all, no more than a special type of scrambled egg enclosed in a coating of coagulated egg – is a question of practice and manual dexterity. The eggs should be seasoned with a small pinch of fine salt and a touch of pepper, and then well beaten until the yolks and whites are thoroughly blended. Heat a little butter – 15 g (½ oz) for 3 eggs – until it is just beginning to turn brown. This will not only give an excellent flavour to the omelette but will also provide the required amount of heat necessary to ensure the correct setting of the eggs. Pour in the beaten, seasoned eggs, shake the pan and stir briskly with a fork to ensure even cooking.

If the omelette is to be stuffed with a garnish, this should be placed in the centre at this stage, and the omelette should then be quickly folded, rolled into shape and turned over on to a serving dish. When the omelette is on the dish and ready for the table draw a piece of butter, held on the point of a knife, over it in order to make its surface glossy.

Omelette Chasseur

3 eggs
1 pinch fine salt
pepper
2 chicken livers, each cut in half
50 g (2 oz) butter
4 tablespoons Sauce Chasseur, page 12
1 pinch chopped fresh parsley

*B*eat the eggs and season. Gently fry the chicken livers in half the butter, drain and mix with one tablespoonful of the Sauce Chasseur. Make the omelette in the usual way (see above) using the remaining butter, and fill and roll with half of the chicken liver mixture. Run a knife lengthways along the top of the omelette and place the rest of the chicken liver mixture in this opening. Sprinkle with chopped fresh parsley.

Surround the omelette with a *cordon* of the remaining Sauce Chasseur.

SERVES 1 OR 2

Omelette Durand

3 eggs
1 pinch fine salt
pepper
15 g (½ oz) mushroom, sliced
15 g (½ oz) artichoke bottom, blanched and sliced
50 g (2 oz) butter
2 slices truffle, cut into julienne
1 tablespoon asparagus tips, sliced
1 tablespoon Sauce Velouté, pages 9–10
4 tablespoons tomato-flavoured Sauce Demi-glace, page 10

*B*eat the eggs and season. Fry the mushroom and artichoke bottom in half the butter until soft, then add this mixture to the beaten eggs.

Make the omelette in the usual way (see left) and fill and roll it with the *julienne* of truffle and sliced asparagus tips mixed with the Sauce Velouté. Surround the finished omelette with a *cordon* of tomato-flavoured Sauce Demi-glace.

SERVES 1 OR 2

Omelette à la Boulonnaise

3 eggs
1 pinch fine salt
pepper
1 herring roe
25 g (1 oz) butter

Maître d'Hôtel Butter
25 g (1 oz) butter, softened
1 teaspoon chopped fresh parsley
salt
pepper
a few drops lemon juice

*B*eat the eggs until whites and yolks are thoroughly blended and season. Fry the herring roe gently in half the butter. Prepare the Maître d'Hôtel Butter by mixing together all the ingredients listed.

Make the omelette in the usual way (see above left) then fill and roll the omelette with the cooked herring roe and a knob of the prepared butter. Draw any remaining Maître d'Hôtel Butter over the top of the omelette before serving.

SERVES 1 OR 2

Omelette au Thon

3 eggs
pepper
25 g (1 oz) canned tuna fish in oil, flaked
20 g (¾ oz) anchovy fillets
65 g (2½ oz) butter

Beat the eggs and season with pepper. Add the flaked tuna fish. Finely pound the anchovy fillets and soften 50 g (2 oz) of the butter. Mix the butter and anchovy fillets together, pass through a fine sieve, melt and reserve.

Make the omelette in the usual way (see page 36) using the remaining butter. Pour 2 tablespoons of melted anchovy butter over the omelette and serve.

SERVES 1 OR 2

Omelette Jurassienne

3 eggs
1 pinch fine salt
pepper
1 pinch chopped fresh chives
1 pinch chopped fresh chervil
1 tablespoon shredded sorrel leaves
15 g (½ oz) butter
25 g (1 oz) streaky bacon, rinded and cut in small bâtons

Beat the eggs, season and add the chopped chives and chervil. Stew the sorrel gently in the butter.

Fry the streaky bacon gently in the omelette pan until the fat runs, add the beaten egg mixture and cook the omelette in the bacon fat. Fill and roll the omelette with the sorrel leaves.

SERVES 1 OR 2

Omelette Mexicaine

3 eggs
1 pinch fine salt
pepper
25 g (1 oz) mushroom, sliced
40 g (1½ oz) butter
10 g (⅓ oz) red pepper, chopped
50 g (2 oz) Fondue de Tomate, page 14

Beat the eggs and season. Gently fry the mushroom slices in half the butter and add these to the egg mixture, along with the chopped red pepper. Make the omelette in the usual way (see page 36), using the rest of the butter, and fill and roll with the thick Fondue de Tomate.

SERVES 1 OR 2

Omelette Clamart

3 tablespoons fresh peas
2 shredded lettuce leaves
50 g (2 oz) butter
3 eggs
1 pinch fine salt
pepper

Cook the peas with the shredded lettuce leaves in half the butter. Meanwhile, beat and season the eggs.

Make the omelette in the usual way (see page 36) using the remaining butter, and fill and roll with 2 tablespoons of peas and lettuce. Slit the top of the omelette and arrange the remaining peas and lettuce in this. Serve immediately. *See photograph on page 39.*

SERVES 1 OR 2

Omelette à la Bruxelloise

3 eggs
1 pinch fine salt
15 g (½ oz) butter
50 g (2 oz) braised chicory (Belgian endive), shredded
2 tablespoons double cream

Cream Sauce
4 tablespoons hot Sauce Béchamel, page 12
½ tablespoon double cream
a few drops lemon juice

Beat the eggs, season and make the omelette in the usual way (see page 36). Fill and roll with the braised chicory, shredded and mixed with the cream. Surround the omelette with a *cordon* of hot Cream Sauce, made by mixing together all the ingredients listed.

SERVES 1 OR 2

Omelette Crécy

3 eggs
1 pinch fine salt
pepper
1 small carrot, peeled and finely sliced
50 g (2 oz) butter
1 small pinch sugar

Cream Sauce
4 tablespoons hot Sauce Béchamel, page 12
½ tablespoon double cream
a few drops lemon juice

Beat the eggs and season. Stew the carrot slices very gently until soft in the butter with a little sugar, then pass half of them through a fine sieve.

Make the omelette in the usual way (see page 36) and fill and roll with the carrot purée. Garnish the omelette with the remaining slices of carrot and surround with a *cordon* of hot Cream Sauce, made by mixing together all the ingredients listed.

SERVES 1 OR 2

Omelette aux Fines Herbes

3 eggs
1 pinch fine salt
pepper
1 tablespoon chopped fresh fines herbes: *parsley, chives, chervil and tarragon*
15 g (½ oz) butter

Beat the eggs, season and add the tablespoon of mixed herbs. (It is quite incorrect to consider an omelette made with only one of these herbs – such as parsley – as an *omelette aux fines herbes*. Authenticity requires the combination specified above.)

Heat the butter in the omelette pan and cook the omelette in the usual way (see page 36).

SERVES 1 OR 2

Omelette Bretonne

3 eggs
1 pinch fine salt
pepper
½ tablespoon shredded onion
½ tablespoon shredded white of leek
½ tablespoon very finely sliced mushroom
20 g (¾ oz) butter
knob of butter

Beat the eggs well until the whites and yolks are thoroughly blended, then season. Stew the vegetables in half the butter and add them to the beaten, seasoned eggs. Heat the rest of the butter in an omelette pan until it just begins to turn brown.

Pour in the egg mixture, shake the pan and stir the egg briskly with a fork to ensure even cooking. Cook to taste, then fold the omelette quickly, roll into an oval shape and turn on to a suitable dish. Draw a knob of butter over the omelette's surface to make it glossy.

SERVES 1 OR 2

Omelette Mousseline

3 eggs
1 small pinch fine salt
1 tablespoon double cream
25 g (1 oz) butter

Separate the eggs and stiffly beat the egg whites. In a basin, mix the egg yolks with the salt and cream. Fold in the stiffly beaten egg whites.

Heat the butter in the omelette pan and pour in the egg mixture when very hot. Shake the pan briskly and keep swirling the eggs quickly from the side of the pan to the centre and back again. When the omelette is evenly set, fold it in the usual way and turn it on to a plate to be served immediately.

SERVES 1 OR 2

Omelette Clamart

FISH & SHELLFISH

Gelée de Poisson

1.5 litres (2½ pints) cold Fumet de Poisson, page 9
75 g (3 oz) fillet of whiting, minced
1 egg white
25 g (1 oz) leaf gelatine, soaked and drained
300 ml (½ pint) dry white wine or Champagne

Skim and decant the cold fish stock, discarding any sediment. Place the whiting and egg white in a thick-bottomed pan and add the stock, mixing well with a whisk or spatula. Slowly bring to the boil, stirring very gently and occasionally to ensure that the bottom of the pan is kept clean. Allow to simmer gently for 15 minutes without disturbance, then add the *leaf gelatine* and simmer for a further 5 minutes. Pass through muslin.

Finally, add the wine when the jelly is almost cold. It is advisable, though, to check the consistency of the jelly while simmering following the addition of the gelatine, as the later addition of the wine will dilute the jelly. This can be done by putting a little on a plate and placing it in the refrigerator until chilled. If the gel is insufficient, or is likely to be after the wine is added, a few extra leaves of soaked gelatine may be used.

MAKES APPROXIMATELY 1.5 LITRES (2½ PINTS)

Court-bouillon au Vinaigre

Whole salmon and large cuts of salmon or salmon trout are usually cooked in a prepared vinegar or wine court-bouillon, started from cold. They should be covered and brought slowly to the boil, then allowed almost to finish cooking over a very gentle heat without further boiling (this will take between 10 and 15 minutes for a 750 g (1 lb 10 oz) piece of salmon). Then remove from the heat and cool fully in the court-bouillon.

1 litre (1¾ pints) water
50 ml (2 fl oz) white wine vinegar
10 g (⅓ oz) coarse salt
125 g (4½ oz) carrot, sliced
100 g (4 oz) onion, sliced
1 sprig thyme
½ bay leaf
20 g (¾ oz) chopped fresh parsley
a few peppercorns

Place all the ingredients in a pan except for the peppercorns. Bring to the boil and simmer gently for about 1 hour. Add the peppercorns 10 minutes before the end, then strain. The court-bouillon is now ready for use.

MAKES APPROXIMATELY 1 LITRE (1¾ PINTS)

Court-bouillon au Vin Blanc

1 litre (1¾ pints) water
1 litre (1¾ pints) white wine
225 g (8 oz) onion, peeled and sliced
40 g (1½ oz) parsley stalks
1 sprig thyme
1 small bay leaf
25 g (1 oz) coarse salt
10 g (¼ oz) peppercorns

Place all the ingredients except for the peppercorns in a pan, bring to the boil and simmer gently for 20 minutes. Then add the peppercorns, simmer for a further 10 minutes and strain. The court-bouillon is now ready for use.

MAKES APPROXIMATELY 1.75 LITRES (3 PINTS)

Farce Fine Pour Poissons

500 g (1¼ lb) fish, such as salmon, trout, whiting or sole,
free from skin and bone
½ pinch salt
½ pinch white pepper
2 large egg whites
625 ml (21 fl oz) double cream

Pound the fish with the seasonings, then add the egg whites one at a time. Beat well with a spatula between additions of egg white, then pass through a fine sieve. Alternatively, process in a food processor.

Place the fish purée in a shallow pan or basin, smooth it over with a spatula and refrigerate for at least 2 hours. Then mix in the cream gradually and carefully until it has been completely incorporated. The forcemeat is now ready to use.

MAKES APPROXIMATELY 750 G (1¾ LB)

Carpe à la Juive

1 medium carp, weighing about 1.5 kg (3 lb 6 oz)
125 g (4½ oz) onion, peeled and finely chopped
50 g (2 oz) shallot, peeled and finely chopped
250 ml (8 fl oz) olive oil
50 g (2 oz) flour
500 ml (18 fl oz) dry white wine
500 ml (18 fl oz) Fumet de Poisson, page 9
1 small pinch cayenne pepper
15 g (½ oz) garlic, peeled and crushed
1 bouquet garni
1 tablespoon coarsely chopped fresh parsley

Cut the carp into steaks, on the bone, about 1 cm (½ inch) thick. Fry the chopped onion and shallot very gently in 100 ml (3½ fl oz) of the oil, without allowing them to colour.

Put the fish steaks, onion and shallot in a fish kettle, cover with the lid and place over a moderate heat to start it cooking in its own juices for a few minutes. Sprinkle with the flour and cook for a few more minutes, without allowing the flour to colour. Then add the white wine and the fish stock.

Season with salt and cayenne pepper and add the garlic, bouquet garni and another 100 ml (3½ fl oz) of oil. Bring to the boil, cover and simmer very gently for 25 minutes.

Remove the pieces of fish and arrange them on a long dish in such a way as to give the appearance of a whole fish. Reduce the cooking liquid to one-third of its original volume, and gradually add the remaining oil, away from the heat, so as to thicken the liquid to the consistency of a sauce. Pour this over the carp and allow it to become quite cold and set.

Sprinkle with the coarsely chopped parsley before serving.

SERVES 6

Grenadins de Brochet à l'Oseille

1.25 kg (2½ lb) fillets of pike, skinned and cut into thick slices
100 g (4 oz) gherkin, cut into thin strips 5 cm (2 inches) long
100 g (4 oz) carrot, peeled, cut into thin strips 5 cm (2 inches)
long and blanched
75 g (3 oz) clarified butter
300 ml (½ pint) fish stock, made using the trimmings of the pike
150 ml (¼ pint) Sauce Velouté, made using
fish stock, pages 9–10
150 g (5 oz) butter

Purée d'Oseille
50 g (2 oz) butter
500 g (1¼ lb) sorrel, stalks removed, washed
50 ml (2 fl oz) thick Sauce Béchamel, page 12
2 tablespoons double cream

Remove the bones from the slices of pike carefully, then *lard* the pike with strips of gherkin and carrot, alternating the two colours. Heat the *clarified butter* in a flameproof dish and put the slices of pike in it to set the flesh.

Add the fish stock, cover loosely with a lid and poach in a hot oven (200°C, 400°F, Gas Mark 6) for about 20 minutes, basting from time to time. When the fish is almost cooked, remove the lid so as to allow it to glaze a little. Drain the fish slices and arrange them in a circle on a serving dish to keep warm.

Strain the cooking liquid, allow it to settle and then skim off the fat. Reduce the liquid to about one-third of its original volume. While the cooking liquid is reducing, make the sorrel purée by heating the butter in a pan, adding the sorrel and cooking it until all the moisture has evaporated. Pass through a sieve and reheat in a pan with the Sauce Béchamel and cream; season with salt and pepper.

When the pike cooking liquid is sufficiently reduced, thicken with the Sauce Velouté made from fish stock, enrich with the butter, and pour the sauce on to the serving dish over the fish slices. Serve accompanied by a little puréed sorrel. *See photograph on page 43.*

SERVES 6

Saumon Froid au Beurre de Montpellier

750 g (1 lb 10 oz) poached middle cut of salmon,
on the bone, cold
600 ml (1 pint) Gelée de Poisson, page 40
175 g (6 oz) truffle
4–6 hard-boiled eggs

Beurre de Montpellier
50 g (2 oz) mixed fresh herbs, to include equal quantities of
parsley, chervil, tarragon, chives and watercress
25 g (1 oz) spinach leaves
20 g ($\frac{3}{4}$ oz) shallot, peeled and finely chopped
25 g (1 oz) gherkins
$\frac{1}{2}$ tablespoon capers, drained
$\frac{1}{2}$ clove garlic, peeled and crushed
4 fillets of anchovy
250 g (9 oz) butter
2 hard-boiled egg yolks
1 raw egg yolk
100 ml (3$\frac{1}{2}$ fl oz) olive oil
salt
1 pinch cayenne pepper

First, prepare the Montpellier butter: blanch the herbs and spinach leaves, refresh, drain and squeeze out all the moisture. Blanch the chopped shallot separately, drain and squeeze. Pound the herbs and shallot together finely.

Add the gherkins, capers, garlic and anchovy fillets and pound to a fine paste or process in a food processor. Add the butter and egg yolks, mix together and then add the oil, drop by drop. Pass through a fine strainer and, if necessary, mix together with a whisk until quite smooth. Season with salt and a small pinch of cayenne. Coat the salmon with this butter as described below, then put the remainder in the refrigerator to harden fully.

Remove the skin from the salmon and discard. Arrange the salmon on a flat dish before coating with Montpellier butter and decorating with cut crescents of truffle in graded sizes to simulate the scales of the fish. Coat with fish aspic, then place on a dish, the bottom of which has also been coated with fish aspic.

Surround the fish with halves of hard-boiled eggs, standing up, and with the yolks facing outwards. Garnish the edge of the dish with an assortment of shapes cut from the remaining very firm Montpellier butter.

SERVES 4–6

Darne de Saumon à la Danoise

6 salmon steaks, about 150–185 g (5–6$\frac{1}{2}$ oz) each
salt

Sauce Bâtarde
25 g (1 oz) butter,
25 g (1 oz) flour
600 ml (1 pint) boiling water
1 pinch salt
4 egg yolks
50 ml (2 fl oz) double cream
a few drops lemon juice
200 g (7 oz) butter, softened
75 g (3 oz) anchovy fillets, pounded

Poach the salmon steaks carefully in lightly salted water. Meanwhile, make the Sauce Bâtarde. Melt the butter in a pan and mix in the flour. Add the boiling water, whisking thoroughly, and add a pinch of salt. Mix in a *liaison* consisting of the egg yolks, cream and lemon juice. Reheat gently to thicken and finish, away from the heat, with the softened butter mixed with the pounded anchovy fillets. Strain finely.

Drain the poached salmon steaks and serve with boiled potatoes and the Sauce Bâtarde.

SERVES 6

Mayonnaise de Saumon

1 lettuce
salt
pepper
1 small piece of salmon, about 1.25 kg (2$\frac{1}{2}$ lb), poached in
Court-bouillon au Vinaigre, page 40, and allowed to cool
300 ml ($\frac{1}{2}$ pint) Sauce Mayonnaise, page 13

To garnish
canned anchovy fillets, capers, olives, hard-boiled eggs, radishes

Cover the bottom of a large salad bowl with lightly seasoned shredded lettuce and put the flaked cold salmon on this, taking care to remove all skin and bone. Mound the salmon pieces into a domed shape, then coat with mayonnaise and decorate with strips of anchovy, capers, stoned olives, slices of hard-boiled egg and thin slices of radish.

SERVES 6–8

Grenadins de Brochet à l'Oseille

Truite Saumonée Froide sur Mousse de Tomates

1 salmon trout weighing about 1.5 kg (3 lb 6 oz)
Court-bouillon au Vin Blanc, page 40
600 ml (1 pint) Gelée de Poisson, page 40

Mousse de Tomates
1 tablespoon chopped onion
15 g ($\frac{1}{2}$ oz) butter
100 ml ($3\frac{1}{2}$ fl oz) dry white wine
300 g (11 oz) very red tomato flesh, coarsely chopped
salt
pepper
1 pinch paprika
1 sprig parsley
300 ml ($\frac{1}{2}$ pint) Sauce Velouté, pages 9–10
25 g (1 oz) leaf gelatine, soaked
100 ml ($3\frac{1}{2}$ fl oz) double cream, lightly beaten

To garnish
fresh tarragon leaves
fresh chervil leaves
hard-boiled egg white

Poach the whole trout in Court-bouillon au Vin Blanc for about 15–20 minutes. Allow to cool in the liquid.

Meanwhile, make the tomato mousse. Fry the onion gently in the butter until golden, moisten with the white wine and reduce by half. Add the tomato flesh, seasoning and parsley. Cover and simmer gently for 25 minutes.

Add the Sauce Velouté and *leaf gelatine*. Allow to boil for 2 minutes and pass through a fine strainer. Adjust the seasoning and allow to cool. When almost cold, add the cream. Pour on to a long serving dish, about 5 cm (2 inches) deep, and leave in the refrigerator to set.

Remove the skin from the fish, then carefully lift the two fillets from the central bone. Arrange the fish fillets side by side on the tomato mousse and decorate with leaves of tarragon and chervil and with hard-boiled egg white. If desired, put the head and tail back at each end of the fish.

Coat the whole fish with fish aspic when it is almost at setting point. Allow the jelly to set and present the dish on a bed of crushed ice.

SERVES 6

Saumon à la Meunière

750 g (1 lb 10 oz) salmon fillet, skinned
salt
pepper
flour
100 g (4 oz) clarified butter
$\frac{1}{2}$ lemon
2 tablespoons blanched and coarsely chopped fresh parsley
100 g (4 oz) butter

Cut the salmon into slices about 2 cm ($\frac{3}{4}$ inch) thick. Season them and coat lightly with flour. Fry quickly on both sides in the very hot *clarified butter*.

When the fish is just cooked, transfer it to a hot serving dish. Squeeze the lemon over the fish, season again and sprinkle the surface with the parsley.

Finally, heat the butter quickly in a pan until it turns brown (or *à la noisette*), then immediately coat the salmon pieces with this. Serve while the butter is still sizzling against the moist parsley.

SERVES 4–6

Truites Persillées

6 trout, cleaned
salt
pepper
flour
75 g (3 oz) clarified butter
juice of 1 lemon
2 tablespoons chopped fresh parsley
100 g (4 oz) butter
25 g (1 oz) fine white breadcrumbs

Season the trout and coat lightly with flour. Fry quickly in the very hot *clarified butter*, turning once. When they are just cooked, arrange the trout on a hot serving dish and sprinkle with lemon juice and chopped parsley.

Cook the second quantity of butter until it starts turning a nut brown colour (or *à la noisette*). Then add the very fine white breadcrumbs and cook until they turn a golden brown colour and are frothing well.

Pour the breadcrumb and butter mixture over the trout and serve immediately.

SERVES 6

Truite Saumonée Froide sur Mousse de Tomates

Truites à la Hussarde

100 g (4 oz) onion, peeled and chopped
200 g (7 oz) butter
450 g (1 lb) Farce Fine Pour Poissons, page 41
6 medium trout, boned and gutted from the back
1 large onion, finely sliced
175 ml (6 fl oz) Chablis
1 bouquet garni
25 g (1 oz) flour

To bone and gut a trout from the back, make two deep incisions down each side of the backbone. Cut the backbone at head and tail, and remove the bone, together with the innards. The cavity left can now be used for stuffing the fish.

Fry the chopped onion gently in 25 g (1 oz) of the butter and mix with the prepared forcemeat. Stuff the trout cavity carefully with this mixture.

Fry the finely sliced onion gently in 25 g (1 oz) of the butter without allowing it to brown. Butter an ovenproof dish, using another 25 g (1 oz) of butter, and cover the bottom of the dish with a layer of fried onion.

Arrange the trout on top and add another 75 g (3 oz) of butter, the wine and the bouquet garni. Poach in a moderate oven (180°C, 350°F, Gas Mark 4) without a lid, for about 45 minutes, basting frequently.

When the trout are cooked, arrange them on a dish and pass the cooking liquid and onion through a fine strainer or blend in a food processor. Lightly thicken this with *beurre manié*, made using the rest of the butter and the flour. Coat the fish with this sauce and brown quickly under the grill.

SERVES 6

Maquereaux à la Boulonnaise

6 mackerel, cut into large sections (on the bone)
2 litres (3½ pints) Court-bouillon au Vinaigre, page 40
30 mussels, poached until opened
400 ml (14 fl oz) Sauce au Beurre, page 14

Poach the mackerel sections in the court-bouillon. When they are cooked, drain, remove the skin and arrange on a dish surrounded by the poached mussels.

Coat with Sauce au Beurre, made using some of the strained court-bouillon instead of water.

SERVES 6

Filets de Maquereau Rosalie

12 mackerel fillets
salt
pepper
flour
200 ml (7 fl oz) olive oil
50 g (2 oz) onion, peeled and chopped
25 g (1 oz) shallot, peeled and chopped
100 g (4 oz) mushrooms, chopped
1 clove garlic, peeled and crushed
1 tablespoon white wine vinegar
1 tablespoon chopped fresh parsley

Season and flour the mackerel fillets and shallow fry them in half the oil. Arrange on an oval serving dish to keep warm. Add the rest of the oil to the pan and quickly fry the onion, shallot, mushroom and garlic. Pour over the fish fillets.

Finally, heat the vinegar in the pan, pour this over the fillets as well and sprinkle with the chopped parsley.

SERVES 6

Fritot de Raie

750 g – 1 kg (1½–2 lb) small, young skate wings
1 tablespoon lemon juice
1 tablespoon olive oil
1 medium onion, peeled and thinly sliced into rings
1 pinch chopped fresh thyme
1 bay leaf
4 parsley stalks
salt
pepper
Pâte à Frire, page 26
oil for deep frying
flour
few sprigs of parsley, fried

Cut the skate wings into small slices and marinate for 3 hours in the lemon juice, oil, onion rings, herbs and seasoning.

Dip the pieces of skate into batter and deep fry in hot oil (190°C, 375°F), then flour the onion rings from the marinade and deep fry also. Drain and arrange the skate on a serviette on a dish with fried parsley on one side and the deep-fried onion rings on the other.

SERVES 4

Harengs à la Calaisienne

6 herrings, boned and gutted from the back
12 herring roes
175 g (6 oz) butter
25 g (1 oz) shallot, peeled and chopped
1 tablespoon chopped fresh parsley
50 g (2 oz) mushroom, chopped
salt
pepper
a few drops lemon juice

Open the herrings from the back and remove the backbones (see page 46, top left). Mix the herring roes with all the other ingredients and stuff the fish, in the cavity left by the removal of backbone and innards, with this mixture.

Enclose each fish in a well-oiled baking paper and cook gently in the oven (160°C, 325°F, Gas Mark 3) for about 20–25 minutes.

Serve the herrings on a dish *en papillote* (still wrapped in their individual paper parcels).

SERVES 6

Merlans à la Dieppoise

4 small whiting
120 ml (4 fl oz) dry white wine
120 ml (4 fl oz) mushroom cooking liquor
25 g (1 oz) butter

White Wine Sauce
300 ml (½ pint) Sauce Velouté made with fish
stock, pages 9–10
1 egg yolk
50 g (2 oz) butter

Dieppoise garnish
100 g (4 oz) shelled prawns, cooked
20 mussels, poached until opened

Slit the whiting along their backs so as to facilitate their cooking. Shallow poach them, covered, with the white wine, *mushroom cooking liquor* and butter in a moderate oven (180°C, 350°F, Gas Mark 4), basting from time to time.

Drain well, reserving the cooking liquid for the white wine sauce. Arrange on a dish and keep warm.

Make the sauce by straining and reducing the reserved cooking liquid to 50 ml (2 fl oz) and heating this in a pan with the fish velouté. Add the egg yolk and reduce by one-third. Finish the sauce with the butter.

Surround the fish with the Dieppoise garnish and cover with the White Wine Sauce.

SERVES 4

Bouillabaisse à la Parisienne

150 ml (¼ pint) olive oil
100 g (4 oz) onion, peeled and chopped
40 g (1½ oz) white of leek, chopped
350 ml (12 fl oz) dry white wine
600 ml (1 pint) water
salt
pepper
1 pinch saffron threads
1 bouquet garni
200 g (7 oz) tomato flesh, roughly chopped
2 cloves garlic, crushed
1.5 kg (3 lb 6 oz) fish, to include sole, red mullet, whiting and
crawfish, trimmed and cleaned
1 litre (1¾ pints) mussels, cleaned
10 g (⅓ oz) coarsely chopped fresh parsley
25 g (1 oz) butter
10 g (⅓ oz) flour
French bread, sliced, toasted and lightly rubbed with garlic

Place half the oil in a deep saucepan, then add the chopped onion and leek and cook gently without allowing the vegetables to colour. Add the wine, water, salt, pepper, saffron, bouquet garni, tomato and garlic, bring to the boil and cook gently for 20 minutes.

Cut the fish into large pieces, place them in a clean pan and put the mussels on top. Add the rest of the oil, sprinkle with the parsley and pour on the reserved cooking liquid and its garnish. Bring back to the boil and cook rapidly for 15 minutes. Remove the bouquet garni and, at the last moment, thicken the cooking liquid slightly by stirring in a *beurre manié* made from the butter and flour.

Arrange the fish and shellfish in a deep dish or in individual serving dishes. Place the slices of toasted French bread lightly rubbed with garlic in separate dishes, and ladle some of the cooking liquid over the bread to soak it thoroughly. *See photograph on page 49.*

SERVES 6

Cabillaud à la Portugaise

125 g (4½ oz) onion, peeled and chopped
100 g (4 oz) butter
6 cod steaks, weighing about 250 g (8 oz) each
salt
pepper
100 ml (3½ fl oz) olive oil
1 small clove garlic, peeled and crushed
2 pinches coarsely chopped fresh parsley
750 g (1½ lb) tomatoes, peeled, depipped and roughly chopped
100 g (4 oz) three-quarters-cooked long-grain rice
200 ml (7 fl oz) dry white wine

Lightly fry the chopped onion gently in 25 g (1 oz) of the butter. Arrange the slices of cod in a shallow pan, season and add the olive oil, lightly fried onion, garlic, parsley, tomato flesh, partially cooked rice and white wine.

Cover the pan and cook quickly for 10 minutes, then remove the lid and cook for a further 8 minutes or so to reduce the liquid and to finish cooking the fish.

Arrange the fish on a serving dish. Pour the cooking liquid over the top and cover with the vegetable and rice mixture.

SERVES 6

Sole Bonne Femme

175 g (6 oz) butter
100 g (4 oz) mushrooms, sliced
2 tablespoons finely chopped shallot
2 pinches chopped fresh parsley
4 small Dover sole, trimmed and with black skin removed
200 ml (7 fl oz) dry white wine
200 ml (7 fl oz) thin Sauce Velouté made with fish stock, pages 9–10

Butter an ovenproof dish, using 25 g (1 oz) of the butter, and sprinkle the bottom with the mushrooms, shallot and parsley. Place the fish on top (white side up), and add the equal quantities of wine and thin fish velouté. Cover and poach in a moderately hot oven (200°C, 400°F, Gas Mark 6) for 12–15 minutes, basting from time to time.

When the sole are cooked, drain off the cooking liquid. Reduce it a little and enrich with the remaining butter. Pour the sauce over the sole and brown quickly under a hot grill.

SERVES 4

Sole Deauvillaise

225 g (8 oz) onion, peeled and finely sliced
150 g (5 oz) butter
4 small Dover sole, trimmed and with black skin removed
300 ml (½ pint) double cream

To garnish
small lightly baked diamonds of Feuilletage, page 28

Fry the onion gently, without allowing it to colour, in 25 g (1 oz) of the butter. Butter an ovenproof dish, using another 25 g (1 oz) of the butter, and add the fried onion, the prepared fish (white side up) and the cream and dot with another 25 g (1 oz) butter. Cover, place in a moderately hot oven (200°C, 400°F, Gas Mark 6) and baste from time to time until cooked (about 12–15 minutes). Place the fish on a serving platter and keep warm.

Pass the cream and onion through a fine strainer and enrich the resulting sauce with the remaining butter. Coat the sole with the sauce and garnish with small lightly baked diamonds of puff pastry.

SERVES 4

Sole à la Florentine

150 g (5 oz) butter
4 small Dover sole, trimmed and with black skin removed
300 ml (½ pint) Fumet de Poisson, page 9
225 g (8 oz) spinach, blanched and roughly chopped

To finish
400 ml (14 fl oz) Sauce Mornay, page 13
75 g (3 oz) grated Parmesan

Butter an ovenproof dish, using 25 g (1 oz) of the butter. Shallow poach the sole (white side up), covered, in a moderately hot oven (200°C, 400°F, Gas Mark 6) with the fish stock and another 50 g (2 oz) of the butter, basting from time to time, for about 12–15 minutes.

Meanwhile, stew the blanched spinach in the remaining butter and transfer it to a suitable serving dish. Drain the cooked sole and place them on top of the spinach.

Coat with the Sauce Mornay, sprinkle with grated cheese and gratinate quickly in a hot oven (220°C, 425°F, Gas Mark 7).

SERVES 4

Bouillabaisse à la Parisienne

Sole à la Rochelaise

100 g (4 oz) butter
50 g (2 oz) onion, peeled and finely chopped
4 small Dover sole, trimmed and with black skin removed
200 ml (7 fl oz) red wine
200 ml (7 fl oz) Fumet de Poisson, page 9

To garnish
8 soft herring roes, poached
16 oysters, poached and bearded
16 mussels, poached and bearded
120 ml (4 fl oz) Sauce Demi-glace, page 10

Butter an ovenproof dish, using 25 g (1 oz) of the butter, and fry the onion gently in another 25 g (1 oz) of butter. Shallow poach the sole, covered with the fried onion, wine and fish stock in a moderately hot oven (200°C, 400°F, Gas Mark 6), basting from time to time until cooked (about 12–15 minutes).

Drain the sole, reserving the cooking liquid, and place on a warmed serving dish, surrounded by the poached herring roes, oysters and mussels. Keep warm.

Reduce the cooking liquid by two-thirds and strain. Add the Sauce Demi-glace and another 50 g (2 oz) of butter. Coat the sole with this sauce and serve.

SERVES 4

Sole Jouffroy

100 g (4 oz) butter
4 small Dover sole, trimmed and with black skin removed
300 ml (½ pint) dry white wine
100 g (4 oz) white mushrooms, sliced

White Wine Sauce
300 ml (½ pint) Sauce Velouté made with fish stock, pages 9–10
1 egg yolk
50 g (2 oz) butter

To garnish
8 small vol-au-vent filled with buttered asparagus tips and topped with a slice of truffle

Butter an ovenproof dish, using 25 g (1 oz) of the butter. Shallow poach the sole (white side up), covered, in a moderately hot oven (200°C, 400°F, Gas Mark 6) with the wine and another 50 g (2 oz) of the butter. Baste from time to time until cooked (about 12–15 minutes).

Meanwhile, fry the mushrooms gently in another 25 g (1 oz) of the butter. When the fish is cooked, drain, reserving the cooking liquid for the sauce. Arrange the sole on a suitable dish, surrounded by slices of mushroom, and keep warm.

Make the wine sauce by straining and reducing the cooking liquid to 50 ml (2 fl oz) and heating this in a pan with the fish velouté and egg yolk. Reduce by one-third and finish by enriching with the butter. Cover the prepared fish with the sauce and brown quickly under a hot grill. Garnish with dainty little vol-au-vent filled with buttered asparagus tips and topped with a slice of truffle.

SERVES 4

Sole Murat

4 small Dover sole, trimmed and with black skin removed
salt
pepper
flour
100 g (4 oz) clarified butter

To garnish
100 g (4 oz) potato, peeled and diced
2 raw artichoke bottoms, diced
50 g (2 oz) butter
salt
pepper
flour
2 large tomatoes, thickly sliced into 4 slices each
1 tablespoon oil
a few drops lemon juice
1 tablespoon roughly chopped fresh parsley
100 g (4 oz) butter

Shallow fry the diced potato then the artichoke in the butter. When cooked, drain and mix together. Season the fish, flour and fry in hot *clarified* butter, turning once.

When they are cooked, place the fish on a hot serving dish and surround with the prepared potato and artichoke bottoms. Season, flour and shallow fry the 8 thick slices of tomato in very hot oil and place two slices on each sole.

Sprinkle the sole with a few drops of lemon juice and the parsley, and cover with the butter which has been cooked until it is brown in colour (or *à la noisette*). Serve immediately.

SERVES 4

Sole à la Rochelaise

Sole Meunière aux Raisins

4 small Dover sole, trimmed and with black skin removed
salt
pepper
flour
100 g (4 oz) clarified butter

To garnish
1 lemon
salt
pepper
1 tablespoon blanched and coarsely chopped fresh parsley
100 g (4 oz) butter
100 g (4 oz) Muscatel grapes, peeled, depipped and well chilled

S eason the fish, lightly coat with flour, and fry in very hot clarified butter, turning just once.

When it is cooked, place the fish on a hot serving dish. Squeeze the lemon over it, season with salt and pepper and sprinkle with the blanched and coarsely chopped parsley. Finally, coat with butter which has been cooked until it is brown in colour (or *à la noisette*). Serve immediately so that the hot butter sizzles against the moist parsley. Surround with the peeled, depipped and well-chilled Muscatel grapes.

SERVES 4

Filets de Sole Lady Egmont

75 g (3 oz) butter
8 fillets of Dover sole, approximately 75 g (3 oz) each
200 ml (7 fl oz) Fumet de Poisson, page 9
75 g (3 oz) mushrooms, sliced
a few drops lemon juice
salt
pepper
5 tablespoons double cream
4 tablespoons asparagus tips, freshly cooked and drained

B utter an ovenproof dish, using a third of the butter. Fold the fillets of sole in half top to bottom, with the head end placed over the narrow end, then place them in the dish and shallow poach them in the fish stock, covered, in a moderately hot oven (200°C, 400°F, Gas Mark 6), basting occasionally. Meanwhile, quickly cook the mushrooms with 25 g (1 oz) of the butter, the lemon juice and seasonings. Drain, reserving the liquor.

When the fish is cooked (after about 12–15 minutes), drain and reserve the cooking liquid. Add this to the reserved mushroom cooking liquor and reduce by half. Add the remaining butter, the cream, the cooked mushrooms and the asparagus tips.

Arrange the fish in an oval gratin dish, cover with the sauce and the garnish, and brown quickly under the grill.

SERVES 4

Filets de Sole Nelson

8 fillets of Dover sole, approximately 75 g (3 oz) each
25 g (1 oz) butter
200 ml (7 fl oz) Fumet de Poisson, page 9

White Wine Sauce
300 ml ($\frac{1}{2}$ pint) Sauce Velouté made with fish stock, pages 9–10
1 egg yolk
50 g (2 oz) butter

To garnish
350 g (12 oz) potatoes, cut into balls the size of large hazelnuts, using a spoon cutter
salt
pepper
50 g (2 oz) butter

F old the fillets of sole in half top to bottom, with the head end placed over the narrow end, then place them in a buttered ovenproof dish and add the fish stock. Cover and shallow poach in a moderately hot oven (200°C, 400°F, Gas Mark 6), basting from time to time.

When the fish is cooked (after about 12–15 minutes), drain, reserving the cooking liquid, and arrange the fillets, overlapping in a circle, on a suitable serving dish to keep warm.

Make the sauce by straining and reducing the cooking liquid to 50 ml (2 fl oz). Heat this in a pan with the fish velouté, add the egg yolk and reduce by one-third. Finish the sauce with the butter.

Coat the fish with this sauce and brown quickly under the grill. Fill the centre of the dish with a pile of potato balls, seasoned and fried in butter.

SERVES 4

Filets de Sole à la Bourguignonne

2 onions, peeled and thinly sliced into rings
150 g (5 oz) butter
100 g (4 oz) mushrooms, sliced
8 fillets of Dover sole, approximately 75 g (3 oz) each
freshly ground black pepper
salt
300 ml (½ pint) red wine
15 g (½ oz) flour

Fry the sliced onion gently in 25 g (1 oz) of the butter. Fry the sliced mushrooms, separately, in another 25 g (1 oz) of the butter. Butter an ovenproof dish, using yet another 25 g (1 oz) of butter, and place the fried onion in the dish with the flat fillets of sole on top. Surround the fish with the mushrooms, sprinkle with pepper and a little salt and add the red wine.

Cover and shallow poach the fish in a moderately hot oven (200°C, 400°F, Gas Mark 6) basting from time to time. When the fillets are cooked (after about 12–15 minutes), drain off the cooking liquid and reduce to one third of its original volume. Thicken with *beurre manié*, made using 25 g (1 oz) of butter and 15 g (½ oz) of flour, and finish with the remaining butter. Adjust the seasoning if necessary. Coat the fillets with the sauce and brown quickly under the grill.

SERVES 4

Filets de Sole Véronique

8 fillets of Dover sole, approximately 75 g (3 oz) each
75 g (3 oz) butter
salt
pepper
200 ml (7 fl oz) Fumet de Poisson, page 9

To garnish
100 g (4 oz) Muscatel grapes, peeled, depipped and well chilled

Lightly flatten the fillets of sole and fold them in half top to bottom, with the head end placed over the narrow end. Butter an ovenproof dish, using 25 g (1 oz) of the butter. Place the fillets in it, season and add the fish stock. Cover and shallow poach in a moderately hot oven (200°C, 400°F, Gas Mark 6).

When the fillets are cooked (after about 12–15 minutes), drain them and reserve the cooking liquid. Return them to the dish to keep warm, arranging them in an overlapping circle.

Reduce the reserved cooking liquid to the consistency of a light syrup and add the remaining butter. Pour this sauce over the fish fillets and brown the sauced fillets quickly in a hot oven (220°C, 425°F, Gas Mark 7) or under the grill.

Just before serving, put the peeled, depipped and well-chilled Muscatel grapes in the centre of the dish.

SERVES 4

Filets de Sole aux Champignons

50 g (2 oz) butter
8 fillets of Dover sole, approximately 75 g (3 oz) each
200 ml (7 fl oz) mushroom cooking liquor
16 very white mushrooms

Mushroom Sauce
100 g (4 oz) tiny button mushrooms
75 g (3 oz) butter
300 ml (½ pint) Sauce Demi-glace, page 10

Butter an ovenproof dish, using 25 g (1 oz) of the butter. Fold the fillets in half top to bottom, with the head end placed over the narrow end, and place them in the dish. Shallow poach them, covered, in the *mushroom cooking liquor*, in a moderately hot oven (200°C, 400°F, Gas Mark 6), basting from time to time. Meanwhile, lightly fry the mushrooms in the remaining 25 g (1 oz) of butter.

When the fish is cooked (after about 12–15 minutes), drain and reserve the cooking liquid. Arrange the fillets of fish in a circle on a suitable serving dish and place the lightly fried mushrooms in the centre. Keep warm.

To make the mushroom sauce, place the reserved cooking liquid in a pan and reduce by half. Meanwhile, fry the tiny button mushrooms gently in 25 g (1 oz) of the butter. Add the Sauce Demi-glace to the reduced cooking liquid and allow to simmer gently for a few minutes. Strain, add the remaining 50 g (2 oz) of butter, and finish by adding the tiny fried mushrooms. Pour over the fillets of sole and serve.

SERVES 4

Filets de Sole Verdi

25 g (1 oz) butter
8 fillets of Dover sole, approximately 75 g (3 oz) each
200 ml (7 fl oz) Fumet de Poisson, page 9

To garnish
175 g (6 oz) macaroni
75 ml (3 fl oz) single cream
50 g (2 oz) grated cheese
125 g (4½ oz) cooked lobster, diced
50 g (2 oz) truffle, diced
300 ml (½ pint) Sauce Mornay, page 13

Butter an ovenproof dish and place the fillets of sole flat in it with the fish stock. Cover and shallow poach in a moderately hot oven (200°C, 400°F, Gas Mark 6), basting from time to time. The fish will cook in 12–15 minutes.

Meanwhile boil the macaroni, drain and cut into very short lengths. Mix these with the cream and the grated cheese. Add the diced lobster and truffle. Place the mixture in a serving dish, arrange the cooked, drained fillets of sole on top, and coat with the Sauce Mornay. Brown quickly in a hot oven (220°C, 425°F, Gas Mark 7) or under the grill.

SERVES 4

Paupiettes de Sole Mexicaine

8 fillets of Dover sole, approximately 75 g (3 oz) each
350 g (12 oz) Farce Fine Pour Poissons, page 41
50 g (2 oz) butter
200 ml (7 fl oz) Fumet de Poisson, page 9
8 large cap mushrooms
150 g (5 oz) tomatoes, peeled, depipped and roughly chopped
1 tablespoon tomato purée
1 small red pepper, diced
300 ml (½ pint) Sauce Béchamel, page 12

Flatten the fillets of sole lightly, coat with the fish forcemeat and roll up into *paupiettes*. Butter an ovenproof dish, using half the butter, and place the paupiettes in the dish. Add the fish stock, cover and shallow poach in a moderately hot oven (200°C, 400°F, Gas Mark 6). Baste from time to time.

Meanwhile, grill the mushrooms and stew the tomato flesh in the remaining butter. Place ½ tablespoon of the stewed tomato flesh in each mushroom and arrange on a serving dish.

When the paupiettes are cooked (after about 20 minutes), drain and stand each one in one of the prepared mushrooms. Add the tomato purée and the diced red pepper to the Sauce Béchamel and pour this over the paupiettes.

SERVES 4

Turbotin Dugléré

1 small turbot, weighing about 1.25 kg (2½ lb), cleaned
200 g (7 oz) butter
900 g (1 lb 14 oz) tomatoes, peeled, depipped and roughly chopped
100 g (4 oz) onion, peeled and chopped
25 g (1 oz) shallot, peeled and chopped
1 clove garlic, peeled and crushed
1 tablespoon roughly chopped fresh parsley
salt
pepper
1 sprig thyme
1 bay leaf
200 ml (7 fl oz) dry white wine
150 ml (¼ pint) Sauce Velouté, made from fish stock, pages 9–10
a few drops lemon juice
cayenne pepper

Split the turbot in half lengthways and cut each half into 6 or so pieces (on the bone). Butter a flameproof dish, using 50 g (2 oz) of the butter. Spread half the tomato flesh, onion, shallot, garlic and parsley over the bottom of the dish and put the pieces of fish on top, arranging them to look like the whole fish. Season and add the rest of the tomato flesh, onion, shallot, garlic and parsley. Add the herbs, another 25 g (1 oz) of the butter cut into small pieces, and the wine.

Bring to the boil, cover and place in a moderate oven (180°C, 350°F, Gas Mark 4). When the fish is cooked (this will take about 25–30 minutes), drain off the cooking liquid into a small saucepan and reduce it by half. Add the Sauce Velouté made from fish stock, the remaining butter, a few drops of lemon juice and a touch of cayenne pepper to the reduced cooking liquid.

Pour this sauce over the fish and serve in its cooking dish, or transfer the fish and vegetables to a serving platter, pour on the sauce and serve.

SERVES 6

Paupiettes de Sole Mexicaine

Turbotin à la Saint-Malo

1 small turbot, weighing about 1.25 kg (2½ lb), cleaned
2 tablespoons oil

Sauce Saint-Malo
100 ml (3½ fl oz) Fumet de Poisson, page 9
1 tablespoon finely chopped shallot
2 tablespoons dry white wine
5 egg yolks
500 g (1¼ lb) butter
½ tablespoon made mustard
a few drops anchovy essence

Cut shallow incisions on both sides of the turbot, season and sprinkle with oil. Grill gently.

Meanwhile make the sauce. Place the fish stock in a pan and reduce by half. Cook the shallot briskly in the white wine. Add the egg yolks to the reduced stock and gradually incorporate the butter, a little piece at a time, as if you were making a Sauce Hollandaise (page 13). Add the cooked shallot, the mustard and the anchovy essence.

Pour the sauce over the fish and serve with a border of small freshly boiled potatoes, skinned, cut in thick slices and fried to a golden brown colour in butter.

SERVES 6

Turbotin Fermière

200 g (7 oz) butter
50 g (2 oz) shallot, peeled and sliced
25 g (1 oz) carrot, peeled and cut into round slices
25 g (1 oz) onion, peeled and cut into rings
sprig of thyme
1 bay leaf
parsley stalks
1 small turbot, weighing about 1.25 kg (2½ lb), cleaned
500 ml (18 fl oz) red wine
100 g (4 oz) mushrooms, sliced
15 g (½ oz) flour

Butter an ovenproof dish, using 25 g (1 oz) of the butter and cover with the prepared vegetables and herbs.

Place the turbot on top of these, add the wine and dot with another 25 g (1 oz) of butter, cut in pieces. Cover the dish and poach gently in a moderate oven (180°C, 350°F, Gas Mark 4)

basting frequently as the turbot cooks.

Meanwhile, fry the mushrooms in another 25 g (1 oz) of butter. When the fish is cooked (after about 25–30 minutes), drain it well, reserving the cooking liquid. Place the fish on a dish, surrounded by the mushrooms, to keep warm.

Strain the reserved cooking liquid and reduce by half. Thicken with *beurre manié*, made using 25 g (1 oz) butter and the flour. Finish the sauce by enriching it with the remaining quantity of butter.

Pour this sauce over the fish and mushrooms and brown quickly under the grill.

SERVES 6

Rougets à la Marseillaise

200 ml (7 fl oz) olive oil
100 g (4 oz) onion, peeled and chopped
400 g (14 oz) tomatoes, peeled, quartered and depipped
1 clove garlic, peeled and crushed
1 pinch saffron threads
salt
pepper
400 ml (14 fl oz) Fumet de Poisson, page 9
6 red mullet, weighing at least 125 g (4½ oz) each
1 loaf French bread, sliced and toasted

Heat the oil in a shallow pan and fry the onion gently for a few minutes with the tomatoes, garlic, saffron, salt, pepper and fish stock.

Cut incisions on both sides of the red mullet and arrange them in the pan with all the other prepared ingredients. Cover them and cook quickly over a fairly fierce heat.

When the fish are cooked (this will take about 5–8 minutes), arrange them in a deep dish on slices of toasted French bread. Reduce the cooking liquid a little with the vegetables and flavourings and pour both over the fish.

SERVES 6

Ecrevisses à la Liégeoise

Rougets au Fenouil

6 red mullet, weighing at least 125 g (4½ oz) each
1½ tablespoons lemon juice
3 tablespoons olive oil
salt
pepper
1 tablespoon chopped fresh fennel
1 large pinch chopped fresh parsley

Cut shallow incisions on both sides of the fish and marinate for 3 hours in the lemon juice, oil, seasoning and herbs. Wrap each fish with a little of the marinade in a piece of lightly oiled greaseproof paper and bake in a moderate oven (180°C, 350°F, Gas Mark 4) for about 15–20 minutes, or until cooked.

Serve the mullet *en papillote* (wrapped in their individual paper parcels).

SERVES 6

Rougets Francillon

6 red mullet, weighing at least 125 g (4½ oz) each
1½ tablespoons lemon juice
1½ tablespoons olive oil
salt
pepper
50 g (2 oz) anchovy fillets
150 g (5 oz) butter, softened
6 slices of bread
6 sprigs parsley, fried

Cut shallow incisions on both sides of the fish and marinate for 20 minutes in the lemon juice, oil and seasoning, then remove from the marinade and grill.

Prepare some anchovy-flavoured butter by pounding the anchovy fillets, mixing with 100 g (4 oz) softened butter and passing through a fine sieve. Cut the slices of bread to the shape and size of the fish, fry them in the remaining butter, and spread with the anchovy butter.

Place a red mullet on each of these croûtons, arrange on a dish and garnish with sprigs of fried parsley. Serve accompanied by Pommes de Terre Pailles, page 144, and Sauce Tomate, page 14. The Sauce Tomate can, if you like, be flavoured with some additional anchovy butter: stir this into the sauce immediately before serving.

SERVES 6

Homard à la Newburg

3 cooked lobsters, weighing 600 g (1 lb 6 oz) each
25 g (1 oz) butter
salt
pepper
150 ml (¼ pint) Sercial Madeira
3 egg yolks
salt
pepper
200 ml (7 fl oz) single cream

Split the lobsters down the middle lengthways and discard the intestine, stomach and gills. Remove the flesh from the shell and claws and cut into fairly thick, even slices.

Melt the butter in a pan, add the slices of lobster, season well and heat on both sides to colour slightly. Add the Madeira and reduce almost completely. Remove from the heat.

Beat the egg yolks with the seasoning, add the cream and pour on to the lobster. Gently heat and shake the pan so that the sauce thickens but does not boil. Serve immediately.

SERVES 6

Homard Clarence

3 cooked lobsters, weighing 600 g (1 lb 6 oz) each
a little Fumet de Poisson, page 9
4 tablespoons double cream
300 ml (½ pint) hot Sauce Béchamel, page 12
1 pinch curry powder
225 g (8 oz) boiled long-grain rice
50 g (2 oz) truffle, very thinly sliced

Split the lobsters down the middle lengthways and discard the intestine, stomach and gills. Remove the flesh from the tail and claws and cut into thick slices on the slant. Keep warm in a pan with a little fish stock.

Remove any flesh from the head along with the creamy parts and the coral and finely pound together with the cream. Pass through a fine sieve. Flavour the béchamel with the curry powder and add this to the sauce.

Fill the half shells two-thirds full with boiled rice and cover this with the slices of lobster, alternating with slices of truffle. Coat lightly with the prepared sauce and reheat.

Serve accompanied by the remaining sauce.

SERVES 6

Homard Clarence

Ecrevisses à la Nage

30 live crayfish
cayenne pepper

Court-bouillon
50 g (2 oz) carrot, peeled and thinly sliced
25 g (1 oz) shallot, peeled and finely sliced
a few parsley stalks
1 pinch chopped fresh thyme
1 bay leaf
300 ml ($\frac{1}{2}$ pint) dry white wine
200 ml (7 fl oz) Fumet de Poisson, page 9
1 pinch salt

P lace all the ingredients for the court-bouillon in a pan, bring to the boil and simmer until all the vegetables are cooked.
While the court-bouillon is simmering, prepare the crayfish. Kill them by piercing the top of the head with a trussing needle behind the beak, on a level with the back of the eyes. Immediately gut them by giving the central flippers a half-twist and pulling gently. This will remove the intestinal tract, which will come out as a fine string. (If this is not done the flesh of the cooked crayfish is inclined to be bitter.) Wash them well, then add the crayfish to the simmering court-bouillon. Cover and simmer gently for 10 minutes, occasionally turning them over. Season with a little cayenne pepper and place the crayfish in a deep serving dish, 'swimming' in the court-bouillon.

SERVES 6–8

Ecrevisses à la Liégeoise

30 live crayfish
court-bouillon as described for Ecrevisses à la Nage, above
100 g (4 oz) butter
1 tablespoon roughly chopped fresh parsley

P repare the crayfish as described in the recipe for Ecrevisses à la Nage, above. Immediately cook the crayfish in the court-bouillon. As soon as they are cooked (see above), remove the crayfish and place in a serving dish to keep warm.
Strain the court-bouillon and reduce it to a quarter of its original volume. Shake in the butter to thicken, pour over the crayfish and sprinkle with the chopped fresh parsley. *See photograph on page 57.*

SERVES 6–8

Moules à la Marinière

300 ml ($\frac{1}{2}$ pint) water
1 medium onion, peeled and sliced
a few parsley stalks
3.4 litres (6 pints) mussels, cleaned
200 ml (7 fl oz) dry white wine
2 heaped tablespoons chopped shallot
200 ml (7 fl oz) Sauce Velouté made with fish stock, pages 9–10
100 g (4 oz) butter
a few drops lemon juice
2 tablespoons chopped fresh parsley

H eat the water in a deep pan with the onion and parsley stalks, bring to the boil and simmer for about 10 minutes. Add the mussels and cook over a high heat, shaking often, until the shells open. Drain them, reserving the cooking liquid, and remove one of the shells from each mussel.
Heat the white wine with the shallot and reduce to one third of its original volume. Add the reserved cooking liquid, the fish-based Sauce Velouté and the butter.
Place the mussels in the sauce and mix gently. Add the lemon juice, place in a deep serving dish and sprinkle with parsley.

SERVES 4

Coquilles Saint-Jacques au Gratin

8 large scallops
300 ml ($\frac{1}{2}$ pint) Court-bouillon au Vin Blanc, page 40
300 ml ($\frac{1}{2}$ pint) Sauce Duxelles, page 12
2 tablespoons dry white wine
50 g (2 oz) mushroom, sliced
2 tablespoons dry white breadcrumbs
50 g (2 oz) melted butter

I f you have bought scallops on the shell, remove the scallops, scrub the four best shells and dry them. (Scallop shells can also be purchased separately.) Poach the scallops for 8–10 minutes in the court-bouillon. When cooked, cut the white and the coral into thick slices.
Coat the bottom of each of the shells with Sauce Duxelles and $\frac{1}{4}$ tablespoon of wine. Place the slices of scallop on top, surround with the slices of raw mushroom and cover with more Sauce Duxelles. Sprinkle with the breadcrumbs and butter and gratinate in a moderately hot oven (200°C, 425°F, Gas Mark 6).

SERVES 4

Coquilles Saint-Jacques au Gratin

MEAT DISHES

Filet de Boeuf à la Berrichonne

1.5 kg (3 lb 6 oz) fillet of beef, trimmed
100 g (4 oz) larding bacon, cut into thin strips approximately
7 cm (3 inches) long
Fonds Brun, page 8
beurre manié

To garnish
braised cabbage cooked with whole rashers of streaky bacon
small glazed onions
large braised chestnuts

*L*ard the fillet with the *larding bacon* and roast it, preferably keeping it slightly rare and pink in the middle: 40 minutes in a hot oven (230°C, 450°F, Gas Mark 8) should be enough.

Place the cooked fillet on a long serving dish and surround it with small mounds of braised cabbage, the whole rashers of bacon (cooked with the cabbage), small glazed onions and large braised chestnuts.

Make a lightly thickened gravy by adding a small quantity of Fonds Brun to the juices from the roasting pan, thickening with *beurre manié* and simmering for a minute or two. Serve the sauce separately.

SERVES 6

Filet de Boeuf Saint-Germain

1.5 kg (3 lb 6 oz) fillet of beef, trimmed
100 g (4 oz) larding bacon, cut into thin strips approximately
7 cm (3 inches) long

To garnish
Purée de Pois Frais, page 119, made very thick
Carottes Glacées, page 126
Pommes de Terre Fondantes (see below)
Sauce Béarnaise, page 13

*L*ard the fillet with the *larding bacon* and roast it, preferably keeping it slightly rare and pink in the middle: 40 minutes in a hot oven (230°C, 450°F, Gas Mark 8) should be enough.

Place the cooked fillet on a long serving dish and surround with the Purée de Pois Frais, made very thick and moulded into small *timbales*, the glazed carrots and the Pommes de Terre Fondantes. These are potatoes cut to the shape of large elongated olives, about 75 g (3 oz) in weight each, that are then fried slowly in butter and turned frequently until they are soft. Finally they are flattened slightly with a fork without being broken. Drain off the fat, replace with fresh butter, cover and leave on the side of the hob until the potatoes have absorbed all the butter. Serve with Sauce Béarnaise.

SERVES 6

Filet de Boeuf Saint-Germain

Filet de Boeuf Macédoine

1.5 kg (3 lb 6 oz) fillet of beef, trimmed
100 g (4 oz) larding bacon, cut into thin strips approximately
7 cm (3 inches) long

To garnish
a macédoine of mixed vegetables
Pommes de Terre Château (see below)

Lard the fillet with the *larding bacon* and roast it, preferably keeping it slightly rare and pink in the middle: 40 minutes in a hot oven (230°C, 450°F, Gas Mark 8) should be enough.

Place the cooked fillet on a long serving dish and surround with the *macédoine* of vegetables and the Pommes de Terre Château. These are potatoes trimmed to a smaller olive shape than that of the Pommes de Terre Fondantes of the previous recipe, seasoned, cooked slowly in *clarified butter* until soft and golden brown, and sprinkled with parsley. Serve with an unthickened gravy made from the cooking juices.

SERVES 6

Filet de Boeuf à la Provençale

1.5 kg (3 lb 6 oz) fillet of beef, trimmed
100 g (4 oz) larding bacon, cut into thin strips approximately
7 cm (3 inches) long
50 g (2 oz) melted butter

To garnish
Tomates Farcies à la Provençale, page 147
Champignons Farcis, page 130
Sauce Provençale, page 14

Lard the fillet with the *larding bacon*. Put it in a deep ovenproof casserole, season and cover it with the melted butter. Cover with a lid and *poêlé* in a hot oven (230°C, 450°F, Gas Mark 8), basting frequently with the butter. To ensure that the fillet is kept slightly rare and pink in the middle, cook for about 50 minutes.

When the meat is nearly cooked, remove the lid and allow it to brown. Then place the meat on a long serving dish and surround with the stuffed tomatoes, arranged alternately with the stuffed mushrooms. Serve with Sauce Provençale.

SERVES 6

Filet de Boeuf Montmorency

1.5 kg (3 lb 6 oz) fillet of beef, trimmed
100 g (4 oz) larding bacon, cut into thin strips approximately
7 cm (3 inches) long
salt
pepper
50 g (2 oz) melted butter

Matignon
50 g (2 oz) carrot, peeled and diced
50 g (2 oz) onion, peeled and diced
25 g (1 oz) celery, diced
50 g (2 oz) streaky bacon, rinded and diced
25 g (1 oz) butter
1 bay leaf
1 sprig thyme
2 tablespoons dry white wine

To finish
300 ml ($\frac{1}{2}$ pint) Fonds Brun, page 8
2 tablespoons Sercial Madeira

To garnish
6 cooked artichoke bottoms, filled with a macédoine of
mixed vegetables
asparagus tips

Lard the fillet with the *larding bacon*. Then prepare the *matignon*: fry the vegetables and bacon gently in the butter and add the herbs. Add the wine and reduce until almost dry.

Place a layer of matignon in a deep heavy ovenproof casserole, just large enough to hold the meat. Put the meat on top of the matignon, season well and coat with melted butter.

Cover with a lid and *poêlé* in a hot oven (230°C, 450°F, Gas Mark 8), basting frequently with the butter. To ensure that the fillet is kept slightly rare and pink in the middle, cook for about 50 minutes. When the meat is nearly cooked, remove the lid and allow it to brown. Place it on a long serving dish, cover and keep warm.

Add the stock to the vegetables, which should not have been allowed to burn. Bring to the boil and simmer for 10 minutes. Strain, remove the fat and reduce by two-thirds. Finally, flavour with Madeira and do not allow to reboil.

Surround the meat with artichoke bottoms filled with a *macédoine* of mixed vegetables arranged alternately with *bouquets* of asparagus tips.

Serve the sauce separately.

SERVES 6

Filet de Boeuf au Madère et aux Champignons

1.5 kg (3 lb 6 oz) fillet of beef, trimmed
100 g (4 oz) larding bacon cut into thin strips approximately
7 cm (3 inches) long
salt
pepper
50 g (2 oz) melted butter

Matignon
50 g (2 oz) carrot, peeled and diced
50 g (2 oz) onion, peeled and diced
25 g (1 oz) celery, diced
50 g (2 oz) streaky bacon, rinded and diced
1 bay leaf
1 sprig thyme
25 g (1 oz) butter
2 tablespoons dry white wine
300 ml (½ pint) Fonds Brun, page 8

Mushroom sauce
100 g (4 oz) tiny button mushrooms
25 g (1 oz) butter
300 ml (½ pint) Sauce Demi-glace, page 10
2 tablespoons Sercial Madeira

To garnish
100 g (4 oz) large mushrooms, fried in butter

Lard the fillet with the *larding bacon*. Then prepare the *matignon*: fry the vegetables gently in a pan for a few minutes with the bacon, herbs and butter. Add the white wine and reduce until almost dry.

Place a layer of matignon in a deep heavy ovenproof casserole just large enough to hold the meat. Put the meat on top of the matignon, season well and coat with melted butter.

Cover with a lid and *poêlé* in a hot oven (230°C, 450°F, Gas Mark 8), basting frequently with the butter. To ensure that the fillet is kept slightly rare and pink in the middle, cook for about 50 minutes. When the meat is nearly cooked, remove the lid and allow it to brown. Place it on a long dish, cover and keep warm.

Meanwhile, add the stock to the matignon vegetables, which should not have been allowed to burn. Bring to the boil and simmer for 10 minutes. Strain, remove the fat, then reduce the liquid by two-thirds.

Prepare the mushroom sauce by first frying the button mushrooms gently in the butter. Remove the mushrooms, reduce the mushroom cooking juices, then add the Sauce Demi-

glace and the reduced juices from the matignon to the reduced mushroom cooking juices and allow all to simmer gently together for a few minutes. Add the Madeira and finish by replacing the fried button mushrooms.

Serve the fillet accompanied by this sauce and garnished with large mushrooms fried gently in butter.

SERVES 6

TOURNEDOS

These are small steaks cut from the thinner middle part of the fillet of beef. They are best when cut approximately 3–4 cm (1¼–1½ inches) thick, and they weigh about 100–125 g (4–4½ oz) each when prepared. They should be trimmed of all fat and membrane and the gristly part on one side should be removed. A nice round shape is an essential part of the appearance of the tournedos and this is best achieved by tying round each one with thin string. This helps the meat to keep its shape while cooking.

Tournedos Bréhan

4 tournedos, about 4 cm (1½ inches) thick and weighing
125 g (4½ oz) each
salt
pepper
125 g (4½ oz) butter
4 artichoke bottoms, fried in butter to a golden brown
8 tablespoons puréed broad beans, heated and mixed with
a little butter and cream
3 tablespoons Sercial Madeira
100 ml (3½ fl oz) Fonds Brun, page 8
8 florets cauliflower, boiled and buttered
8 small potatoes, boiled, buttered and sprinkled with
chopped fresh parsley

Season the tournedos, then shallow fry in 50 g (2 oz) of the butter for 3–4 minutes on each side if liked rare, 4–5 minutes medium rare, 6–8 minutes for well done. Place on a dish and on top of each tournedos place an artichoke bottom filled with the purée of broad beans. Keep warm.

Pour off the fat from the pan and deglaze with the Madeira and stock. Reduce until slightly syrupy then blend in the remaining butter.

Arrange the prepared cauliflower and potatoes around the tournedos. Strain the sauce and serve separately.

SERVES 4

Tournedos Favorite

4 tournedos, about 4 cm (1½ inches) thick and weighing
125 g (4½ oz) each
salt
pepper
125 g (4½ oz) butter
3 tablespoons Sercial Madeira
100 ml (3½ fl oz) Jus de Veau Lié, page 9

To garnish
4 slices bread, cut into rounds with a plain pastry cutter
50 g (2 oz) clarified butter
4 slices foie gras
salt
pepper
flour
25 g (1 oz) butter
4 slices truffle
buttered asparagus tips
Pommes de Terre Noisettes (see below)

Season the tournedos and shallow fry in 50 g (2 oz) butter (see page 65 for timing instructions). Keep warm. Pour off the fat from the pan and deglaze with the Madeira and Jus de Veau Lié, then blend in the rest of the butter.

Arrange each tournedos on a round croûton of bread, fried in *clarified butter*. Season, flour and lightly fry the slices of foie gras in the butter and place these on the tournedos, with a slice of truffle on top. Strain the sauce and serve separately.

Serve with buttered asparagus tips and Pommes de Terre Noisettes. These are made by cutting out balls of potato the size of large hazelnuts using a spoon cutter. They are then seasoned and fried in butter until they are soft inside and golden brown on the outside.

SERVES 4

Tournedos aux Champignons

4 tournedos, about 4 cm (1½ inches) thick and weighing
125 g (4½ oz) each
salt
pepper
75 g (3 oz) butter
200 g (7 oz) small mushrooms
50 ml (2 fl oz) mushroom cooking liquid
100 ml (3½ fl oz) Sauce Demi-glace, page 10

Season the tournedos and shallow fry in 50 g (2 oz) of the butter (see page 65 for timing instructions). Fry the mushrooms separately in the remaining butter. Arrange the tournedos in a circle and put the mushrooms in the centre, placing a handsome mushroom on each steak.

Deglaze the pan with the *mushroom cooking liquid*, add the Sauce Demi-glace and strain. Pour the sauce over the mushrooms in the centre of the dish.

SERVES 4

Tournedos à la Catalane

50 g (2 oz) onion, peeled and finely chopped
1 small red pepper, skinned, deseeded, and cut into short julienne
1 tablespoon oil
225 g (8 oz) tomatoes, peeled, depipped and roughly chopped
1 pinch chopped fresh parsley
4 tournedos, about 4 cm (1½ inches) thick and weighing
125 g (4½ oz) each
salt
pepper
50 g (2 oz) butter
3 tablespoons dry white wine
200 ml (7 fl oz) thin Sauce Tomate, page 14

Fry the onion with the pepper gently in the oil and add the prepared tomato. Simmer until the mixture is fairly stiff and finish with the parsley.

Season the tournedos and shallow fry in the butter (see page 65 for timing instructions). Pour off the fat from the pan, deglaze with the wine and sauce, strain, and surround the tournedos with this sauce.

Place a little of the hot tomato, pepper and parsley mixture in the centre of each tournedos.

SERVES 4

Tournedos à la Catalane

Tournedos Castillane

4 tournedos, about 4 cm (1½ inches) thick and weighing
125 g (4½ oz) each
salt
pepper
125 g (4½ oz) butter
3 tablespoons dry white wine
100 ml (3½ fl oz) Fonds Brun, page 8

To garnish
4 slices bread, cut into rounds about the same size as the
tournedos with a plain pastry cutter
50 g (2 oz) clarified butter
deep fried onion rings
4 small tartlet cases filled with Fondue de Tomate, page 14

Season the tournedos and shallow fry in 50 g (2 oz) of the butter (see page 65 for timing instructions). Keep warm. Pour off the fat from the pan and deglaze with the wine and stock. Reduce until slightly syrupy then blend in the remaining butter; strain and serve this sauce separately.

Arrange each tournedos on a round croûton of bread fried in *clarified butter*. Surround with deep fried onion rings and serve with a small tartlet case filled with Fondue de Tomate.

SERVES 4

Tournedos à la Sarde

4 tournedos, about 4 cm (1½ inches) thick and weighing
125 g (4½ oz) each
salt
pepper
50 g (2 oz) butter

To garnish
Tomates Farcies à la Provençale, page 147
Concombres Farcies, page 136
Croquettes de Riz Safrané, page 145
thin Sauce Tomate, page 14

Season the tournedos and shallow fry in the butter (see page 65 for timing instructions). Arrange on a round dish, surrounded by stuffed tomatoes and cucumbers. Fill the centre with croquettes of rice and serve with thin tomato sauce.

SERVES 4

Tournedos à la Provençale

4 tournedos, about 4 cm (1½ inches) thick and weighing
125 g (4½ oz) each
salt
pepper
25 g (1 oz) butter
1 tablespoon olive oil

To garnish
4 slices bread, cut into rounds with a plain pastry cutter
50 g (2 oz) clarified butter
Tomates Farcies à la Provençale, page 147
Champignons Farcis, page 130
Sauce Provençale, page 14

Season the tournedos and shallow fry in a mixture of butter and oil (see page 65 for timing instructions).

Fry the slices of bread in the *clarified butter*, place a tournedos on top of each slice, and arrange them neatly on a dish. Place a stuffed half tomato on each tournedos and surround with stuffed mushrooms.

Serve the Sauce Provençale separately.

SERVES 4

Tournedos à l'Estragon

1 small bunch of tarragon
50 ml (2 fl oz) Fonds Brun, page 8
4 tournedos, about 4 cm (1½ inches) thick and weighing
125 g (4½ oz) each
salt
pepper
50 g (2 oz) butter
12 blanched fresh tarragon leaves
150 ml (¼ pint) Jus de Veau Lié, page 9

Infuse the bunch of tarragon in the stock for 5 minutes, then strain and reduce by half.

Season the tournedos and shallow fry in the butter (see page 65 for timing instructions). Place three leaves of tarragon on each tournedos. Keep warm.

Pour off the fat from the pan and deglaze with the Jus de Veau Lié. Add the reduced and flavoured stock, then strain and serve separately.

SERVES 4

Tournedos Roumanille

4 small tournedos, about 3 cm (1¼ inches) thick and weighing
100 g (4 oz) each
salt
pepper
2 tablespoons olive oil
2 large tomatoes, cut in half and grilled
300 ml (½ pint) Sauce Mornay, page 13
1 tablespoon tomato purée

To garnish
4 large black olives, stoned
4 anchovy fillets
1 large aubergine, sliced and fried

Season the tournedos and shallow fry in the oil (see page 65 for timing instructions: deduct ½ minute from each, as small tournedos are used). Grill the tomatoes and place each tournedos on half a grilled tomato. Colour the Sauce Mornay with the tomato purée, coat the prepared tournedos with this sauce, and brown quickly in a hot oven (220°C, 425°F, Gas Mark 7) or under the grill.

Arrange the prepared tournedos on a dish. Put a large olive wrapped in an anchovy fillet on each one, and surround with crisply fried slices of aubergine.

S<small>ERVES</small> 4

Tournedos Cendrillon

25 g (1 oz) truffle, chopped
4 large artichoke bottoms, cooked
4 tournedos, about 4 cm (1½ inches) thick and weighing
125 g (4½ oz) each
salt
pepper
125 g (4½ oz) butter
100 ml (3½ fl oz) Fonds Brun, page 8

Purée Soubise
225 g (8 oz) onion, peeled and sliced
65 g (2½ oz) butter
100 ml (3½ fl oz) thick Sauce Béchamel, page 12
salt
pepper
1 pinch caster sugar
50 ml (2 fl oz) cream

First prepare the onion purée. Blanch the sliced onions and drain thoroughly. Stew in 25 g (1 oz) of the butter, without colouring them, and add the Sauce Béchamel, salt, pepper and sugar. Cover, place in a moderate oven (160°C, 325°F, Gas Mark 3) and cook gently for about 30 minutes. When the onions are cooked, pass through a fine sieve, reheat and add the remaining butter and the cream.

Mix the onion purée with the chopped truffle. Fill the artichoke bottoms with this mixture and brown them quickly in a hot oven or under the grill.

Season the tournedos and shallow fry in 50 g (2 oz) of the butter (see page 65 for timing instructions). Place each one on one of the artichoke bottoms and arrange on a serving dish.

Pour off the fat from the pan and deglaze with the stock, reduce until slightly syrupy and blend in the remaining butter. Strain and serve separately.

S<small>ERVES</small> 4

Entrecôte Mirabeau

4 sirloin steaks, weighing about 200 g (7 oz) each
salt
pepper
25 g (1 oz) clarified butter
100 g (4 oz) anchovy fillets
125 g (4½ oz) butter, softened
100 g (4 oz) black olives, stoned
1 tablespoon fresh tarragon leaves, blanched

Season the steaks, brush with *clarified butter* and grill for 2–3 minutes on each side if liked rare, 4 minutes medium rare, 5–6 minutes for well-done. Meanwhile prepare an anchovy butter by pounding half the anchovy fillets to a paste, mixing with the butter and passing through a fine sieve. Arrange the cooked steaks on a serving dish.

Garnish the steaks with the remaining anchovy fillets, arranged trellis fashion, the black olives and the tarragon. Serve accompanied by the anchovy-flavoured butter.

S<small>ERVES</small> 4

Entrecôte à la Forestière

4 sirloin steaks, weighing about 200 g (7 oz) each
salt
pepper
100 g (4 oz) butter
125 g (4½ oz) mushrooms, preferably morels
125 g (4½ oz) potatoes, cut into large dice
4 slices lean bacon, rinded and well trimmed
1 tablespoon chopped fresh parsley
2 tablespoons dry white wine
50 ml (2 fl oz) Fonds Brun, page 8

Season the steaks, then shallow fry in 50 g (2 oz) of the butter for 2–3 minutes on each side if liked rare, 4 minutes medium rare, 5–6 minutes for well done. Arrange them on a serving dish to keep warm.

At the same time, fry the mushrooms and the potatoes separately in another 25 g (1 oz) of butter each. Grill the bacon. Arrange the vegetables and bacon around the steaks and sprinkle with the parsley.

Deglaze the pan with the wine and the stock, pass through a fine strainer and serve the sauce separately.

SERVES 4

Entrecôte à la Lyonnaise

4 sirloin steaks, weighing about 200 g (7 oz) each
salt
pepper
125 g (4½ oz) butter
200 g (7 oz) onion, peeled and finely sliced
½ tablespoon Glace de Viande, page 9
1 tablespoon chopped fresh parsley
100 ml (3½ fl oz) dry white wine
a few drops white wine vinegar
50 ml (2 fl oz) Sauce Demi-glace, page 10

Season the steaks and shallow fry in half the butter (see left for timing instructions). Arrange them on a serving dish to keep warm.

At the same time, fry the onion separately in another 25 g (1 oz) of the butter. Add the meat glaze and sprinkle with the parsley. Arrange the onion along the sides of the steaks.

Deglaze the pan in which the steak was cooked with the white wine and vinegar. Reduce by two-thirds and add the Sauce Demi-glace. Pass through a fine strainer, shake in the remaining butter, and pour over the garnished steaks.

SERVES 4

Entrecôte à la Hongroise

4 sirloin steaks, weighing about 200 g (7 oz) each
75 g (3 oz) butter
100 g (4 oz) streaky bacon, rinded, diced and blanched
100 g (4 oz) onion, peeled and chopped
1 pinch paprika
100 ml (3½ fl oz) dry white wine
50 ml (2 fl oz) Sauce Velouté made with Fonds Blanc de Volaille, pages 9–10

Season and shallow fry the sirloin steaks in 50 g (2 oz) of the butter (see above for timing instructions). Arrange them on a serving dish to keep warm.

At the same time, fry the bacon separately in another 25 g (1 oz) of butter. Add the onion and fry together until well coloured. Then add the paprika and wine and reduce by two-thirds. Add the Sauce Velouté and cook gently for 7–8 minutes.

Arrange the cooked steaks on a serving dish, cover with the prepared sauce and surround with small boiled potatoes.

SERVES 4

Entrecôte Tyrolienne

4 sirloin steaks, weighing about 200 g (7 oz) each
salt
pepper
25 g (1 oz) clarified butter
200 g (7 oz) onion, peeled and finely sliced
25 g (1 oz) butter
100 ml (3½ fl oz) Sauce Poivrade, page 10

To garnish
Fondue de Tomate, page 14

Season the steaks, brush with *clarified butter* and grill (see page 69 for timing instructions). Meanwhile, fry the onion in the butter and add the Sauce Poivrade. Pour this mixture over the steaks when ready, then surround the steaks with a *cordon* of Fondue de Tomate.

SERVES 4

Entrecôte à la Forestière

Paupiettes de Boeuf Fontanges

1 kg (2 lb) sirloin steak in one piece
8 thin slices salt pork fat
25 g (1 oz) butter
1 large onion, peeled and sliced
1 large carrot, peeled and sliced
400 ml (14 fl oz) Fonds Brun, page 8
1 bouquet garni
1 teaspoon arrowroot

Pork forcemeat
150 g (5 oz) lean pork, chopped
150 g (5 oz) pork fat, chopped
1 pinch fine salt
ground white pepper
1 pinch mixed spice
1 tablespoon chopped fresh parsley
1 tablespoon brandy
1 egg white

To garnish
8 Croquettes de Pommes de Terre, page 140
purée of white haricot beans

Wipe the steak and cut off any excess fat. Cut the meat into 8 slices, each weighing about 100 g (4 oz), and flatten each to a rectangle about 10 cm (4 inches) long by 5 cm (2 inches) wide. Season the beef slices on one side.

The forcemeat should be prepared next. Pound together the chopped lean pork and the pork fat, then season with salt, pepper, mixed spice and parsley. Moisten with the brandy and add enough egg white to bind the mixture.

Spread the beef slices with the forcemeat on the seasoned side and roll up. Wrap each paupiette in a slice of salt pork fat, and tie with fine string to keep it in shape.

Fry the paupiettes in a flameproof casserole in the butter until the pork fat is lightly browned, then remove and fry the onion and the carrot in the same fat until just beginning to brown. Place the paupiettes on top of the vegetables and add enough stock to come halfway up the paupiettes. Add the bouquet garni and cover with a tight-fitting lid. Braise in a moderate oven (180°C, 350°F, Gas Mark 4) for approximately 1½ hours, or until cooked. Twenty minutes before the end of the cooking time, remove the lid and take away the strings and the pork fat slices. Baste frequently with the braising liquid from this point onwards, so as to glaze the surface of the paupiettes.

Place the paupiettes in a circle on a warmed serving dish. To make the sauce, pass the braising liquid through a fine strainer. Dilute the arrowroot with a little cold water, and use this to thicken the sauce. Place a Croquette de Pommes de Terre on top of each paupiette, fill the centre of the dish with a purée of white haricot beans and surround all with the sauce.

SERVES 8

Goulash à la Hongroise

125 g (4½ oz) lard or olive oil
1.25 kg (2½ lb) chuck steak, cut into 100 g (4 oz) cubes
200 g (7 oz) onion, peeled and cut into large dice
salt
1 teaspoon paprika
500 g (1¼ lb) tomatoes, peeled, depipped and quartered
300 ml (½ pint) water
500 g (1¼ lb) small potatoes, peeled and quartered

Heat the lard or oil in a flameproof casserole and fry the beef and onion over a moderate heat until the onion has become lightly coloured. Season with salt and paprika and continue to cook for a few more minutes. Add the tomatoes and 100 ml (3½ fl oz) of the water. Cover with a lid and cook gently for 1½ hours in a moderate oven (160°C, 325°F, Gas Mark 3), stirring from time to time.

Then add the quartered potatoes and the remaining water. Continue cooking in the same oven without a lid, basting frequently, until the meat and potatoes are tender.

SERVES 6

Beefsteak à la Hambourgeoise

750 g (1½ lb) fillet steak, trimmed
4 egg yolks
75 g (3 oz) onion, peeled and chopped
25 g (1 oz) butter
salt
pepper
grated nutmeg
flour
clarified butter for frying

To garnish
150 g (5 oz) onion, peeled and finely sliced
25 g (1 oz) butter

hop the fillet steak finely and mix in the egg yolks. Cook the chopped onion without colouring it in the butter, add to the meat and season with the salt, pepper and a little grated nutmeg.

Mould into round, flat cakes using a little flour, and fry on both sides in the *clarified butter*. They are cooked when little beads of blood appear on the surface. Meanwhile, fry the onion for the garnish to a golden brown in the butter.

Arrange the steaks on a serving dish and place the fried onion on top.

SERVES 4

Carbonnades de Boeuf à la Flamande

1.25 kg (2½ lb) chuck steak or topside, cut into small
thinnish slices
salt
pepper
2 tablespoons olive oil
600 g (1 lb 6 oz) onion, peeled and finely sliced
50 g (2 oz) butter
1 bouquet garni
2 tablespoons plain flour
800 ml (1¼ pints) brown ale or stout
800 ml (1¼ pints) Fonds Brun, page 8
50 g (2 oz) brown sugar

eason the beef and fry quickly on both sides in the oil. At the same time, shallow fry the onions in the butter.

Put the beef and onions in alternate layers in a shallow ovenproof casserole and add the bouquet garni. Stir the flour into the saucepan in which the beef was fried and brown lightly. Gradually add the beer and stock, stirring continuously until the mixture thickens. Add the sugar and bring to the boil, still stirring. Strain the sauce over the beef and onions, cover with a lid and cook gently in a moderate oven (160°C, 325°F, Gas Mark 3) for 2½–3 hours, or until the beef is tender.

SERVES 6

Estouffade de Boeuf à la Provençale

1.5 kg (3 lb) stewing steak (chuck, blade or shin)
225 g (8 oz) lean salt belly of pork, diced
100 g (4 oz) butter
225 g (8 oz) onions, peeled and quartered
salt
pepper
50 g (2 oz) flour
1 clove garlic, peeled and crushed
1 litre (1¾ pints) dry white wine
1 litre (1¾ pints) Fonds Brun, page 8
450 g (1 lb) tomatoes, crushed
1 bouquet garni
225 g (8 oz) button mushrooms
225 g (8 oz) black olives, stoned

ipe the meat and trim off any excess fat. Cut the meat into cubes, each weighing approximately 100 g (4 oz). Fry the diced salt belly of pork in a large flameproof casserole in 65 g (2½ oz) of the butter until brown, then remove and put it to one side. Place the quartered onions and the beef in the same pan, season with salt and pepper, and fry until brown on all sides. Drain off any surplus fat.

Replace the pork, sprinkle with the flour, add the crushed garlic, and continue to cook for a few minutes longer. Add the white wine and brown stock and stir well. Then add the tomatoes and bouquet garni, bring to the boil, cover and cook in a moderate oven (180°C, 350°F, Gas Mark 4) for 2½–3 hours, or until the beef is tender. Meanwhile, fry the button mushrooms very gently in the remaining butter.

Remove the casserole from the oven when the meat is tender. Place a sieve over a large mixing bowl and tip the stew out into it. Allow to drain for a few minutes, then carefully remove the pieces of beef and pork. Place them in a clean flameproof casserole dish together with the fried mushrooms.

Tip the drained sauce into a pan and allow to rest for a few minutes until all the fat rises to the surface, then skim well. Adjust the consistency of the sauce, either by reducing it if it is too thin or by adding a little more brown stock if it is too thick. Check the seasoning and pass through a fine strainer on to the meat. Add the olives and simmer the stew very gently together on top of the stove for 15 minutes before serving.

SERVES 8

Queue de Boeuf Cavour

50 g (2 oz) butter
3 onions, peeled and sliced
3 carrots, peeled and sliced
1 clove garlic, peeled and crushed
1 bouquet garni
100 g (4 oz) pork rind, blanched
2 oxtails, jointed, weighing in total about 2.5 kg (5½ lb)
salt
pepper
1 litre (1¾ pint) Fonds Brun, page 8
300 ml (½ pint) dry white wine
25 g (1 oz) arrowroot
100g (4 oz) mushrooms, fried in butter
Purée de Marrons, page 139

Butter a flameproof braising pan and cover the bottom with the sliced vegetables, herbs and pork rind. Put the pieces of oxtail on top, season, cover with a lid and place in a hot oven (240°C, 475°F, Gas Mark 9) for 15 minutes.

Remove from the oven, moisten with a little stock and reduce this to a glaze on top of the stove. Almost cover with the rest of the stock and the white wine. Cover with the lid, place in a moderate oven (160°C, 325°F, Gas Mark 3) and braise gently for 3½–4 hours, or until the meat is tender.

Drain off the fat from the cooking liquid, then thicken the cooking liquid with the arrowroot, diluted in a little cold water. Pass this sauce through a fine strainer. Put the sections of oxtail in a clean pan and cover with the sauce. Add the mushrooms and simmer gently in the same oven for another 15 minutes.

Serve the oxtail and its garnish in a deep dish. Serve a dish of chestnut purée separately.

SERVES 8

Tripes à la Lyonnaise

1 kg (2¼ lb) dressed tripe
salt
100 g (4 oz) butter
250 g (9 oz) onions, peeled and sliced
pepper
1 tablespoon white wine vinegar
1 tablespoon chopped fresh parsley

Tripe is usually sold as dressed tripe, which in effect means that it is part-cooked. For this recipe the tripe needs to be completely cooked before you start. To cook dressed tripe completely, simmer gently in salted water for about 1½ hours or until the tripe is tender to the knife.

Drain and dry the cooked tripe and cut it into large strips. Heat 75 g (3 oz) of the butter in a frying pan and fry the tripe quickly in the butter until golden brown. Fry the onion separately in the remaining butter until golden brown. Add it to the tripe, season and toss tripe and onions together in the pan until both are well coloured.

Transfer the tripe and onions to a deep dish. Deglaze the pan with the vinegar and sprinkle over the tripe. Finally, sprinkle with chopped parsley.

SERVES 8

Côtes de Veau au Basilic

1 large bunch basil leaves
150 g (5 oz) butter
4 veal cutlets
salt
pepper
4 tablespoons dry white wine
4 tablespoons Glace de Viande, page 9

First prepare some basil-flavoured butter. Blanch the basil leaves for 2 minutes, drain, refresh and squeeze dry. Pound finely, then mix in 75 g (3 oz) of the butter and pass through a fine sieve.

Season the veal cutlets, shallow fry in the remaining butter and place on a dish. Keep warm. Deglaze the pan with the white wine and add the meat glaze. Take the pan off the heat and shake in the basil-flavoured butter.

Coat the cutlets with this sauce.

SERVES 4

Côtes de Veau en Cocotte à la Paysanne

4 veal cutlets
salt
pepper
225 g (8 oz) streaky bacon, rinded and cut in lardons
100 g (4 oz) butter
16 button onions
450 g (1 lb) small potatoes, peeled and thickly sliced
6 tablespoons Fonds Brun, page 8

*P*lace the seasoned cutlets and *lardons* of bacon in a flameproof casserole and brown them in 50 g (2 oz) of the butter, colouring the cutlets on both sides.

Fry the button onions separately and gently in the remaining butter until lightly browned and add these to the casserole along with the potatoes. Cover with the lid and continue to cook in a moderately hot oven (190°C, 375°F, Gas Mark 5) for about 30–40 minutes, or until tender. Add the stock a few minutes before removing from the oven.

Serve the cutlets straight from the casserole dish.

S<small>ERVES</small> 4

Côtes de Veau à la Fermière

4 veal cutlets
salt
pepper
50 g (2 oz) butter
6 tablespoons Fonds Brun, page 8

To garnish
Garnish à la Fermière
100 g (4 oz) carrot, peeled and cut into paysanne
100 g (4 oz) turnip, peeled and cut into paysanne
50 g (2 oz) onion, peeled and cut into large dice
50 g (2 oz) celery, cut into paysanne
50 g (2 oz) butter
salt
1 pinch sugar

*S*tart by preparing the Fermière garnish. Fry all of the prepared vegetables gently for a few minutes in the butter with the salt and sugar.

Season the cutlets and fry gently in the butter in a flameproof casserole. Add the garnish, cover with a lid and continue to cook in a moderately hot oven (190°C, 375°F, Gas Mark 5) for 30–40 minutes or until the cutlets are tender.

Just before serving, moisten with the stock and serve the cutlets straight from the casserole.

S<small>ERVES</small> 4

Filet de Veau au Paprika

1.5 kg (3 lb 6 oz) fillet of veal, trimmed
100 g (4 oz) larding bacon, cut into thin strips 7 cm
(3 inches) long
paprika
salt
50 g (2 oz) lard or butter
200 g (7 oz) onion, peeled, sliced and blanched
300 ml ($\frac{1}{2}$ pint) double cream

To garnish
Chou-fleur au Gratin, page 134, prepared as florets
100 g (4 oz) boiled ham, chopped
paprika

*L*ard the veal, sprinkle generously with paprika, season with salt and shallow fry in hot lard or butter.

Cover the bottom of an ovenproof casserole, just large enough to hold the meat, with a layer of the sliced and blanched onions. Place the meat on top and cover with a lid. *Poêlé* the meat in a hot oven (220°C, 425°F, Gas Mark 7), basting frequently with the fat, for approximately 1 hour or until just cooked. Place the veal fillet on a serving plate and keep warm.

Meanwhile, prepare the florets of Chou-fleur au Gratin, coating them as described with Sauce Mornay; to accompany this particular dish, though, the Sauce Mornay should contain chopped ham and be flavoured with paprika. Brown the sauced cauliflower in a hot oven or under the grill before serving.

Deglaze the meat and onion pan with the cream and pass through a fine strainer. Serve this sauce separately.

S<small>ERVES</small> 6

Poitrine de Veau aux Céleris

75 g (3 oz) butter
3 kg (7 lb) breast of veal, boned (about 2.5 kg (5½ lb)
after boning)
1 litre (1¾ pints), Fonds Blanc, page 9
5–6 heads of celery, trimmed and blanched

Pork forcemeat
1 tablespoon chopped onion
1 tablespoon chopped shallot
50 g (2 oz) butter
200 g (7 oz) mushrooms, finely chopped
salt
pepper
1½ tablespoons chopped fresh parsley
1 tablespoon chopped fresh tarragon
450 g (1 lb) sausage meat
100 g (4 oz) white breadcrumbs
1 egg
1 pinch mixed spice

*F*irst prepare the forcemeat. Fry the onion and shallot gently in the hot butter, and add the mushrooms. Fry gently until all the moisture has evaporated, season and add the chopped herbs. Add the sausage meat, breadcrumbs, egg and mixed spice and check the seasoning; mix all these ingredients together, stuff the breast and sew up with coarse thread.

Heat the butter in a flameproof braising pan, season the veal and colour it lightly on both sides. Add the stock and braise slowly, basting frequently, in a moderate oven (180°C, 350°F, Gas Mark 4) for 2 hours.

The breast should now be about two-thirds cooked. Remove it and place in a clean pan. Surround with the heads of celery, cover with the strained braising liquid and return to the same oven for about 1 hour. Remove the lid just before the end of the cooking time and allow the meat to brown.

Arrange the breast on a serving dish surrounded by the celery heads, cut into portions. Remove the fat from the braising liquid and reduce to the desired quantity and consistency. Serve the sauce separately.

SERVES 10–12

Sauté de Veau Marengo

1.5 kg (3 lb 6 oz) stewing veal, cut into small pieces
salt
pepper
100 ml (3½ fl oz) oil
125 g (4½ oz) onion, peeled and chopped
1 clove garlic, peeled and crushed
200 ml (7 fl oz) dry white wine
1 litre (1¾ pints) Fonds Brun, page 8
1½ kg (3 lb) tomatoes, peeled, depipped and roughly chopped
1 bouquet garni
24 button onions
40 g (1½ oz) butter
24 button mushrooms
2 pinches roughly chopped fresh parsley

To garnish
8 slices white bread, cut into heart shapes
clarified butter or oil

*S*eason and shallow fry the pieces of veal in very hot oil until well coloured on all sides. Add the onion and garlic and fry until golden brown.

Drain off the oil, add the white wine and reduce a little. Add the stock, tomatoes and bouquet garni and cook gently in a moderate oven (160°C, 325°F, Gas Mark 3) for 1½ hours.

Meanwhile, fry and colour the button onions gently in the butter. When the onions are coloured, add the button mushrooms and fry lightly. When the veal is cooked, transfer it to a clean pan with the fried button onions, the mushrooms and the parsley. Reduce the sauce by one-third and pass it through a fine strainer over the veal and vegetables. Simmer for 15 minutes and remove any fat.

Place in a deep dish and garnish with small heart-shaped croûtons of bread fried in *clarified butter* or oil.

SERVES 8

Sauté de Veau Marengo

Blanquette de Veau à l'Ancienne

1.5 kg (3 lb 6 oz) stewing veal, cut into cubes
enough Fonds Blanc to cover the veal, page 9
salt
1 carrot, peeled
1 onion, peeled and stuck with 1 clove
1 leek
1 bouquet garni
65 g (2½ oz) butter
75 g (3 oz) flour
100 g (4 oz) white mushrooms, chopped, or mushroom
trimmings, white pieces only
24 button onions, peeled
24 button mushrooms
juice of ½ lemon
5 egg yolks
100 ml (3½ fl oz) cream
grated nutmeg
2 tablespoons chopped fresh parsley

Cover the veal with stock and add just a little salt. Bring to the boil slowly, stirring frequently, and skim carefully. Add the vegetables and bouquet garni and simmer gently for 1½ hours, or until tender.

Now prepare a velouté. Make a *roux* with the butter and flour and gradually add 1.25 litres (2¼ pints) of the cooking liquid from the veal. Add the chopped mushrooms and allow to simmer gently for 15 minutes, skimming the sauce as necessary.

Cook the button onions in lightly salted water for 6 minutes. Simmer the button mushrooms separately in water with a few drops of lemon juice for 3 minutes. Drain the pieces of veal and place in a clean pan with the cooked button onions and mushrooms.

Finish the sauce at the last moment with a *liaison*, consisting of the egg yolks, cream and a few more drops of lemon juice. Adjust the seasoning and add a little grated nutmeg.

Strain the sauce over the veal, reheat without boiling and place in a deep serving dish. Sprinkle with the chopped parsley.

SERVES 8

Ris de Veau à la Cévenole

3 pairs veal sweetbreads
75 g (3 oz) onion, peeled and sliced
50 g (2 oz) carrot, peeled and sliced
50 g (2 oz) butter
1 bouquet garni
salt
pepper
Fonds Blanc, page 9
arrowroot

To garnish
6 slices brown bread, cut to the shape of cockscombs
50 g (2 oz) clarified butter
glazed button onions
Purée de Marrons, page 139

Soak the sweetbreads under cold running water for 2–3 hours to remove all the blood. Drain and put them in a pan. Cover with cold water, heat and bring to the boil. Pour off the liquid, rinse and cool under cold water. Remove all gristle and connective tissue, then place between two clean cloths, pressed between two plates, until quite cold.

Stew the vegetables gently in the butter for a few minutes in a flameproof casserole. Add the bouquet garni, seasoning and enough stock almost to cover the vegetables, then reduce the stock to a glaze. Place the sweetbreads on top of the vegetables and add more stock, to come half way up the sweetbreads. Heat to boiling point. Baste the sweetbreads, cover the casserole and cook in a moderate oven (180°C, 350°F, Gas Mark 4) for 1 hour, basting from time to time. Remove the lid about 10 minutes before the end of the cooking time, baste and allow the sweetbreads to glaze to a light brown.

Fry the cockscombs of brown bread in the *clarified butter*. Arrange the braised sweetbreads on a dish with glazed button onions and the croûtons of fried bread. Serve accompanied by the chestnut purée and the braising liquid, lightly thickened with a little arrowroot.

SERVES 6

Ris de Veau à la Cévenole, Purée de Marrons

Ris de Veau au Gratin

3 pairs veal sweetbreads
75 g (3 oz) onion, peeled and sliced
50 g (2 oz) carrot, peeled and sliced
75 g (3 oz) butter
1 bouquet garni
salt
pepper
Fonds Blanc, page 9
300 ml ($\frac{1}{2}$ pint) reduced Sauce Duxelles, page 12
150 g (5 oz) button mushrooms, sliced
25 g (1 oz) breadcrumbs
50 g (2 oz) melted butter
a few drops lemon juice
1 tablespoon chopped fresh parsley

Soak the sweetbreads under cold running water for 2–3 hours to remove all the blood. Drain and put them in a pan. Cover with cold water, heat and bring to the boil. Pour off the liquid, rinse and cool under cold water. Remove all gristle and connective tissue then place between two clean cloths, pressed between two plates, until quite cold.

Stew the vegetables gently in 50 g (2 oz) butter for a few minutes in a flameproof casserole. Add the bouquet garni, seasoning, enough stock to cover the vegetables, then reduce the stock to a glaze. Place the sweetbreads on top of the vegetables, and add more stock to come halfway up the sides of the sweetbreads. Heat to boiling point. Baste the sweetbreads, cover the casserole and cook in a moderate oven (180°C, 350°F, Gas Mark 4) for 1 hour, basting from time to time. Remove the lid about 10 minutes before the end of the cooking time, baste and allow the sweetbreads to glaze to a light brown.

Cut the braised sweetbreads into slices and reform, in an ovenproof gratin dish, in their original shape, spreading a spoonful of the reduced Sauce Duxelles between each slice.

Fry the button mushrooms gently in the remaining butter. Surround the sweetbreads with the mushrooms, then cover the sweetbreads with some more Sauce Duxelles. Sprinkle the sweetbreads with breadcrumbs and melted butter and gratinate quickly in a hot oven (220°C, 425°F, Gas Mark 7) until the breadcrumb mixture is golden brown.

Sprinkle with a few drops of lemon juice and chopped parsley before serving.

SERVES 6

Foie de Veau aux Raisins

40 g (1$\frac{1}{2}$ oz) sultanas
40 g (1$\frac{1}{2}$ oz) currants
8 slices calf's liver
salt
pepper
50 g (2 oz) butter
2 tablespoons red wine vinegar
1 pinch brown sugar
150 ml ($\frac{1}{4}$ pint) Sauce Demi-glace, page 10

Pick over and wash the sultanas and currants. Soak them well in advance in warm water to allow them to swell.

Season the liver and shallow fry in the butter, then arrange on a round dish. Keep warm. Deglaze the pan with the vinegar and add the sugar and Sauce Demi-glace. Reduce the sauce to the desired consistency and pass through a fine strainer.

Add the drained sultanas and currants to the sauce and simmer for a few more minutes. Pour over the liver and serve.

SERVES 4

Rognons de Veau Robert

3 calf's kidneys
salt
pepper
100 g (4 oz) butter
100 ml (3$\frac{1}{2}$ fl oz) brandy
1 teaspoon made mustard
$\frac{1}{2}$ tablespoon lemon juice
1 pinch chopped fresh parsley

Trim the kidneys, leaving a thin layer of their suet. Season them and fry quickly in 50 g (2 oz) of the butter in a flameproof *cocotte* to brown slightly on all sides. Cover and place in a hot oven (220°C, 425°F, Gas Mark 7) for 20 minutes.

Transfer the kidneys to a warmed dish. Deglaze the cocotte with the brandy and reduce by half. Meanwhile, cut the kidneys into very thin slices, cover and keep warm.

To the reduced brandy add the mustard and the remaining butter. Add the lemon juice and the parsley. Mix together with a fork, then add the prepared slices of kidney along with any juices which have drained from them. Reheat everything together but do not allow to boil, and serve immediately.

SERVES 6

Foie de Veau aux Raisins

Rognons de Veau en Cocotte

3 calf's kidneys
salt
pepper
75 g (3 oz) butter
100 g (4 oz) streaky bacon, rinded, diced and blanched
125 g (4½ oz) mushrooms, quartered
125 g (4½ oz) potatoes, peeled, trimmed to the shape of
olives and blanched
3 tablespoons Fonds Brun, page 8

Trim and season the kidneys, leaving them covered with a thin layer of their suet. Place 50 g (2 oz) of the butter in a flameproof *cocotte*, heat it, add the seasoned kidneys and fry till slightly brown on all sides.

Meanwhile, fry the blanched bacon separately in the remaining butter, then add the quartered mushrooms and fry together. Surround the kidneys with the fried bacon and mushrooms and the blanched potatoes, cover and complete the cooking in a moderately hot oven (200°C, 400°F, Gas Mark 6) for 30 minutes.

At the last minute, moisten with the stock and serve straight from the cocotte.

SERVES 6

Cervelle au Beurre Noir

8 pairs calf's brains
1.5 litres (2½ pints) boiling Court-bouillon au Vinaigre, page 40
salt
pepper
175 g (6 oz) butter
2 tablespoons chopped fresh parsley
2 tablespoons white wine vinegar

Place the brains under gently running cold water so as to extract as much of the blood as possible, then carefully remove all of the membrane and connective tissue which surrounds them. Place once again under gently running water to soak out any remaining blood.

To cook them, place in the boiling Court-bouillon au Vinaigre and allow to poach gently for about 25–30 minutes.

Cut the cooked brains into thick slices and arrange on a dish. Season with salt and pepper. Cook the butter to a dark brown colour (or *à la noisette* to a more than usual degree), and then add

the parsley to it at the last minute. Pour over the brains. Swill out the pan in which the butter was cooked with the vinegar and pour this over the buttered brains.

SERVES 8

Côtelettes d'Agneau à la Réforme

16 lamb cutlets, well trimmed
salt
pepper
flour
100 g (4 oz) melted butter
150 g (5 oz) white breadcrumbs
50 g (2 oz) lean ham, very finely chopped
100 g (4 oz) clarified butter

Sauce Réforme
250 ml (8 fl oz) Sauce Poivrade, page 10
250 ml (8 fl oz) Sauce Demi-glace, page 10
25 g (1 oz) gherkins, cut into short julienne
1 hard-boiled egg white, cut into short julienne
20 g (¾ oz) mushroom, cut into short julienne and cooked in butter
20 g (¾ oz) truffle, cut into short julienne
20 g (¾ oz) cooked salted ox tongue, cut into short julienne

Lightly flatten the cutlets to about 5 mm (¼ inches) thick and season. Coat them in flour and dip in the melted butter, then in the breadcrumbs mixed with the chopped ham.

Flatten carefully with the flat of a knife to ensure that the crumb mixture sticks to the cutlets, and shallow fry in the *clarified butter* for about 2 minutes on each side or until light golden in colour.

Serve accompanied by Sauce Réforme. This is made by combining the Sauces Poivrade and Demi-glace and adding the gherkin, hard-boiled egg white, mushroom, truffle and tongue all cut into short *julienne*. Serve the sauce separately.

SERVES 8

Côtelettes d'Agneau à la Réforme

Côtelettes d'Agneau à la Navarraise

8 lamb cutlets, well trimmed
salt
pepper
100 g (4 oz) lean boiled ham, chopped
100 g (4 oz) mushrooms, fried in butter and chopped
15 g ($\frac{1}{2}$ oz) red pepper, cooked and chopped
150 ml ($\frac{1}{4}$ pint) very thick Sauce Béchamel, page 12
25 g (1 oz) Parmesan, grated
50 g (2 oz) melted butter

To garnish
4 large tomatoes, halved
oil
200 ml (7 fl oz) Sauce Tomate, page 14

Season and grill the cutlets on one side only. Coat the cooked sides with a mixture of ham, mushrooms, red pepper and very thick béchamel, arranged in a dome shape.

Place the cutlets on an ovenproof dish, uncooked sides downwards, and sprinkle with the grated Parmesan and the melted butter. Put in a hot oven (230°C, 450°F, Gas Mark 8) for about 8–10 minutes, both to complete the cooking and to gratinate the cutlets.

When they are ready, arrange in a circle on a dish, placing each cutlet on half a large tomato, seasoned and shallow fried in oil. Surround with a *cordon* of tomato sauce.

SERVES 4

Epaule d'Agneau à la Boulangère

1 shoulder of lamb, weighing about 2 kg (4$\frac{1}{2}$ lb), boned
salt
pepper
250 g (9 oz) onions, peeled and sliced
50 g (2 oz) butter
1.25 kg (2$\frac{1}{2}$ lb) potatoes, peeled and sliced
2 pinches chopped fresh parsley

Season the inside of the shoulder of lamb, then roll and tie it carefully with string. Place it in a roasting tray in a hot oven (220°C, 425°F, Gas Mark 7) for 30 minutes, to brown and partly cook it.

Place the shoulder in an ovenproof dish and surround with the sliced onions, fried in the butter without being coloured,

and the sliced potatoes. Sprinkle with the fat from the roasting tray and return to the same oven, basting frequently, for another 1$\frac{1}{2}$ hours or until the juices that run when the meat is pricked with a trussing needle are colourless.

When the meat is cooked, remove the string and sprinkle with the chopped parsley.

SERVES 8

Epaule d'Agneau aux Navets

1 shoulder of lamb, weighing about 2 kg (4$\frac{1}{2}$ lb), boned
200 g (7 oz) onion, peeled and sliced
200 g (7 oz) carrot, peeled and sliced
1 clove garlic, peeled and crushed
100 g (4 oz) butter
salt
pepper
1 bouquet garni
900 ml (1$\frac{1}{2}$ pints) Fonds Brun, page 8
1 kg (2 lb) turnips, peeled and trimmed to the shape of large olives
1 pinch caster sugar
20 button onions, peeled
$\frac{1}{2}$ tablespoon tomato purée
15 g ($\frac{1}{2}$ oz) arrowroot

Pork forcemeat
200 g (7 oz) onion, peeled and chopped
50 g (2 oz) butter
450 g (1 lb) pork sausage meat
1 tablespoon chopped fresh parsley
1 pinch powdered thyme
150 g (5 oz) breadcrumbs
1 egg
salt
pepper

First of all prepare the forcemeat. Fry the onion in the butter without allowing it to colour, then let it cool. Add the onion to the sausage meat and mix together with the herbs, breadcrumbs and egg, and a little seasoning as needed.

Stuff the boned shoulder of lamb with the pork forcemeat, roll and tie carefully with string. Fry the vegetables and garlic in 25 g (1 oz) of the butter, allowing them to brown slightly, and place with the bouquet garni in the bottom of a flameproof braising pan, just large enough to hold the meat. Season the meat and fry it in another 25 g (1 oz) of the butter to brown it on

MEAT DISHES

all sides. Place on top of the vegetables, moisten with a little stock and cover with the lid. Place over a moderate heat and cook until the stock is reduced to a glaze. Add the rest of the stock, to come about halfway up the meat this time, and bring to the boil. Place the braising pan in a moderate oven (180°C, 350°F, Gas Mark 4) for about 3 hours, basting frequently.

Meanwhile, fry the turnips gently with the sugar in another 25 g (1 oz) of the butter, and fry the button onions to colour lightly in the remainder of the butter.

When the meat is three-quarters cooked (after about 2 hours 10 minutes), remove the shoulder and place it in a shallow pan. Surround with the lightly browned turnips and onions.

Remove the fat from the braising liquid and strain the liquid over the meat and vegetables. Cover, return to the oven and complete the cooking. When ready, remove the string and place the shoulder in a deep dish surrounded by its garnish. Keep warm.

Skim the braising liquid of all fat, add the tomato purée and reduce carefully to about 600 ml (1 pint). Thicken with the arrowroot diluted with a little water, season to taste and pass through a fine strainer. Pour some of the sauce over the shoulder of lamb and its garnish and serve the rest separately.

SERVES 8–10

Gigot d'Agneau Chivry

1 leg of lamb weighing about 2 kg (4½ lb)
salt
pepper
flour

Sauce Chivry
2 good pinches each chopped fresh tarragon, parsley, chervil,
pimpernel, chives and shallot, mixed
50 g (2 oz) butter, softened
120 ml (4 fl oz) dry white wine
600 ml (1 pint) Sauce Velouté, pages 9–10, heated to
boiling point

Season and flour the leg of lamb and tie it up carefully in a clean piece of cloth. Place in lightly salted boiling water and poach gently, allowing 25 minutes per 450 g (1 lb).

Meanwhile, make the Sauce Chivry. First prepare a flavoured butter: cover half the herbs and shallot with cold water, bring to the boil quickly, then drain and cool in cold water. Squeeze the herbs to remove as much liquid as possible, then pound to a fine purée and mix with the softened butter.

Now bring the wine to the boil in a pan, add the remainder of the herbs and shallot, and allow to infuse for 10 minutes. Strain and add to the Sauce Velouté. Finish, away from the heat, by mixing in the prepared herb butter.

Remove the leg of lamb from the cooking liquid when ready. Place on a dish and serve accompanied by the Sauce Chivry.

SERVES 8

Gigot d'Agneau à la Liégeoise

1 leg of lamb, weighing about 2 kg (4½ lb)
salt
pepper
50 g (2 oz) melted butter
500 ml (18 fl oz) Fonds Brun, page 8
5 juniper berries, finely crushed
50 ml (2 fl oz) gin, flaming

Mirepoix
50 g (2 oz) carrot, peeled and diced
50 g (2 oz) onion, peeled and diced
25 g (1 oz) celery, diced
50 g (2 oz) streaky bacon, diced
25 g (1 oz) butter
1 bay leaf
1 sprig thyme

Before *poêling* the meat, first prepare the *mirepoix*. Fry the vegetables and bacon gently in the butter and add the herbs.

Place a layer of mirepoix in a deep heavy flameproof *cocotte* just large enough to hold the piece of meat. Put the meat on top of the mirepoix, season well and coat with melted butter.

Cover with a lid and place in a moderately hot oven (200°C, 400°F, Gas Mark 6) basting frequently, for about 2 hours. When the meat is cooked, remove it and keep warm. Add the stock to the vegetables, which should not have been allowed to burn. Bring to the boil and simmer for 10 minutes. Strain, remove the fat and reduce by two-thirds. Add the finely crushed juniper berries and the flaming gin. Return the gigot to the cocotte, pour over the sauce and serve.

SERVES 8

Carré d'Agneau Soubise

a best end of neck of lamb, weighing about 1.25 kg (2½ lb)
salt
pepper
150 g (5 oz) butter
225 g (8 oz) onion, peeled, finely sliced and blanched
150 ml (¼ pint) boiling Sauce Béchamel, page 12

*S*eason the best end of neck and fry gently in 50 g (2 oz) of the butter until golden brown. Fry the onion separately in another 25 g (1 oz) of the butter without browning.

Transfer the lamb to an ovenproof casserole and surround with the lightly fried onion. Cover with a lid and place in a moderately hot oven (190°C, 375°F, Gas Mark 5) for 45 minutes.

Transfer the meat to a dish and keep warm. Add the boiling béchamel to the onion, mix together and pass through a fine sieve. Reheat this onion purée or soubise and finish with the remaining butter.

Place the meat on a suitable dish and accompany with the soubise in a sauceboat.

SERVES 4

Carré d'Agneau Marly

a best end of neck of lamb, weighing about 1.25 kg (2½ lb)
salt
pepper
50 g (2 oz) butter
450 g (1 lb) mange-tout peas, broken into small pieces
1 pinch caster sugar
1 tablespoon water
250 g (9 oz) flour
100 ml (3½ fl oz) water

*S*eason the best end of neck and fry quickly in the butter to a golden brown colour. Transfer it to an ovenproof casserole and add the mange-tout peas, sugar, a little more salt and the tablespoon of water.

Cover with the lid and seal with a band of stiff paste (*repère*) made by mixing together the flour and water. Cook in a moderately hot oven (190°C, 375°F, Gas Mark 5) for 1 hour.

SERVES 4

Carré d'Agneau Mireille

450 g (1 lb) unbaked Pommes de Terre Anna, page 142
225 g (8 oz) raw artichoke bottoms, sliced
a best end of neck of lamb, weighing about 1.25 kg (2½ lb)
salt
pepper
50 g (2 oz) butter

*I*n a shallow, oval ovenproof dish large enough to hold the lamb comfortably, prepare a layer of unbaked Pommes de Terre Anna, according to the recipe on page 142, but incorporating the artichoke bottoms as well as the sliced potatoes.

Place in a hot oven (220°C, 425°F, Gas Mark 7) for 20 minutes. Meanwhile season the best end of lamb and brown it quickly in the butter.

Place it on top of the potatoes and return to the oven to complete the cooking of potatoes and lamb together. Turn the temperature down to 180°C, 350°F, Gas Mark 4 and cook for a further 45 minutes, basting frequently. Serve from the dish.

SERVES 4

Sauté d'Agneau Chasseur

2 kg (4½ lb) best end of neck and/or shoulder of lamb,
trimmed of fat
salt
pepper
50 g (2 oz) butter
2 tablespoons olive oil
200 ml (7 fl oz) dry white wine
300 ml (½ pint) Sauce Chasseur, page 12
2 tablespoons chopped fresh parsley

*C*ut the meat into 50 g (2 oz) cubes, season and shallow fry in the butter and oil on all sides for about 20 minutes, or until completely cooked.

Remove the pieces of lamb and place them on a dish to keep warm. Drain off the fat and deglaze the pan with the white wine. Reduce by half and add the Sauce Chasseur. Replace the pieces of lamb in this sauce and keep hot, without boiling, for 5 minutes.

Place in a *timbale* or deep serving dish and sprinkle generously with the chopped parsley.

SERVES 8

Navarin Printanier

100 g (4 oz) clean fat, such as strained dripping
2.5 kg (5½ lb) breast, cutlets, neck and shoulder of lamb, cut in
pieces weighing about 75 g (3 oz) each
salt
pepper
1 pinch caster sugar
50 g (2 oz) flour
1.5 litres (2½ pints) Fonds Brun, page 8
3 tablespoons tomato purée
1 clove garlic, peeled and crushed
1 large bouquet garni
300 g (11 oz) small new carrots, peeled
300 g (11 oz) small new turnips, peeled
50 g (2 oz) butter
20 button onions
500 g (1¼ lb) small new potatoes
150 g (5 oz) fresh peas
150 g (5 oz) French beans, trimmed and cut into
diamond shapes

Heat the fat in a flameproof casserole and add the pieces of lamb. Season, add the sugar and fry quickly until brown on all sides. Drain off almost all of the fat, sprinkle with the flour and cook for a few more minutes.

Add the stock and the tomato purée, garlic and bouquet garni. Bring to the boil, stirring continuously, cover with a lid and transfer to a moderate oven (180°C, 350°F, Gas Mark 4) for about 1 hour, or until almost tender. Meanwhile, fry the carrots and turnips quickly in the butter until lightly browned.

Transfer the meat to a clean ovenproof casserole and add the carrots, turnips, button onions, potatoes, peas and beans. Skim off the fat from the sauce, check the seasoning, adjusting if necessary, and strain over the meat and vegetables. Cover with a lid and return to the same oven for approximately 45 minutes more, or until everything is tender, basting frequently with the sauce.

Before serving, remove any remaining fat, place in a deep serving dish and serve very hot.

SERVES 10

Daube à l'Avignonnaise

750 g (1½ lb) leg of mutton, cut into cubes weighing
75 g (3 oz) each
200 g (7 oz) larding bacon, cut into strips 7 cm (3 inches) long
150 g (5 oz) unsmoked streaky bacon, cut thinly and rinded
200 g (7 oz) onion, peeled and chopped
2 cloves garlic, peeled and crushed
250 g (9 oz) unsmoked streaky bacon, diced and blanched
250 g (9 oz) fresh pork rind, blanched and cut into
2.5 cm (1 inch) squares
1 pinch dried thyme
1 pinch powdered bay leaf
1 large bouquet of parsley stalks wrapped around a strip of
dried orange peel
Fonds Brun, page 8
250 g (9 oz) flour
100 ml (3½ fl oz) water

Marinade
1 bottle red wine
100 ml (3½ fl oz) olive oil
1 carrot, peeled and sliced
1 onion, peeled and sliced
4 cloves garlic, peeled
1 sprig thyme
1 bay leaf
a few parsley stalks

Lard each piece of mutton with a strip of *larding bacon* and marinate for 2 hours with all the marinade ingredients. Drain the mutton, reserving the marinade.

Cover the bottom and sides of a flameproof casserole with thin slices of streaky bacon, reserving a few for the top. Inside this, arrange the mutton, the chopped onion mixed with the garlic, the diced and blanched bacon and the pork rind in alternate layers, lightly seasoning each layer of mutton and finally sprinkling all with dried thyme and powdered bay leaf. Place the *bouquet* of parsley stalks and orange peel in the centre.

Strain the marinade and add to the casserole, along with enough stock to cover. Finish with the remaining slices of bacon, replace the lid and seal the casserole with a band of *repère* (see page 86 and Glossary). Bring to the boil, then place in a moderate oven (160°C, 325°F, Gas Mark 3) for 5 hours.

At the end of the cooking time, discard the bouquet of parsley stalks and orange peel, and skim off any fat from the surface of the cooking liquid. Serve from the casserole.

SERVES 6

Cassoulet

1 kg (2 lb) haricot beans, soaked overnight
3 litres (5½ pints) water
1 carrot, peeled
1 onion, peeled and stuck with 1 clove
2 bouquet garnis
3 cloves garlic, peeled
300 g (11 oz) fresh pork rind, blanched
300 g (11 oz) belly of pork, blanched
300 g (11 oz) whole garlic sausage
400 g (14 oz) boned shoulder of mutton, cut into pieces weighing
about 40 g (1½ oz) each
400 g (14 oz) boned breast of mutton, cut into pieces weighing
about 40 g (1½ oz) each
50 g (2 oz) lard
250 g (9 oz) onion, peeled and chopped
2 cloves garlic, peeled and crushed
3 tablespoons tomato purée
salt
25 g (1 oz) breadcrumbs

*P*lace the haricot beans in a pan with the water and the carrot, onion, 1 bouquet garni, garlic and blanched pork rind. Bring to the boil, skim, cover and simmer gently for 1 hour.

Add the blanched belly of pork and whole garlic sausage and continue cooking until the beans are cooked but still firm.

Fry the diced boned shoulder of mutton and the breast of mutton in the lard, in a flameproof casserole. Drain off half the fat, add the chopped onion and crushed garlic and continue frying until everything is lightly browned.

Now add enough of the cooking liquid from the beans to cover the meat, plus the tomato purée and the other bouquet garni. Season, cover and place in a cool oven (150°C, 300°F, Gas Mark 2) to bake very gently, for at least 1½ hours.

Cover the bottom of a deep ovenproof casserole with the pork rind and fill with alternate layers of the mutton and sauce, the beans, the belly pork cut into cubes and slices of garlic sausage. Sprinkle with the breadcrumbs and gratinate in a moderate oven (180°C, 350°F, Gas Mark 4) for 1 hour, basting from time to time with a little of the remaining cooking liquid from the beans.

SERVES 10

Brochettes de Rognons d'Agneau

8 lamb's kidneys
salt
pepper
75 g (3 oz) butter
200 g (7 oz) large mushrooms, thickly sliced
200 g (7 oz) sliced streaky bacon, rinded, blanched and
cut into squares
25 g (1 oz) melted butter
25 g (1 oz) white breadcrumbs

*S*kin the kidneys and cut them into round slices about 5 mm (¼ inch) thick. Season with salt and pepper and fry quickly in 50 g (2 oz) of very hot butter just to set the flesh. Fry the mushrooms gently in the remaining butter.

Impale the slices of kidney on skewers, alternating with squares of blanched bacon and slices of fried mushroom. Brush the skewers with melted butter, sprinkle with the breadcrumbs and grill. Serve immediately.

SERVES 4

Rognons d'Agneau Vert-Pré

8 lamb's kidneys
salt
pepper

To garnish
Pommes de Terre Pailles, page 144
a few sprigs watercress

*S*kin the kidneys and open out by cutting through them from the convex side without actually separating the two halves. Impale them crossways on a skewer to keep them open, then season and grill.

Arrange on an oval dish with straw potatoes at the sides and sprigs of watercress at either end.

SERVES 4

Cassoulet

Rognons Turbigo

4 lamb's kidneys
salt
pepper
50 g (2 oz) butter
100 ml (3½ fl oz) dry white wine
150 ml (¼ pint) Sauce Demi-glace, page 10
½ tablespoon tomato purée
cayenne pepper

To garnish
100 g (4 oz) button mushrooms
25 g (1 oz) butter
8 small chipolata sausages, grilled

Skin the kidneys and cut in half lengthways. Season and fry quickly in 50 g (2 oz) of hot butter, tossing frequently. Fry the mushrooms for the garnish separately in 25 g (1 oz) butter.

Drain the kidneys well and arrange in a circle in a deep dish. Place the small fried mushrooms and grilled chipolatas in the centre of the dish.

Deglaze the pan with the white wine and reduce. Flavour the Sauce Demi-glace with the tomato purée and add this to the reduction. Season with a touch of cayenne pepper, and strain this sauce over the kidneys.

SERVES 4

Carré de Porc à la Soissonnaise

2 kg (4½ lb) best end of loin of pork
salt
pepper
olive oil
1.5 kg (3 lb) white haricot beans, cooked and drained

Season the pork, place in a flameproof casserole and sprinkle with a little oil for basting. Roast in a hot oven (220°C, 425°F, Gas Mark 7) for about 25 minutes per 450 g (1 lb).

When the meat is three-quarter cooked (after about 1¼ hours), surround it with the cooked haricot beans. Finish cooking the meat together with the beans, reducing the temperature if either meat or beans begin to burn, and basting the beans frequently with the fat from the pork. When the meat is cooked, remove from the oven and serve from the casserole.

SERVES 6–8

Carré de Porc à la Paysanne

2 kg (4½ lb) best end of loin of pork
salt
pepper
olive oil
225 g (8 oz) onion, peeled and sliced
50 g (2 oz) butter
1 kg (2 lb) medium-sized potatoes, peeled and quartered
1 tablespoon roughly chopped fresh parsley

Season the pork, place in a flameproof casserole and sprinkle with a little oil for basting. Roast in a hot oven (220°C, 425°F, Gas Mark 7) for about 25 minutes per 450 g (1 lb). Fry the onions gently in the butter.

When the meat is half-cooked (after about 50 minutes), surround the pork with the gently fried onions and the quartered potatoes. Lightly season the vegetables and complete the cooking of meat and vegetables together, basting frequently and reducing the temperature if either meat or vegetables begin to burn.

When both meat and vegetables are cooked, remove from the oven, sprinkle with the parsley and serve the dish direct from the casserole.

SERVES 6–8

Jambon aux Fèves de Marais

1 small whole raw ham, weighing about 4–4.5 kg (9–10 lb)
400 ml (14 fl oz) Fino sherry
250 g (9 oz) flour
100 ml (3½ fl oz) water
icing sugar

To garnish
broad beans, cooked, skinned and buttered
1 tablespoon chopped fresh savory

Soak the ham in cold water for 6 hours and remove the aitch bone. Place it in a large pot with plenty of cold water, but no seasoning or flavouring. Bring to the boil and simmer very gently for 3–3½ hours, allowing 20 minutes per 450 g (1 lb).

Remove the ham from the liquid 30 minutes before the end of the cooking time. Remove the skin and trim off excess fat. Place in a braising pan just large enough to hold it and add the dry sherry.

Cover with a tight-fitting lid, seal with a band of *repère* (see page 86 and Glossary) and place in a cool oven (150°C, 300°F, Gas Mark 2) for 1 hour, to complete the cooking and to allow the ham to become impregnated with the sherry.

Cover the surface of the cooked ham with icing sugar, using a sugar sifter, and glaze in a very hot oven or under the grill.

Place on a suitable dish and serve with a dish of very fresh broad beans, boiled, their skins removed and buttered, mixed with a little chopped savory. Serve with the braising sherry from the ham, well skimmed of fat and reduced.

SERVES 10–12

Jambon aux Laitues

1 small whole raw ham, weighing about 4–4.5 kg (9–10 lb)
400 ml (14 fl oz) Sercial Madeira
250 g (9 oz) flour
100 ml (3½ fl oz) water
icing sugar

To garnish
braised lettuce
Sauce Demi-glace, page 10

Soak the ham in cold water for 6 hours and remove the aitch bone. Place it in a large pot with plenty of cold water, but no seasoning or flavouring. Bring to the boil and simmer very gently for 2½–3 hours, allowing 20 minutes per 450 g (1 lb).

Remove the ham from the liquid 30 minutes before the end of the cooking time. Remove the skin and trim off excess fat. Place in a braising pan just large enough to hold it and add the dry Madeira.

Cover with a tight-fitting lid, seal with a band of *repère* (see page 86 and Glossary) and place in a cool oven (150°C, 300°F, Gas Mark 2) for 1 hour, to complete the cooking and to allow the ham to become impregnated with the Madeira.

Cover the surface of the cooked ham with icing sugar, using a sugar sifter, and glaze in a very hot oven or under the grill.

Place on a suitable dish and surround with halves of braised lettuce. Serve accompanied by a light Sauce Demi-glace, page 10, finished with the reduced braising Madeira in place of the final addition of Fonds Brun.

SERVES 10–12

Jambon à la Bayonnaise

1 small whole raw ham, weighing about 4–4.5 kg (9–10 lb)
400 ml (14 fl oz) Sercial Madeira
200 g (9 oz) flour
100 ml (3½ fl oz) water
icing sugar

To garnish
Sauce Demi-glace, page 10
450 g (1 lb) long grain rice made into Riz Pilaff, page 145,
with 150 g (5 oz) diced tomato flesh, 20 cooked button mushrooms
and 20 small cooked chipolatas added half way through
the cooking

Soak the ham in cold water for 6 hours and remove the aitch bone. Place it in a large pot with plenty of cold water, but no seasoning or flavouring. Bring to the boil and simmer very gently for 2½–3 hours, allowing 20 minutes per 450 g (1 lb).

Remove the ham from the liquid 30 minutes before the end of the cooking time. Remove the skin and trim off excess fat. Place in a braising pan just large enough to hold it and add the dry Madeira.

Cover with a tight-fitting lid, seal with a band of *repère* (see page 86 and Glossary) and place in a cool oven (150°C, 300°F, Gas Mark 2), for 1 hour, to complete the cooking and allow the ham to become impregnated with the Madeira.

Cover the surface of the cooked ham with icing sugar, using a sugar sifter, and glaze in a very hot oven or under the grill.

Serve accompanied by a light Sauce Demi-glace, page 10, finished with the reduced braising Madeira in place of the final addition of Fonds Brun.

Place the ham on a suitable dish and serve with the sauce, passed round separately, and a dish of the specially prepared Riz Pilaff.

SERVES 10–12

Mousse Froide de Jambon

500 g (1¼ lb) lean cooked ham, chopped
200 ml (7 fl oz) cold Sauce Velouté, pages 9–10
salt
pepper
150 ml (¼ pint) Gelée Ordinaire, melted, below
400 ml (14 fl oz) double cream, lightly whipped
more Gelée Ordinaire, below

Finely pound the chopped ham or work thoroughly in a food processor, then add the cold Sauce Velouté. Pass through a fine sieve.

Put the resultant purée in a basin and adjust the seasoning. Gradually add the melted aspic jelly and finally fold in the lightly whipped cream.

Pour the mousse into a suitable mould, containing a set layer of clear aspic jelly in the bottom if the mousse is to be demoulded before serving. Place in the refrigerator to set. If the mousse is to be served from the mould, cover the surface with a layer of aspic jelly and place in the refrigerator to set.

SERVES 8

Gelée Ordinaire

2 litres (3½ pints) cold Fonds Blanc, page 9
225 g (8 oz) lean beef, minced
1 egg white
1 teaspoon chopped fresh chervil
1 teaspoon chopped fresh tarragon
25 g (1 oz) leaf gelatine, soaked and drained

Skim the cold stock and decant, discarding any sediment. Place the minced beef, egg white and herbs in a thick-bottomed pan and add the cold stock, mixing well with a whisk or spatula. Slowly bring to the boil, stirring very gently and occasionally to ensure that the bottom of the pan is kept clean. Allow to simmer gently for 45 minutes without disturbance, then add the *leaf gelatine* and simmer for a further 5 minutes. Pass through a muslin cloth.

If wished, the consistency of the jelly may be checked during the 5 minute simmering period following the addition of the gelatine. This can be done by putting a little of the liquid jelly on a plate and placing it in the refrigerator until chilled. If the gel is insufficient a few extra leaves of soaked gelatine may be used.

MAKES APPROXIMATELY 1.5 LITRES (2½ PINTS)

Boudins Noirs à la Normande

450 g (1 lb) black pudding
75 g (3 oz) butter
250 g (9 oz) dessert apples, peeled, cored and thickly sliced

Cut the black pudding into slices and sauté them in half the butter, tossing frequently. Fry the sliced apples separately in the remaining butter. Combine all the ingredients in the same pan and toss well to mix together, then tip into a deep, warmed earthenware dish for service.

SERVES 4

Saucisses au Vin Blanc

12 fine fresh sausages
225 g (8 oz) butter
120 ml (4 fl oz) dry white wine
6 slices bread, crusts removed
1 egg yolk
a few drops lemon juice
1 tablespoon Glace de Viande, page 9

Fry the sausages quickly in 50 g (2 oz) of the butter to colour, then poach them gently, covered, in the white wine for about 15 minutes.

Meanwhile, fry the slices of bread in 100 g (4 oz) of the butter. When the sausages are cooked, arrange them on top of these croûtons.

Reduce the wine by two-thirds, then remove from the heat. When the wine has ceased boiling, add the egg yolk, lemon juice, meat glaze and remaining butter. Stir this sauce well without reheating and pour over the sausages.

SERVES 6

Mousse Froide de Jambon, Salade Aurore

POULTRY & GAME

Poularde Sylvana

1 large oven-ready chicken, weighing about 1.75–2.25 kg
(4–5 lb)
50 g (2 oz) butter
250 g (9 oz) button mushrooms
250 g (9 oz) flour
100 ml (3½ fl oz) water

To garnish
250 g (9 oz) peas
10 button onions
1 small lettuce, shredded
1 bouquet garni, comprising fresh parsley stalks, chervil and
thyme
1 pinch sugar
1 pinch salt
50 g (2 oz) butter

Season the chicken inside and out. Cook the butter until it is brown or *à la noisette*, then fry the mushrooms in it. Stuff the chicken with the mushrooms, truss well and roast in a moderately hot oven (200°C, 400°F, Gas Mark 6) for about 45 minutes, so it is nicely coloured but only half-cooked.

Meanwhile, place the peas in a pan with the rest of the ingredients for the garnish. Add 2 tablespoons water, cover with a lid and half-cook, tossing from time to time.

Place the half-cooked chicken in an ovenproof casserole, surround with the garnish, cover with the lid and seal with a band of *repère* (see page 86 and Glossary). Place in the same oven for another 45 minutes or so to finish cooking.

Remove the trussing string and serve the chicken from the casserole. If required, it may be accompanied by a good chicken gravy, made using Fonds Blanc de Volaille, page 9.

SERVES 4–6

Poularde à l'Estragon

1 large oven-ready chicken, weighing about 1.75–2.25 kg
(4–5 lb)
100 g (4 oz) salt pork fat
enough Fonds Blanc de Volaille to cover, page 9
1 bunch of fresh tarragon, separated into stalks and leaves
salt
pepper
2 teaspoons arrowroot
1 tablespoon chopped fresh tarragon

Cover the bird in thin slices of salt pork fat and tie carefully. Place it in a pan just large enough to hold it and add enough chicken stock to cover. Bring rapidly to the boil, skim, add the tarragon stalks, tied in a bouquet, cover with a lid and allow to poach gently with only a barely discernible movement of the liquid for about 1–1½ hours. The way to tell when the bird is cooked is to pierce the thick part of the leg just above the drumstick with a needle: the juice should run perfectly clear and white. Meanwhile, blanch the tarragon leaves.

Remove the fat and arrange the cooked chicken on a dish, decorate the breast with a wreath of the blanched tarragon leaves; cover and keep hot. Strain 800 ml (1 pint 8 fl oz) of the cooking liquid into a pan and reduce it by half. Blend the arrowroot with a little cold water, then stir it into the hot reduced stock. Bring back to the boil and stir until it thickens and clears. Finish the sauce with the chopped tarragon, season to taste and serve separately.

SERVES 6

Poularde à la Grecque

1 large oven-ready chicken, weighing about 1.75–2.25 kg
(4–5 lb)
400 g (14 oz) Riz à la Grecque, page 145, three-quarters
cooked only
salt
pepper
75 g (3 oz) carrot, peeled and finely sliced
75 g (3 oz) onion, peeled and finely sliced
50 g (2 oz) celery, finely sliced
1 bay leaf
1 sprig thyme
1 clove garlic, crushed
4 rashers streaky bacon
75 g (3 oz) butter, melted
350 ml (12 fl oz) Fonds Brun, page 8
5 g (1 teaspoon) arrowroot

Stuff the chicken with the Riz à la Grecque and truss. Season well. Layer the vegetables and herbs in the bottom of a deep, heavy ovenproof casserole, then place the chicken on top of these, cover it with the bacon and pour over the melted butter. Cover with the lid and place in a moderately hot oven (190°C, 375°F, Gas Mark 5). After 45 minutes of cooking time remove the bacon and place at the sides of the chicken. Cook for a further 60 minutes or until the chicken is ready, basting frequently with the butter.

Remove the lid for the last 15 minutes of the cooking time, adding 50 ml (2 fl oz) of the stock and use this, together with the butter in the pan, to carry on basting the chicken so as to glaze and colour it a light brown.

Remove the chicken when cooked, cover and keep warm.

Add the remaining stock to the pan and simmer gently for 5 minutes, then drain off the liquid and skim off the fat. Lightly thicken the liquid with the arrowroot blended with a little cold water, cook for 1 minute and season as necessary. Pass through a fine strainer.

Remove the trussing string from the chicken and coat with a little of the sauce. Serve the rest of the sauce separately.

SERVES 4—6

Poularde à la Languedocienne

1 large oven-ready chicken, weighing about 1.75–2.25 kg
(4–5 lb), trussed
salt
pepper
75 g (3 oz) carrot, peeled and finely sliced
75 g (3 oz) onion, peeled and finely sliced
50 g (2 oz) celery, finely sliced
1 clove garlic, crushed
1 bay leaf
1 sprig thyme
4 rashers streaky bacon
75 g (3 oz) butter, melted
350 ml (12 fl oz) Fonds Brun, page 8
5 g (1 teaspoon) arrowroot
2 tablespoons Sercial Madeira

To garnish
very small skinned tomatoes lightly cooked in a little olive oil
round slices of aubergine, floured and fried in olive oil
thick slices of ceps or mushrooms fried in olive oil

Season the chicken. Layer a deep heavy ovenproof casserole with the vegetables and herbs, then place the chicken on top of these. Cover with the bacon and pour over the melted butter. Cover with the lid and place in a moderately hot oven (190°C, 375°F, Gas Mark 5). After 45 minutes of cooking time remove the bacon and place at the sides of the chicken. Cook for a further 60 minutes or until the chicken is ready. Baste frequently.

Remove the lid for the last 15 minutes of the cooking time, adding 50 ml (2 fl oz) of the stock and use this, together with the butter in the pan, to carry on basting the chicken so as to glaze and colour it a light brown.

Remove the chicken when cooked, cover and keep warm.

Add the remaining stock to the pan and simmer gently for 5 minutes, then drain off the liquid and skim off the fat. Lightly thicken the liquid with the arrowroot blended with a little cold water, cook for 1 minute and season as necessary. Pass through a fine strainer and finish the sauce with the dry Madeira. Do not reboil after the addition of the Madeira.

Remove the trussing string from the chicken and coat with a little of the sauce. Surround with neat *bouquets* of the garnish. Serve the rest of the sauce separately.

SERVES 4—6

Poularde Printanière

1 large oven-ready chicken, weighing about 1.75–2.25 kg
(4–5 lb)
salt
pepper
75 g (3 oz) carrot, peeled and finely sliced
75 g (3 oz) onion, peeled and finely sliced
1 clove garlic, crushed
1 bay leaf
1 sprig thyme
4 rashers streaky bacon
50 g (2 oz) butter, melted
100 ml (3½ fl oz) Fonds Brun, page 8

Beurre Printanier
50 g (2 oz) carrot, peeled and sliced
50 g (2 oz) turnip, peeled and sliced
100 g (4 oz) onion, peeled and sliced
Fonds Blanc, page 9
100 g (4 oz) butter
1 pinch chopped fresh parsley
1 pinch chopped fresh tarragon
1 pinch chopped fresh basil
1 pinch fresh thyme

Printanier garnish
50 g (2 oz) small new carrots, peeled
50 g (2 oz) small new turnips, peeled
50 g (2 oz) peas, shelled
50 g (2 oz) French beans, trimmed
10 small new onions, peeled
50 g (2 oz) butter

First prepare the Beurre Printanier. Stew the vegetables in a very little stock with a small knob of butter until tender and dry. When cold, pound the cooked vegetables with the herbs and the rest of the butter and pass through a fine sieve.

Place the Beurre Printanier inside the chicken and truss, closing all apertures carefully. Season the chicken well. Layer the vegetables and herbs in a deep heavy ovenproof casserole. Place the chicken on top of the vegetables and herbs, then cover with the bacon and pour over the melted butter. Cover with the lid and cook in a moderately hot oven (190°C, 375°F, Gas Mark 5) for about 50 minutes or until half-cooked.

Meanwhile prepare the garnish. Blanch the vegetables and drain well. Lightly colour the onions in the butter.

Transfer the half-cooked chicken to a clean ovenproof casserole and surround with the garnish. Deglaze the first casserole with the stock, strain and skim off the fat. Pass this liquid through a fine strainer over the chicken and garnish, then cover. Replace in the oven to complete cooking, for another 50 minutes or so. Remove the trussing string and serve chicken and garnish straight from the casserole.

SERVES 4–6

Poularde à la Niçoise

1 large oven-ready chicken, weighing about 1.75–2.25 kg
(4–5 lb), trussed
75 g (3 oz) carrot, peeled and finely sliced
75 g (3 oz) onion, peeled and finely sliced
50 g (2 oz) celery, finely sliced
1 clove garlic, crushed
1 bay leaf
1 sprig thyme
4 rashers streaky bacon
75 g (3 oz) butter, melted
350 ml (12 fl oz) Fonds Brun page 8
5 g (1 teaspoon) arrowroot

To garnish
cooked and buttered French beans
very small skinned tomatoes, lightly cooked in a little butter
black olives, stoned

Season the chicken. Layer a deep heavy ovenproof casserole with the vegetables and herbs, then place the chicken on top of these. Cover it with the bacon and pour over the melted butter. Cover with the lid and place in a moderately hot oven (190°C, 375°F, Gas Mark 5). After 45 minutes of cooking time place the bacon at the sides of the chicken. Cook for a further 60 minutes or until ready. Baste frequently.

Remove the lid for the last 15 minutes of the cooking time, adding 50 ml (2 fl oz) of the stock and use this, together with the butter in the pan, to carry on basting the chicken so as to glaze and colour it a light brown.

Remove the chicken when cooked, cover and keep warm.

Add the remaining stock to the pan and simmer gently for 5 minutes, then drain off the liquid and skim off the fat. Lightly thicken the liquid with the arrowroot blended with a little cold water, cook for 1 minute and season as necessary. Strain.

Remove the trussing string from the chicken and coat with a little of the sauce and surround with the French beans, tomatoes and black olives. Serve the rest of the sauce separately.

SERVES 4–6

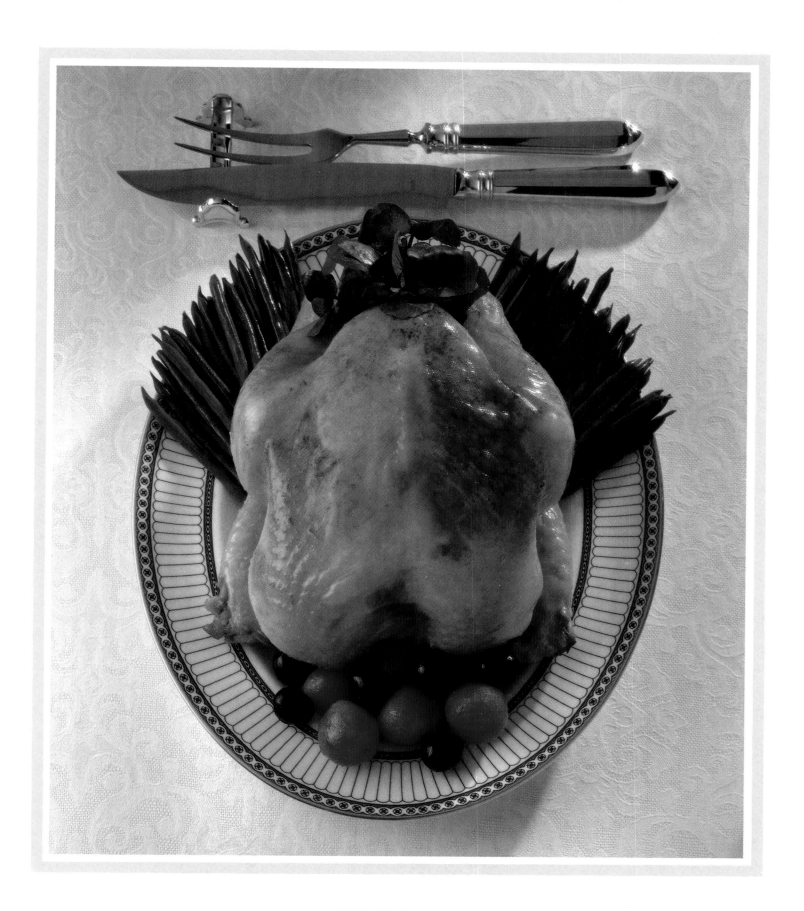

Poularde à la Niçoise

Poulet Sauté Algérienne

1 oven-ready chicken, weighing about 1.5 kg (3 lb 6 oz), jointed
salt
pepper
50 g (2 oz) butter
100 ml (3½ fl oz) dry white wine
½ clove garlic, peeled and crushed
200 g (7 oz) tomatoes, peeled, depipped and roughly chopped

To garnish
350 g (12 oz) sweet potato, peeled, trimmed to the shape of large
olives and gently fried in butter
350 g (12 oz) chayote (custard marrow), peeled, trimmed to the
shape of large olives and gently fried in butter

Season the chicken pieces. Heat the butter in a shallow flameproof casserole, just large enough to hold all the chicken pieces, and fry quickly to brown all over. Cover the casserole with the lid and place in a moderately hot oven (200°C, 400°F, Gas Mark 6) until completely cooked, removing the most tender pieces after only a few minutes and leaving those that take longer to cook for up to 10–15 minutes.

Remove the chicken pieces and keep warm. Drain off the fat and deglaze the pan with the wine. Add the garlic and the tomato flesh. Cook together for a minute or so.

Arrange the chicken in a deep serving dish, coat with the sauce and surround with the prepared garnish.

SERVES 4

Poulet Sauté Beaulieu

1 oven-ready chicken, weighing about 1.5 kg (3 lb 6 oz), jointed
100 g (4 oz) butter
150 g (5 oz) small new potatoes, or a larger potato cut into
small pieces
150 g (5 oz) small artichoke hearts, quartered
12 black olives, stoned
6 tablespoons dry white wine
a few drops lemon juice
4 tablespoons Fonds Blanc, page 9

Season the chicken pieces, heat half the butter in a shallow flameproof casserole and fry the chicken quickly to brown all over. Meanwhile, fry the potatoes and artichoke hearts gently in the remaining butter until just tender. Add to the

chicken, cover the pan and place in a moderately hot oven (200°C, 400°F, Gas Mark 6) for 10–15 minutes or until just cooked, removing the most tender pieces after a few minutes.

Arrange the chicken, potato and artichoke in the casserole and add the olives. Add the wine, lemon juice and stock.

Cover with the lid and allow to heat in the same oven for a further 5 minutes. Serve straight from the casserole dish.

SERVES 4

Poulet Sauté à la Bourguignonne

125 g (4½ oz) unsmoked streaky bacon, diced and blanched
8 button onions, peeled
100 g (4 oz) mushrooms, cut in quarters
75 g (3 oz) butter
1 oven-ready chicken, weighing about 1.5 kg (3 lb 6 oz), jointed
salt
pepper
1 clove garlic, peeled and crushed
200 ml (7 fl oz) good quality red burgundy
1 generous pinch flour

Fry the bacon, onions and mushrooms gently in 50 g (2 oz) of the butter in a flameproof casserole until golden brown. Remove the bacon and vegetables and keep warm.

Season the pieces of chicken, then fry them in the same casserole until golden brown, then add the bacon and vegetables. Cover with a lid and finish cooking in a moderately hot oven (190°C, 375°F, Gas Mark 5) for about 20 minutes, removing the most tender pieces after a few minutes.

Arrange the chicken and garnish in a deep serving dish and keep warm. Meanwhile, remove the fat from the pan, add the garlic and wine, and reduce by half. Mix the remaining butter with a generous pinch of flour and add this to the sauce to thicken it.

Pour the sauce over the chicken and serve.

SERVES 4

Poulet Sauté à la Bourguignonne

Poulet Sauté Boivin

1 oven-ready chicken, weighing about 1.5 kg (3 lb 6 oz), jointed
salt
pepper
125 g (4½ oz) butter
12 button onions, peeled
3 artichoke hearts, blanched and quartered
24 pieces of potato, cut to the size and shape of hazelnuts
150 ml (¼ pint) Fonds Blanc, page 9
a few drops lemon juice
50 ml (2 fl oz) Glace de Viande, page 9
½ tablespoon coarsely chopped fresh parsley

S eason the chicken pieces and brown quickly in 50 g (2 oz) of the butter in a flameproof casserole. Meanwhile, brown the button onions separately in another 25 g (1 oz) of butter. Add these to the chicken, along with the blanched and quartered artichoke hearts and the small pieces of potato. Cover with a lid and cook in a moderately hot oven (190°C, 375°F, Gas Mark 5) for about 20 minutes until just cooked, removing the most tender pieces after a few minutes.

Arrange the cooked chicken and vegetables in a deep dish. Deglaze the pan with the white stock and lemon juice. Add the meat glaze and the remaining butter. Pour this sauce over the chicken and vegetables and sprinkle with the chopped parsley.

SERVES 4

Poulet Sauté à la Bretonne

1 oven-ready chicken, weighing about 1.5 kg (3 lb 6 oz), jointed
salt
pepper
75 g (3 oz) butter
100 g (4 oz) white of leek, sliced
50 g (2 oz) onion, peeled and sliced
100g (4 oz) mushrooms, sliced
100 ml (3½ fl oz) double cream
100 ml (3½ fl oz) Sauce Velouté, pages 9–10

S eason the chicken pieces and fry gently in 25 g (1 oz) of the butter in a flameproof casserole to stiffen the flesh, but do not allow to brown. At the same time, fry the leek and onion separately in another 25 g (1 oz) of butter. Add these to the chicken, cover with a lid and place in a moderately hot oven (190°C, 375°F, Gas Mark 5) for about 20 minutes, removing

the most tender pieces after a few minutes. Meanwhile, fry the mushrooms gently in the remaining butter and add these to the chicken about 5 minutes before the end of the cooking time.

When the chicken is cooked, arrange it in a deep serving dish. Add the cream and Sauce Velouté to the vegetables in the pan and reduce by half. Pour this sauce and the vegetables over the chicken and serve.

SERVES 4

Poulet Sauté Chasseur

1 oven-ready chicken, weighing about 1.5 kg (3 lb 6 oz), jointed
salt
pepper
25 g (1 oz) butter
1 tablespoon olive oil
125 g (4½ oz) mushrooms, sliced
3 shallots, peeled and finely chopped
100 ml (3½ fl oz) dry white wine
25 ml (1 fl oz) brandy
100 ml (3½ fl oz) Sauce Demi-glace, page 10
1 tablespoon tomato purée
1 pinch chopped fresh tarragon
1 pinch chopped fresh chervil
1 tablespoon coarsely chopped fresh parsley

S eason the chicken pieces and fry in the butter and oil until cooked. Arrange the chicken in a deep serving dish, cover and keep warm.

Quickly fry the mushrooms in the same pan and add the shallots. Cook for another 30 seconds, then add the wine and brandy and reduce by half. Flavour the Sauce Demi-glace with the tomato purée and add this to the pan, together with the tarragon and chervil. Mix all together.

Pour this sauce over the chicken, sprinkle with the parsley and serve.

SERVES 4

Poulet Sauté au Fenouil

1 oven-ready chicken, weighing about 1.5 kg (3 lb 6 oz), jointed
salt
pepper
40 g (1½ oz) butter
4 tablespoons double cream
2 heads fennel, quartered
300 ml (½ pint) Sauce Mornay, page 13

Season the pieces of chicken and fry gently in the butter in a flameproof casserole to stiffen the flesh, but do not allow to brown. Remove the chicken pieces and deglaze the pan with the cream. Replace the chicken.

Trim the fennel quarters into large oval shapes and blanch well in boiling salted water until nearly cooked. Drain and add to the chicken.

Cover with the lid and finish cooking both chicken and fennel in a moderately hot oven (190°C, 375°F, Gas Mark 5) for about 20 minutes. Remove the most tender pieces of chicken after a few minutes.

Arrange the pieces of fennel around an oval dish, with the pieces of chicken in the centre. Flavour the Sauce Mornay with the cooking juices and cream in the pan, and pour this sauce over the chicken and fennel. Brown quickly under the grill.

SERVES 4

Poulet Sauté à la Marseillaise

50 g (2 oz) green pepper, finely sliced
3 small tomatoes, peeled and quartered
3 tablespoons olive oil
1 oven-ready chicken, weighing about 1.5 kg (3 lb 6 oz), jointed
salt
pepper
1 clove garlic, peeled and crushed
100 ml (3½ fl oz) dry white wine
a few drops lemon juice
1 tablespoon coarsely chopped fresh parsley

Fry the pepper and tomatoes very lightly in half the oil. Season the chicken pieces and fry gently in the remaining oil. When the chicken is half cooked, add the crushed garlic and the lightly fried pepper and tomatoes. Continue to fry all together.

When the chicken is fully cooked, drain off the fat and add the white wine and lemon juice. Reduce until almost dry.

Arrange the chicken in a deep serving dish with the cooking vegetables on top and sprinkle with parsley.

SERVES 4

SUPRÊMES DE VOLAILLE

This is the name given to the breast of the chicken with its skin removed, divided into 2 along the breastbone, then removed from the carcass. Suprêmes then only require a little trimming to give a neat and tidy shape. Generally speaking, they are best when cut from a young chicken of 1.25–1.5 kg (2 lb 12 oz–3 lb 6 oz) giving a weight of between 125–150 g (4½–5 oz) for each Suprême.

Suprêmes de Volaille Boitelle

75 g (3 oz) butter
4 chicken breasts, skinned
250 g (9 oz) mushrooms, sliced
salt
pepper
juice of ¼ lemon
1 tablespoon chopped fresh parsley

Butter a shallow ovenproof dish, using 25 g (1 oz) of the butter, and place the chicken breasts and mushrooms in it. Season and sprinkle with a few drops of lemon juice. Cover and cook gently in a moderate oven (190°C, 375°F, Gas Mark 5) for about 20 minutes.

When they are cooked, transfer the chicken breasts to a serving dish and arrange the mushrooms in the centre. Shake the remaining butter into the cooking liquid and add a few more drops of lemon juice.

Pour this sauce over the breasts and sprinkle with parsley.

SERVES 4

Suprêmes de Volaille aux Fonds d'Artichauts

4 chicken breasts, skinned
salt
pepper
50 g (2 oz) clarified butter
4 artichoke bottoms, sliced
75 g (3 oz) butter
1 tablespoon chopped fresh parsley
150 ml ($\frac{1}{4}$ pint) Fonds Brun, page 8
1 tablespoon Glace de Viande, page 9

Season the chicken breasts and shallow fry in hot *clarified butter*. Arrange on a serving dish and keep warm. Meanwhile, fry the sliced artichoke bottoms gently in 25 g (1 oz) of the butter. Place next to the chicken breasts on the serving dish, and sprinkle the artichoke bottoms with the chopped parsley. Cook the rest of the butter until brown or *à la noisette*, then pour this over the chicken breasts.

Deglaze the pan in which the breasts were cooked with the brown stock. Add the meat glaze and cook all together for a few minutes to thicken and reduce slightly. Serve this sauce separately.

SERVES 4

Suprêmes de Volaille à la Florentine

4 chicken breasts, skinned
salt
pepper
50 g (2 oz) melted butter
a few drops lemon juice
450 g (1 lb) spinach, washed
salt
25 g (1 oz) butter
300 ml ($\frac{1}{2}$ pint) Sauce Mornay, page 13

Season the chicken breasts and place them in a shallow pan with the melted butter. Turn them gently in the butter to set the flesh, then add a few drops of lemon juice and cover tightly with the lid. Place in a very hot oven (240°C, 475°F, Gas Mark 9) for about 15 minutes.

Meanwhile, cook the spinach in plenty of boiling salted water, refresh, drain and squeeze out all the water. Chop the spinach finely and warm thoroughly in the butter, then place in a serving dish.

Arrange the cooked chicken breasts on top of the spinach and keep warm. Add the chicken cooking juices to the Sauce Mornay, then coat the breasts with this and brown quickly under the grill.

SERVES 4

Suprêmes de Volaille à la Hongroise

4 chicken breasts, skinned
paprika
salt
50 g (2 oz) clarified butter
150 ml ($\frac{1}{4}$ pint) double cream

Sauce Hongroise
25 g (1 oz) butter
50 g (2 oz) onion, peeled and chopped
salt
paprika
200 ml (7 fl oz) Sauce Velouté, pages 9–10

To serve
Riz Pilaff, page 145, cooked with tomato as described below

First prepare the Sauce Hongroise. Melt the butter in a pan, add the chopped onion and fry gently without allowing it to brown. Season with salt and paprika, add the Sauce Velouté and simmer gently for a few minutes.

Season the chicken breasts with the paprika and salt and shallow fry to a light brown colour in the hot *clarified butter*. Deglaze the pan with the cream, add the Sauce Hongroise and pour over the chicken breasts to serve.

Serve with Riz Pilaff, cooked with 100 g (4 oz) diced tomato flesh added half way through the cooking time.

SERVES 4

Suprêmes de Volaille aux Fonds d'Artichauts

Suprêmes de Volaille Orly

4 chicken breasts, skinned
Pâte à Frire, page 26

Marinade
2 tablespoons olive oil
1 tablespoon lemon juice
1 small onion, peeled and finely chopped
a few parsley stalks

To garnish
fried parsley
Sauce Tomate, page 14

*M*arinate the chicken breasts in the marinade ingredients for 1 hour. Dry the breasts on a cloth, dip them in the batter and deep fry quickly.

Arrange the chicken breasts on a serviette on a dish, and garnish with the fried parsley. Serve with a sauceboat of Sauce Tomate.

SERVES 4

Suprêmes de Volaille Pojarski

4 chicken breasts, skinned
125 g (4½ oz) breadcrumbs, soaked in milk, then squeezed dry
125 g (4½ oz) butter, at room temperature
100 ml (3½ fl oz) double cream
salt
pepper
grated nutmeg
flour
50 g (2 oz) clarified butter

*F*inely chop the chicken breasts and add the prepared breadcrumbs, the butter and the cream. Season with salt, pepper and nutmeg and mix well.

Mould this mixture into the shape of 4 chicken breasts and coat with flour. Shallow fry in *clarified butter* and serve immediately.

SERVES 4

Poussins à la Polonaise

4 poussins
25 g (1 oz) melted butter

Forcemeat
75 g (3 oz) fresh pork fat, finely chopped
150 g (5 oz) chicken livers
15 g (½ oz) shallot, peeled and finely chopped
1 pinch finely chopped mushroom trimmings
½ bay leaf
1 pinch thyme
salt
pepper
mixed spice
75 g (3 oz) breadcrumbs, soaked in milk, then squeezed dry
25 g (1 oz) butter, softened
1 tablespoon chopped fresh parsley

To garnish
15 g (½ oz) fine white breadcrumbs
75 g (3 oz) butter
a few drops lemon juice

*B*egin by preparing the forcemeat. Heat the fresh pork fat in a shallow pan until it begins to render, then add the chicken livers with all the seasonings and flavourings down to and including the mixed spice. Fry quickly to stiffen and cook the livers, but leave them slightly underdone so that they give a pink colour to the resultant forcemeat. Allow to cool. Pound in a mortar until smooth, pass through a fine sieve, then beat further in a basin; alternatively, work to a smooth paste in a food processor. Add the soaked and squeezed breadcrumbs to the forcemeat, along with the butter and the chopped parsley. Mix well together.

Stuff the poussins with this mixture and truss. Season, place in a roasting pan, coat with the melted butter and place in a hot oven (220°C, 425°F, Gas Mark 7) and allow to brown quickly for a few minutes. Then transfer them to an ovenproof casserole, cover and finish cooking in an oven of the same temperature for a further 30 minutes.

To make the garnish, cook the fine white breadcrumbs in the butter until golden brown. Sprinkle the cooked poussins with a few drops of lemon juice and coat with the fried breadcrumbs.

SERVES 4

Dindonneau à la Jardinière

1 young, oven-ready turkey, weighing about 4 kg (9 lb)
salt
100 g (4 oz) butter
225 g (8 oz) salt pork fat, cut in thin slices
800 ml (1 pint 6 fl oz) Fonds Brun, page 8
½ tablespoon arrowroot

Matignon

100 g (4 oz) carrot, peeled and cut in small thin slices
100 g (4 oz) onion, peeled and cut in small thin slices
75 g (3 oz) celery, cut in small thin slices
100 g (4 oz) raw ham or unsmoked bacon, chopped
1 bay leaf, finely crushed
½ tablespoon finely chopped fresh thyme
75 g (3 oz) butter
150 ml (5 fl oz) dry white wine

Garnish à la Jardinière

150 g (5 oz) carrot, peeled and trimmed to the shape of olives
150 g (5 oz) turnip, peeled and trimmed to the shape of olives
a little Fonds Blanc, page 9
50 g (2 oz) butter
150 g (5 oz) shelled peas
150 g (5 oz) fresh flageolet beans
150 g (5 oz) French beans, trimmed and cut into diamond shapes
1 cauliflower, divided into florets
300 ml (½ pint) Sauce Hollandaise, page 13

First prepare the *matignon* by cooking the vegetables, ham or bacon and herbs in the butter until a light brown colour. Then add the white wine and reduce until almost dry.

Season the turkey with the salt and fry quickly in 75 g (3 oz) of the butter on all sides to a golden brown. Butter a large double sheet of greaseproof paper with the remaining butter, place the turkey in the centre, then cover it with the prepared matignon and the slices of salt pork fat. Pull the paper over the bird from all sides, seal well, then place in a deep ovenproof dish. Place in a moderate oven (180°C, 350°F, Gas Mark 4) and cook slowly for 3–3½ hours or until fully cooked. Reduce the temperature slightly if the paper colours too quickly.

Meanwhile prepare the à la Jardinière garnish. Cook the carrot and turnip in a little lightly seasoned white stock with a small knob of butter and allow to glaze. Cook the peas, flageolet beans, French beans and cauliflower florets separately in salted water then drain and lightly butter.

When the turkey is cooked, remove it from the paper, then remove and reserve the matignon. Place the turkey on a large

dish surrounded by all the vegetables arranged in *bouquets*. Cover and keep warm. Discard the paper and salt pork fat and place the cooking juices and reserved matignon in a pan together with the brown stock. Reduce by half, skim off all the fat and slightly thicken with the arrowroot, blended with a little cold water. Check the seasoning, pass through a fine strainer and pour a little of this gravy over the turkey before serving. Serve the rest of the gravy separately. Each bouquet of cauliflower should be coated with Sauce Hollandaise before serving, and any remaining Hollandaise served separately.

SERVES 8–10

Caneton Braisé aux Navets

1 duck, weighing about 1.75–2.75 kg (4–6 lb)
75 g (3 oz) butter
150 ml (¼ pint) dry white wine
300 ml (½ pint) Sauce Espagnole, page 10
300 ml (½ pint) Fonds Brun, page 8
1 bouquet garni
450 g (1 lb) turnips, peeled and trimmed to large oval shapes
1 pinch sugar
20 button onions

In a flameproof casserole, brown the duck in 50 g (2 oz) of the butter and remove it. Drain off the butter and reserve for later. Deglaze the pan with the white wine. Reduce well, then add the Sauce Espagnole, the brown stock and the bouquet garni. Put the duck back in the casserole, cover and braise in a moderate oven (180°C, 350°F, Gas Mark 4) basting from time to time.

Meanwhile, use the reserved butter to fry the pieces of turnip gently until brown but not soft. Add the sugar and turn up the heat to glaze them. Fry the button onions separately in the remaining 25 g (1 oz) of butter until half-cooked.

When the duck is half-cooked (after about 1 hour) transfer it to a clean casserole, then surround with the turnips and onions, and strain the cooking liquid over duck and vegetables. Return to the same oven for a further 1 hour, to complete the cooking.

Place the duck on a dish surrounded by the vegetables and keep warm. Skim the fat from the sauce and check for seasoning. Pour a little of the sauce over the duck and vegetables and serve the rest separately.

SERVES 4

Caneton au Champagne

1 oven-ready duck, weighing about
1.75–2.75 kg (4–6 lb)
salt
pepper
50 g (2 oz) butter
75 g (3 oz) carrots, peeled and finely sliced
75 g (3 oz) onion, peeled and finely sliced
50 g (2 oz) celery, finely sliced
1 sprig thyme
1 bay leaf, finely crushed
300 ml ($\frac{1}{2}$ pint) Brut Champagne
150 ml (5 fl oz) Fonds Brun, page 8
1 teaspoon arrowroot

Season and brown the duck in the butter in a flameproof casserole, then remove. Add the vegetables and herbs to the casserole and put the duck on top of these. Cover and place in a moderate oven (180°C, 350°F, Gas Mark 4) for about $1\frac{1}{4}$–$1\frac{3}{4}$ hours, keeping the bird slightly underdone. Baste with the butter from time to time, and remove the lid for the last 10 minutes or so to brown the duck. Remove the duck and place on a serving dish to keep warm.

Add the Champagne to the juices, vegetables and herbs in the casserole and reduce by two-thirds. Then add the brown stock, simmer for a few minutes and skim off all the fat. Lightly thicken this sauce with the arrowroot blended with a little cold water, cook for 1 minute and check the seasoning, adjusting as necessary. Pass through a fine strainer. Serve the duck and sauce separately.

SERVES 4

Côtelettes de Chevreuil aux Cerises

8 venison cutlets
salt
pepper
2 tablespoons olive oil
8 slices stale pain d'épice
50 g (2 oz) butter
450 g (1 lb), cherries, stoned and poached

Sauce Venaison
40 g ($1\frac{1}{2}$ oz) redcurrant jelly, melted
75 ml (3 fl oz) double cream
300 ml ($\frac{1}{2}$ pint) Sauce Poivrade, page 10

Season and shallow fry the cutlets quickly in very hot oil, keeping them slightly underdone. Cut the pieces of stale *pain d'épice* into heart shapes and fry them gently in the butter until lightly coloured. Alternate the cutlets and these croûtons on a serving dish, and keep warm.

Prepare the Sauce Venaison by mixing the melted redcurrant jelly with the cream and adding this, at the last moment and away from the heat, to the Sauce Poivrade.

Fill the centre of the dish with the poached cherries and coat these with some of the Sauce Venaison. Serve the rest separately.

SERVES 4

Côtelettes de Chevreuil au Genièvre

8 venison cutlets
salt
pepper
2 tablespoons olive oil
8 slices white bread
50 g (2 oz) clarified butter
50 ml (2 fl oz) gin
4 juniper berries, crushed
150 ml ($\frac{1}{4}$ pint) double cream
a few drops lemon juice
150 ml ($\frac{1}{4}$ pint) Sauce Poivrade, page 10

To garnish
Sauce aux Pommes, page 14

Season and shallow fry the cutlets in very hot oil, keeping them slightly underdone. Cut the pieces of bread into heart shapes and fry them in the *clarified butter*. Alternate the cutlets and croûtons in a serving dish.

Deglaze the pan with the gin, and flame it by igniting the liquid in the pan with a match. Add the juniper berries and the cream when the flames have died down and reduce by half. Add a few drops of lemon juice and the Sauce Poivrade, pass through a fine strainer and pour over the cutlets.

Serve accompanied by a sauceboat of hot Sauce aux Pommes.

SERVES 4

Filets Mignons de Chevreuil, Sauce Venaison

4 small fillets of venison
100 g (4 oz) larding bacon, cut into thin strips 5 cm
(2 inches) long
salt
pepper
50 g (2 oz) butter

Sauce Venaison
40 g (1½ oz) redcurrant jelly, melted
85 ml (3 fl oz) double cream
300 ml (½ pint) Sauce Poivrade, page 10

*T*rim the fillets carefully and finely *lard* with the *larding bacon*. Season and shallow fry in the butter. Prepare the sauce by mixing the melted redcurrant jelly with the cream and adding this, away from the heat, to the Sauce Poivrade.

Arrange the venison fillets on a dish and coat with the Sauce Venaison.

SERVES 4

Noisettes de Chevreuil Romanoff

8 large, thick slices peeled cucumber
50 g (2 oz) butter
100 g (4 oz) Purée de Champignons, page 130
8 venison noisettes
salt
pepper
2 tablespoons olive oil

To garnish
Cèpes à la Crème, page 132
Sauce Poivrade, page 10

*H*ollow out the slices of cucumber on one side and fry very gently in the butter in a covered pan. When they are cooked, fill the hollowed side of each with a stiff mushroom purée. Keep warm.

Season and shallow fry the noisettes quickly in very hot oil and arrange in a circle on a serving dish, placing each on one of the prepared pieces of cucumber.

Fill the centre of the dish with a garnish of Cèpes à la Crème and serve accompanied by Sauce Poivrade.

SERVES 4

Selle de Chevreuil à la Crème

¼ saddle of venison, weighing about 2 kg (4½ lb), trimmed
150 g (5 oz) larding bacon, cut into thin strips 7 cm
(3 inches) long
salt
pepper
400 ml (14 fl oz) double cream
4 juniper berries, crushed
50 ml (2 fl oz) Glace de Viande, page 9, melted

Marinade
100 g (4 oz) carrot, peeled and sliced
100 g (4 oz) onion, peeled and sliced
40 g (1½ oz) shallot, peeled and sliced
25 g (1 oz) celery, sliced
2 cloves garlic, peeled and chopped
25 g (1 oz) parsley stalks
1 sprig thyme
½ bay leaf
salt
6 peppercorns
1 litre (1¾ pints) dry white wine
300 ml (½ pint) white wine vinegar
100 ml (3½ fl oz) olive oil

*L*ard the venison with the *larding bacon* and season with salt and pepper. Place half the dry marinade ingredients in a deep dish, just large enough to hold the meat and the marinade. Put the meat on top, cover with the remaining dry marinade ingredients, and add the wine, vinegar and oil. Place in the refrigerator for 2–3 days, turning from time to time.

When you are ready to cook the meat, remove it from the marinade and dry it well. Scatter the vegetables from the marinade on the bottom of a roasting pan and place the meat on top. Start to roast in a hot oven (230°C, 450°F, Gas Mark 8) for the first 20 minutes or so, then reduce to 190°C, 375°F, Gas Mark 5 for another 50–60 minutes. Monitor cooking time and temperature carefully to ensure that the venison is served slightly rare and pink in the middle. Baste from time to time.

Remove the saddle of venison as soon as it is cooked and deglaze the pan with a little of the liquid from the marinade. Allow this to reduce to almost nothing, remove any fat and then add the cream and the crushed juniper berries. Reduce again by one-third, finish with the melted meat glaze and pass through a fine strainer.

Serve the saddle of venison accompanied by a sauceboat of this sauce.

SERVES 8

Selle de Chevreuil Briand

¼ saddle of venison, weighing about 2 kg (4½ lb), trimmed
150 g (5 oz) larding bacon, cut into thin strips 7 cm
(3 inches) long
salt
pepper
400 ml (14 fl oz) Fonds de Gibier, page 8
15 g (½ oz) arrowroot
redcurrant jelly

Marinade
100 g (4 oz) carrot, peeled and sliced
100 g (4 oz) onion, peeled and sliced
40 g (1½ oz) shallot, peeled and sliced
25 g (1 oz) celery, sliced
2 cloves garlic, peeled and chopped
25 g (1 oz) parsley stalks
1 sprig thyme
½ bay leaf
6 peppercorns
1 litre (1¾ pints) dry white wine
300 ml (½ pint) white wine vinegar
100 ml (3½ fl oz) olive oil

To garnish
450 g (1 lb) pears, peeled, cored and quartered
300 ml (½ pint) dry red wine
1 cinnamon stick, broken in half
1 strip lemon rind
100 g (4 oz) sugar

*L*ard the venison with the *larding bacon* and season with salt and pepper. Place half the dry marinade ingredients in a deep dish, just large enough to hold the meat and the marinade. Put the venison on top, cover with all the remaining dry marinade ingredients and add the wine, vinegar and oil. Place in the refrigerator for 12 hours, turning from time to time.

Meanwhile, prepare the garnish. Poach the pears in the red wine, diluted with a little water to cover and flavoured with cinnamon, lemon rind and sugar.

Remove the meat from the marinade and dry the surfaces well. Scatter the herbs and vegetables from the marinade on the bottom of a roasting pan and place the meat on top. Start to roast in a hot oven (230°C, 450°F, Gas Mark 8) for the first 20 minutes or so, then reduce to 190°C, 375°F, Gas Mark 5 for another 50–60 minutes. Monitor cooking time and temperature carefully to ensure that the venison is served slightly rare and pink in the middle. Baste from time to time.

When the venison is cooked, place it on a dish with the garnish of pears at each end. Add the game stock to the roasting pan and simmer very gently for 10 minutes. Strain the sauce, remove the fat and thicken lightly with arrowroot blended with a little cold water.

Serve the saddle accompanied by a sauceboat of the thickened sauce and some redcurrant jelly.

SERVES 8

Selle de Chevreuil au Genièvre

¼ saddle of venison, weighing about 2 kg (4½ lb), trimmed
150 g (5 oz) larding bacon, cut into thin strips 7 cm
(3 inches) long
salt
pepper
100 ml (3½ fl oz) gin
4 juniper berries, crushed
200 ml (7 fl oz) double cream
a few drops lemon juice
200 ml (7 fl oz) Sauce Poivrade, page 10

To garnish
Sauce aux Pommes, page 14

*L*ard the venison with *larding bacon* and season well. Start to roast in a hot oven (230°C, 450°F, Gas Mark 8) for the first 20 minutes or so, then reduce to 190°C, 375°F, Gas Mark 5 for another 50–60 minutes. Monitor cooking time and temperature carefully to ensure that the venison is served slightly rare and pink in the middle. Baste from time to time.

When the venison is cooked, remove it, deglaze the pan with the gin and flame it by igniting the liquid in the pan with a match. When the flames have died down, add the crushed juniper berries and cream and reduce by half. Finish with a few drops of lemon juice and the Sauce Poivrade and pass through a fine strainer.

Serve the saddle accompanied by this sauce and a dish of Sauce aux Pommes.

SERVES 8

Selle de Chevreuil Briand

Selle de Chevreuil Grand-Veneur

¼ saddle of venison, weighing about 2 kg (4½ lb), trimmed
salt
pepper
150 g (5 oz) bacon fat, sliced thinly

Marinade
100 g (4 oz) carrot, peeled and sliced
100 g (4 oz) onion, peeled and sliced
40 g (1½ oz) shallot, peeled and sliced
40 g (1½ oz) celery
2 cloves garlic, peeled and chopped
25 g (1 oz) parsley stalks
1 sprig thyme
½ bay leaf
6 peppercorns
1 litre (1¾ pints) dry white wine

To garnish
600 ml (1 pint) Sauce Poivrade, page 10
Croquettes de Pommes de Terre, page 140
40 g (1½ oz) redcurrant jelly
85 ml (3 fl oz) double cream
Purée de Marrons, page 139
French beans, cooked and buttered

Season the saddle and marinate in all the marinade ingredients for 2 hours. Dry it well, cover with slices of bacon fat and start to roast in a hot oven (230°C, 450°F, Gas Mark 8) for the first 20 minutes or so, then reduce to 190°C, 375°F, Gas Mark 5 for another 50–60 minutes. Monitor cooking time and temperature carefully to ensure that the venison is served slightly rare and pink in the middle. Baste from time to time.

When the meat is ready, remove the bacon fat, cover the bottom of the serving dish with half the Sauce Poivrade, place the meat on top and arrange the croquette potatoes around it.

Make a Sauce Venaison by mixing the melted redcurrant jelly with the cream and adding this, at the last moment and away from the heat, to the remaining Sauce Poivrade. Hand this sauce round separately in a sauceboat. Serve the venison accompanied by a dish of chestnut purée and another dish of freshly cooked and buttered French beans.

SERVES 8

Civet de Lièvre à la Flamande

1 hare, to include liver
200 ml (7 fl oz) red wine vinegar
75 g (3 oz) butter
25 g (1 oz) flour
1 litre (1¾ pints) red wine
salt
pepper
25 g (1 oz) brown sugar
1 bouquet garni
500 g (1¼ lb) onions, peeled and sliced

To garnish
6 slices white bread
50 g (2 oz) clarified butter
redcurrant jelly

Cut the hare into pieces and reserve the liver. Pound the liver to a purée and pass through a fine sieve or purée in a food processor, then mix the liver with the vinegar.

Fry the pieces of hare in half the butter in a deep flameproof casserole until stiffened and brown on all sides. Sprinkle with the flour and cook for a few minutes longer. Add the red wine, the puréed liver and vinegar, season with salt and pepper and add the brown sugar and bouquet garni. Cover and leave to simmer very gently. Meanwhile, fry the onions without browning in the remaining butter and add to the casserole.

As soon as the hare is cooked, after about 2½ hours, tip the contents of the casserole into a large sieve. Transfer the pieces of hare to a clean pan and pass the cooking liquid and onion through a fine sieve on to the hare. Reheat thoroughly.

Cut the slices of bread into heart shapes and fry in *clarified butter*. Spread one side of these croûtons with redcurrant jelly and use them to garnish the hare, which should be served in a deep dish.

SERVES 6

Civet de Lièvre de la Mère Jean

1 hare, to include blood and liver
150 g (5 oz) unsmoked streaky bacon, cubed
2 tablespoons olive oil
750 g (1¾ lb) onions, peeled and sliced
50 g (2 oz) butter
3 tablespoons flour
1 bouquet garni
1 clove garlic, peeled and crushed
100 ml (3½ fl oz) cream

Marinade
salt
pepper
4 tablespoons Armagnac
1 bottle good red wine

Cut the hare into pieces, reserving the blood and liver. Place the pieces of hare in a basin with the marinade ingredients. Place in the refrigerator and allow to marinate for 24 hours, turning from time to time.

Fry the bacon in the olive oil in a flameproof casserole. Fry the onion, separately, in the butter and reserve for use later. Sprinkle the flour on to the bacon and cook together for 2 minutes, stirring all the time.

Remove the pieces of hare from the marinade, dry them well and add to the casserole. Stir and allow to cook until they have stiffened and browned. Now add the reserved marinade, bouquet garni, crushed garlic and fried onions.

Cover and simmer very gently for about 2½ hours. When cooked, transfer the pieces of hare to a clean pan. Add the blood and the reserved liver, cut into thick slices, to the sauce. When the liver is cooked, add it to the pieces of hare. Check the seasoning of the sauce.

Strain the sauce over the hare and liver. Reheat without boiling and finish with the cream.

SERVES 6

RÂBLE DE LIÈVRE

Correctly speaking, the saddle of hare comprises the whole of the back of the hare from the beginning of the neck to the tail with the bones of the ribs being trimmed back so that the saddle can then sit level in the roasting tray. However, it is more usual these days for the saddle to exclude the ribs (thus corresponding to a saddle of lamb) and the following recipes use this shortened version.

Râble de Lièvre, Sauce Groseilles au Raifort

2 saddles of hare
100 g (4 oz) larding bacon, cut into thin strips 5 cm
(2 inches) long
salt
pepper

Sauce Groseilles au Raifort
50 ml (2 fl oz) port
1 pinch ground nutmeg
1 pinch cinnamon
200 ml (7 fl oz) melted redcurrant jelly
2 tablespoons finely grated horseradish

Lard the saddles of hare with the *larding bacon*, season and roast them in a very hot oven (240°C, 475°F, Gas Mark 9) for about 30 minutes.

To prepare the Sauce Groseilles au Raifort, heat the port in a pan with the nutmeg and cinnamon and reduce by one-third. Add the melted redcurrant jelly and the finely grated horseradish. Mix well.

Place the saddles on a suitable serving dish and serve, accompanied by the sauce.

SERVES 4

Râble de Lièvre à la Navarraise

2 saddles of hare
100 g (4 oz) larding bacon, cut into thin strips 5 cm
(2 inches) long
salt
pepper
350 g (12 oz) onions, peeled and sliced
50 g (2 oz) garlic, peeled and crushed
100 g (4 oz) butter
20 g ($\frac{3}{4}$ oz) flour
200 ml (7 fl oz) Fonds Blanc, page 9
1 pinch chopped fresh thyme
1 bay leaf
8 large mushrooms

Marinade
100 g (4 oz) carrot, peeled and sliced
100 g (4 oz) onion, peeled and sliced
40 g (1$\frac{1}{2}$ oz) shallot, peeled and sliced
25 g (1 oz) celery, sliced
2 cloves garlic, peeled and crushed
1 sprig thyme
$\frac{1}{2}$ bay leaf
6 peppercorns
400 ml (14 fl oz) good quality red wine

*L*ard the saddles with the *larding bacon* and season. Marinate for a few hours with all the marinade ingredients, then drain, reserving the marinade, and dry well. Scatter the vegetables from the marinade on the bottom of a roasting pan, put the hare on top and roast in a very hot oven (240°C, 475°F, Gas Mark 9) for about 30 minutes.

Meanwhile, fry the sliced onion and garlic gently in 50 g (2 oz) of the butter until soft. Sprinkle with the flour, cook gently for a few more minutes and add the stock. Add the herbs and simmer gently.

Pass this mixture through a fine sieve or purée in a food processor and reduce over a gentle heat until thick. Grill the mushrooms and fill them with this thick purée.

Arrange the cooked saddles on a dish, surrounded by the prepared mushrooms. Quickly deglaze the roasting pan with the reserved liquid from the marinade and pass it through a fine strainer. Reduce to about 100 ml (3$\frac{1}{2}$ fl oz) and finish with the remaining butter.

Serve the saddle accompanied by this sauce.

SERVES 4

Terrine de Lièvre

1 hare, prepared according to the instructions given in
the method, below
50 g (2 oz) larding bacon, cut into thin strips approximately
5 cm (2 inches) long
salt
mixed spice
100 ml (3$\frac{1}{2}$ fl oz) brandy
200 g (7 oz) lean ham, cut into thickish strips approximately
10 cm (4 inches) long
200 g (7 oz) salt pork fat, cut into thickish strips approximately
10 cm (4 inches) long
300 g (11 oz) salt pork fat, cut into very thin slices
1 bay leaf
Gelée Ordinaire, page 92, flavoured with the hare trimmings and
brandy

Forcemeat
150 g (5 oz) lean veal
150 g (5 oz) lean pork
750 g (1 lb 10 oz) fresh pork fat
salt
pepper
mixed spice
3 eggs

*B*one out the saddle and legs of the hare and remove the tendons. *Lard* the fillets from the top of the saddle and the best parts only of the hind legs with the strips of *larding bacon*. Season with salt and mixed spice and place to marinate with the brandy, ham and salt pork fat strips for 5–6 hours. Turn occasionally to obtain even marination.

Use the rest of the boned hare flesh to make a forcemeat. Chop the hare and other meats and the fat separately, then place them together in a mortar or food processor with the seasonings. Pound or purée finely, adding the eggs one by one and then, finally, the brandy from the marinade. Pass all through a fine sieve.

Line a deep ovenproof terrine with thin salt pork fat slices, then fill with alternate layers of the forcemeat, the marinated hare and ham and salt pork fat strips. Finish with a layer of forcemeat. When the terrine is full, fold over any ends of fat and cover with any remaining salt pork fat, plus a pinch more of mixed spice and a bay leaf. Cover the terrine with a lid.

Place the terrine in a shallow roasting tray, pour in enough hot water to half-fill the tray, then cook in a moderate oven (180°C, 350°F, Gas Mark 4) for about 2 hours, or until the fat that rises to the surface is completely clear. A trussing needle

Râble de Lièvre à la Navarraise

may be used to ascertain whether the terrine is cooked: it should come out evenly hot along its entire length when withdrawn after being inserted in the centre and left for a moment or two. Add more water to the roasting tray during the cooking as and when necessary.

To serve the terrine from its cooking dish, cover and fill the terrine with flavoured jelly a few minutes after taking it out of the oven. Then press it by covering with a chopping board, with a weight positioned on top, while it cools. When cold and set, remove any fat from the surface and trim neatly.

For presenting the terrine as a whole demoulded item, allow to cool, then turn the terrine out of the dish. Trim it neatly. Clean the cooking dish, set a layer of the flavoured jelly in the bottom, then replace the unmoulded terrine on top and surround with more jelly. When well set, demould the terrine once again onto a serving dish and surround with cut shapes of the same jelly.

MAKES APPROXIMATELY 2 KG (4½ LB)

Lapin aux Pruneaux

1 rabbit
salt
pepper
50 g (2 oz) butter
500 g (1¼ lb) prunes, soaked, stones removed
3 tablespoons redcurrant jelly

Marinade
100 g (4 oz) carrot, peeled and sliced
100 g (4 oz) onion, peeled and sliced
40 g (1½ oz) shallot, peeled and sliced
25 g (1 oz) celery, sliced
2 cloves garlic, peeled and crushed
25 g (1 oz) parsley stalks
1 sprig thyme
½ bay leaf
6 peppercorns
600 ml (1 pint) dry white wine
150 ml (¼ pint) white wine vinegar
100 ml (3½ fl oz) olive oil

Cut the rabbit into pieces and marinate for 24 hours in all the marinade ingredients.

Drain the pieces of rabbit, reserving the marinade, dry them well and season. Fry in the butter in a flameproof casserole, and brown well on all sides. Meanwhile, strain the marinade into a separate pan and reduce to half its original volume.

Add the reduced marinade together with a little water if necessary to just cover the rabbit, season and add the prunes. Cover and cook gently in a moderate oven (180°C, 350°F, Gas Mark 4) for about 2 hours.

When the rabbit is cooked, add the redcurrant jelly to the sauce and transfer to a deep dish to serve.

SERVES 3–4

Sauté de Lapin Portugaise

2 young rabbits, jointed
salt
pepper
olive oil
125 g (4¼ oz) onion, peeled and chopped
1 clove garlic, peeled and crushed
200 ml (7 fl oz) dry white wine
1 litre (1¾ pints) Fonds Brun, page 8
2 kg (4½ lb) tomatoes, peeled, depipped and roughly chopped
1 bouquet garni
2 pinches roughly chopped fresh parsley

Season and shallow fry the rabbit in very hot oil in a flameproof casserole until well coloured on all sides. Add the onion and garlic and allow to colour. Drain off the oil, add the white wine and allow to reduce a little. Then add the stock, half the tomatoes and the bouquet garni. Cook gently in a moderate oven (180°C, 350°F, Gas Mark 4) for 1½ hours or until all the rabbit pieces are tender.

Remove the rabbit pieces and transfer to a clean flameproof casserole. Pass the cooking sauce and vegetables through a fine strainer over the rabbit pieces, then add the remaining tomatoes and the parsley. Simmer gently for a further 20 minutes, before serving direct from the casserole.

SERVES 8

Canard Sauvage au Porto

1 wild duck, preferably a mallard
salt
pepper
melted clean fat, such as lard
150 ml (5 fl oz) port
15 g ($\frac{1}{2}$ oz) arrowroot

Season the duck, place in a roasting pan and coat with the melted fat. Roast in a hot oven (230°C, 450°F, Gas Mark 8) for 20 minutes, basting frequently. (Wild duck should be served underdone.) Meanwhile, use the trimmings and giblets to make a little stock.

At the end of the cooking time, drain off the fat, deglaze the pan with the port and reduce by half. Remove any further fat, add 150 ml (5 fl oz) of the duck stock prepared from trimmings and giblets, and thicken with the arrowroot blended with a little cold water. Season, then pass through a fine strainer.

Serve the duck accompanied by this sauce.

SERVES 2 OR 3

Faisan à la Normande

1 pheasant
salt
pepper
75 g (3 oz) butter
6 medium dessert apples
100 ml (3$\frac{1}{2}$ fl oz) single cream

Season and fry the pheasant in 50 g (2 oz) of the butter for about 6 minutes, until golden brown on all sides.

Meanwhile, peel the apples, cut them in quarters and slice. Sauté them quickly in the remaining butter. Put a layer of these on the bottom of an ovenproof casserole, place the pheasant on top and surround it with the remaining apple slices. Sprinkle with the cream, season and cover closely with the casserole lid. Cook in a hot oven (220°C, 425°F, Gas Mark 7) for 30–35 minutes or until just cooked.

Serve the pheasant and apples direct from the casserole.

SERVES 4

Faisan Titania

2 pheasants
salt
pepper
50 g (2 oz) melted butter
225 g (8 oz) black grapes, skinned and depipped
2 oranges, peeled and segmented
3 tablespoons Fonds de Gibier, page 8
3 tablespoons pomegranate juice

Matignon
50 g (2 oz) carrot, peeled and finely sliced
50 g (2 oz) onion, peeled and finely sliced
25 g (1 oz) celery, finely sliced
50 g (2 oz) streaky bacon, diced
25 g (1 oz) butter
1 bay leaf
1 sprig thyme
2 tablespoons dry white wine

Before *poêling* the pheasant, first prepare the *matignon*. Fry the vegetables and bacon gently in the butter and add the herbs. Then deglaze the pan with the wine.

Place a layer of matignon in a heavy ovenproof *cocotte* just large enough to hold the birds. Put them on top of the matignon, season well and coat with melted butter.

Cover with a lid and cook in a moderately hot oven (200°C, 400°F, Gas Mark 6), basting frequently, for 1 hour or until the birds are just cooked. Place them in a warmed ovenproof serving dish and surround with the grapes and orange segments.

Add the game stock and pomegranate juice to the juices left from the cooking of the pheasant. Skim off any fat and strain the sauce over the pheasants. Heat all through for about 5 minutes in the same oven, then serve immediately.

SERVES 6–8

Faisan à la Georgienne

1 pheasant
30 fresh green walnuts, peeled and halved
500 ml (18 fl oz) white grape juice
100 ml (3½ fl oz) orange juice
50 ml (2 fl oz) Malmsey Madeira or dessert Muscat wine
50 ml (2 fl oz) strong green tea
50 g (2 oz) butter
salt
pepper
200 ml (7 fl oz) Sauce Espagnole, page 10

Truss the pheasant and place in an ovenproof casserole with the walnuts, grape juice, orange juice, wine, tea, butter and seasonings. Cover with a lid and place in a moderately hot oven (190°C, 375°F, Gas Mark 5) for about 35–40 minutes. Remove the lid after this time and allow the bird to brown and finish cooking.

When the pheasant is cooked, cut the trussing string, place on a suitable serving dish and surround with the halved walnuts. Keep warm. Pass the cooking liquid through a fine strainer, add the Sauce Espagnole and reduce by half.

Lightly coat the pheasant and walnuts with this sauce, and serve the rest of the sauce in a sauceboat.

SERVES 4

Salmis de Faisan

1 pheasant
4 rashers streaky bacon, rinded
2 tablespoons brandy
2 tablespoons Glace de Viande, page 9, melted
250 ml (8 fl oz) dry white wine
25 g (1 oz) shallot, peeled and chopped
pepper
150 ml (¼ pint) Sauce Espagnole, page 10
150 ml (¼ pint) Fonds de Gibier, page 8
10 button mushrooms
75 g (3 oz) butter
20 slices truffle

Cover the pheasant with the rashers of bacon and roast in a moderately hot oven (190°C, 375°F, Gas Mark 5) for about 30 minutes, so that it is slightly underdone but not excessively so. Remove from the oven and cut into 6 pieces: 2 legs, 2 wings

and the breast cut in 2 lengthways. Discard the skin from all the pieces and trim these neatly.

Place the pieces of pheasant in a small pan, heat then pour the brandy over the top and flame it by igniting with a match. When the flames have died down, add the melted meat glaze, cover and keep warm.

Pound the carcass and trimmings and place in a pan with the wine, shallot and pepper. Allow to reduce to almost nothing, then add the Sauce Espagnole and game stock and simmer for 10 minutes. Meanwhile, fry the mushrooms gently in 25 g (1 oz) of the butter and reserve.

Pass the mixture of Sauce Espagnole and game stock through a fine sieve, pressing firmly on the carcass. Reduce by one-third, skimming as necessary, and strain again. Finish with the remaining butter.

Add the fried mushrooms and slices of truffle to the prepared pheasant and cover with the sauce. Place in a deep dish and serve hot.

SERVES 4

Sauté de Faisan au Suc d'Ananas

1 plump pheasant, jointed
salt
pepper
50 g (2 oz) butter
50 ml (2 fl oz) brandy
a few drops lemon juice
2–3 tablespoons fresh pineapple juice

Season the pheasant and heat the butter in a flameproof casserole just large enough to hold all the pieces of pheasant. When it is very hot, put in the pieces of pheasant and brown them quickly on all sides. Cover with a lid and place in a moderately hot oven (190°C, 375°F, Gas Mark 5) for about 30–40 minutes, or until completely cooked.

Arrange the cooked pheasant in a deep serving dish and keep warm. Deglaze the pan with the brandy and flame by igniting with a match. When the flames have died down, add the lemon juice and, at the last moment, the fresh pineapple juice. Pour this over the pheasant and serve immediately.

SERVES 4

Faisan à la Georgienne

Perdreaux à la Bourguignonne

2 young partridges
salt
pepper
75 g (3 oz) butter
50 g (2 oz) carrot, finely sliced
50 g (2 oz) onion, finely sliced
25 g (1 oz) celery, finely sliced
25 g (1 oz) bacon, finely sliced
1 clove garlic, crushed
1 pinch dried thyme
1 bay leaf
12 button onions
1 pinch sugar
12 button mushrooms
300 ml ($\frac{1}{2}$ pint) red wine
50 ml (2 fl oz) Sauce Demi-glace, page 10

Truss and season the partridges. Heat 50 g (2 oz) of the butter in a deep flameproof casserole and, when it is very hot, add the partridges and brown them quickly on all sides. Add the vegetables, bacon, garlic and herbs. Cover with a lid and place in a hot oven (220°C, 425°F, Gas Mark 7) for about 25–30 minutes, until three-quarters cooked.

Meanwhile, fry the button onions in 15 g ($\frac{1}{2}$ oz) of the butter and glaze with a pinch of sugar. Fry the mushrooms in the remaining butter.

Transfer the three-quarters cooked partridges to a clean ovenproof casserole with the glazed onions and fried mushrooms. Deglaze the pan in which the partridges were cooked with the red wine, reduce by two-thirds and add the Sauce Demi-glace. Pass through a fine strainer and skim.

Pour this sauce over the partridges, cover with the lid and return to the same oven for 10 more minutes to finish cooking. Cut the trussing strings and serve direct from the casserole.

SERVES 2

Perdreaux en Estouffade

2 young partridges
salt
pepper
50 g (2 oz) butter
50 ml (2 fl oz) brandy
50 ml (2 fl oz) Fonds de Gibier, page 8
250 g (9 oz) flour
100 ml ($3\frac{1}{2}$ fl oz) water

Matignon
50 g (2 oz) carrot, peeled and diced finely
50 g (2 oz) onion, peeled and diced finely
25 g (1 oz) celery, chopped finely
50 g (2 oz) bacon, rinded and chopped
$\frac{1}{2}$ bay leaf
1 small sprig thyme
1 crushed juniper berry
25 g (1 oz) butter
1 tablespoon dry white wine

Season the partridges, dot with half the butter and brown, uncovered, in a hot oven (220°C, 425°F, Gas Mark 7).

Meanwhile, prepare the *matignon* by frying all the vegetables and flavourings together gently in the butter in a covered pan. Add the white wine and reduce until almost dry.

Place 2 tablespoons of the matignon in a small ovenproof casserole just large enough to hold the partridges. Add the browned partridges and cover with 2 more tablespoonsful of matignon. Add the remaining butter and the brandy. Flame by igniting the contents of the casserole with a match and, when the flames have died down, add the game stock.

Cover with the lid and seal the edges with a band of *repère* (see page 86 and Glossary). Place in the same oven for 25 more minutes, then serve direct from the casserole.

SERVES 2

Perdrix aux Choux

2 old partridges
salt
pepper
75 g (3 oz) butter
1 small cabbage, blanched and shredded
4 rashers streaky bacon, rinded and blanched
4 carrots, peeled
2 small smoked pork sausages
150 ml ($\frac{1}{4}$ pint) Fonds Blanc, page 9

To garnish
150 ml ($\frac{1}{4}$ pint) Sauce Demi-glace, page 10, finished with well-
reduced Fonds de Gibier in place of Fonds Brun
6 chipolata sausages, grilled

Truss the partridges and season. Heat 50 g (2 oz) of the butter in a deep flameproof casserole and, when it is very hot, add the partridges and brown them quickly on all sides.

Add the cabbage, bacon, carrots, sausages and stock, cover with a lid and place in a moderate oven (180°C, 350°F, Gas Mark 4) to braise. Remove the bacon, carrots and sausages after about 1 hour, leaving the cabbage and partridges to finish cooking together for another hour or so.

Slice the carrots and sausages and cut the bacon into squares. Butter a clean deep ovenproof casserole using the remaining butter, then line with the slices of sausage and carrot and the squares of bacon, and cover these with a layer of cabbage. Remove the trussing strings from the partridges and place in the centre of the casserole. Cover with the remaining cabbage and return to the same oven for 5 minutes or so to reheat.

Turn the casserole upside down on to a round serving dish and allow any liquid to drain and be discarded before removing the casserole dish and 'demoulding' the birds and vegetables. Surround with a little game-flavoured Sauce Demi-glace and the grilled chipolata sausages.

Serves 2

Cailles à la Dauphinoise

50 g (2 oz) butter
4 vine leaves
4 quail
4 thinly cut rashers streaky bacon, rinded
4 thin slices boiled ham

Purée de Pois Frais
450 g (1 lb) fresh peas, shelled
1 pinch sugar
salt
1 lettuce, tied together with a few parsley stalks
50 g (2 oz) butter
salt
pepper

First prepare the purée of peas. Cook the peas in just enough boiling water to cover them, together with the sugar, salt, lettuce and parsley stalks. When they are cooked, drain and pass the peas and lettuce through a sieve, and leave the cooking liquid to reduce to a glaze. Add the butter to the puréed peas, season, stir in the glazed cooking liquid, and reduce to a thick consistency.

Butter the vine leaves and wrap each quail in a buttered vine leaf, then in a rasher of streaky bacon. Secure the vine leaves and bacon by trussing with string. Roast in a very hot oven (240°C, 475°F, Gas Mark 9) for 10 minutes. Remove the trussing strings.

Cover the bottom of an ovenproof dish with the slices of boiled ham, place the puréed peas on top and smooth over the surface of the purée.

Arrange the quail on top of the purée, pressing them halfway into it. Return to the same oven for a further 10 minutes and serve from the dish.

Serves 2

Cailles à la Grecque

8 quail
salt
pepper
50 g (2 oz) butter

To garnish
Riz à la Grecque, page 145
6 tablespoons Fonds de Gibier, page 8

Season and place the quail in an ovenproof casserole with the butter, cover and cook in a very hot oven (240°C, 475°F, Gas Mark 9) for 20 minutes.

Half-fill a deep serving dish with Riz à la Grecque and place the quails on top. Deglaze the casserole with the game stock, remove any fat, pour over the quail and serve.

SERVES 4

Pigeonneaux à la Printanière

3 plump young wood pigeons
salt
pepper
75 g (3 oz) butter
Fonds Brun, page 8
150 ml (5 fl oz) Sauce Demi-glace, page 10
1 bouquet garni

Garnish à la Printanière
125 g (4½ oz) small new carrots, peeled and trimmed
125 g (4½ oz) small new turnips, peeled and trimmed
20 small new onions, peeled
125 g (4½ oz) asparagus tips, blanched

Season and fry the pigeons on all sides in the butter until browned. Transfer the pigeons to an ovenproof casserole. Deglaze the pan with a little stock and add this, the Sauce Demi-glace, bouquet garni and all the garnishing vegetables except the asparagus tips to the casserole containing the pigeons.

Finish cooking the pigeons with the vegetables in a moderate oven (160°C, 325°F, Gas Mark 3) for about 1 hour or until the pigeons are tender. Add the blanched asparagus tips 5 minutes before the end of the cooking time.

Serve the pigeons surrounded by the vegetables.

SERVES 6

Pigeonneaux au Sauternes

3 plump young wood pigeons
salt
pepper
50 g (2 oz) melted butter
300 ml (½ pint) Sauternes
3 tablespoons Glace de Viande, page 9

Matignon
50 g (2 oz) carrot, peeled and finely sliced
50 g (2 oz) onion, peeled and finely sliced
25 g (1 oz) celery, finely sliced
50 g (2 oz) streaky bacon, diced
25 g (1 oz) butter
1 bay leaf
1 sprig thyme
2 tablespoons dry white wine

Before *poêling* the birds, prepare the *matignon*. Fry the vegetables and bacon gently in the butter and add the herbs. Then add the white wine and reduce until almost dry.

Place a layer of matignon in a heavy ovenproof *cocotte* just large enough to hold the birds. Put these on top of the matignon, season well and coat with melted butter.

Cover with a lid and place in a moderately hot oven (200°C, 400°F, Gas Mark 6) basting frequently for about 1 hour or until the pigeons are cooked. When they are cooked, transfer the birds to a serving dish and keep warm.

Deglaze the pan with the Sauternes and reduce by two-thirds. Add the meat glaze and pass through a fine strainer. Cover the pigeons with the prepared sauce and serve.

SERVES 6

Cailles à la Grecque

VEGETABLE DISHES

Artichauts Cavour

12 very small, tender artichokes
2 litres (3½ pints) Fonds Blanc, page 9
75 g (3 oz) melted butter
50 g (2 oz) Parmesan, grated
50 g (2 oz) Gruyère, grated
2 hard-boiled eggs, chopped
25 g (1 oz) butter
a few drops anchovy essence
1 tablespoon chopped fresh parsley

Trim off any tough or fibrous leaf ends to produce artichokes the shape and size of an egg. Cook them until tender in boiling Fonds Blanc, then drain well and squeeze dry.

Dip the artichokes in melted butter, then in a mixture of grated Parmesan and Gruyère. Arrange in a circle on an ovenproof dish and brown in a hot oven (220°C, 425°F, Gas Mark 7).

Meanwhile, fry the chopped hard-boiled eggs in the butter and, while the butter is still foaming, add the anchovy essence and parsley. Pour this over the browned artichokes and serve.

SERVES 4–6

Coeurs d'Artichauts Clamart

50 g (2 oz) butter
12 small young artichokes, trimmed down to the heart and each heart cut into 6
12 small carrots, peeled and quartered
450 g (1 lb) fresh peas, shelled
1 bouquet garni
10 g (⅓ oz) flour

Butter a small ovenproof *cocotte*, using 25 g (1 oz) of the butter. Arrange the artichoke hearts in the cocotte with the carrots and peas. Add the bouquet garni, a little water and a pinch of salt. Cover and cook slowly in a moderate oven (160°C, 325°F, Gas Mark 3) for about 50 minutes.

When the artichoke hearts are cooked, remove the bouquet garni and drain off and reserve the cooking liquid. Make a *beurre manié*, using the rest of the butter and the flour, and add this to the cooking liquid. Simmer briefly to thicken. Pour the thickened cooking liquid over the vegetables and serve as they are, direct from the cocotte.

SERVES 6–8

Purée d'Artichauts

15 tender young artichokes
salt
450 g (1 lb) medium potatoes, peeled
200 g (7 oz) butter

Trim the artichokes of all fibrous green leaf ends, remove the spiny filaments of the central choke and half-cook by boiling in salted water for about 10 minutes. Meanwhile, boil the potatoes in salted water until soft.

Drain the artichokes and finish cooking them in a covered pan in a third of the butter. Drain the potatoes when cooked and mash them thoroughly.

Pass the buttery artichokes through a fine sieve, return to the pan and add the mashed potato. Finish the purée with another third of the butter. Cook the remaining butter until brown (or *à la noisette*) and add this to the purée just before serving. *See photograph on page 129.*

SERVES 6–8

Artichauts Cavour

Fonds d'Artichauts Stanley

100 g (4 oz) butter
2 large onions, peeled, sliced and blanched
150 g (5 oz) raw ham, sliced
16 artichoke bottoms, trimmed
150 ml (¼ pint) dry white wine
150 ml (¼ pint) thin Sauce Béchamel, page 12
250 ml (8 fl oz) double cream
100 g (4 oz) lean boiled ham, diced

Butter a shallow saucepan, using 25 g (1 oz) of the butter, and arrange the onions and raw ham on the bottom. Place the artichoke bottoms on top, cover the pan closely and allow the artichoke bottoms to cook gently in their own juices for a few minutes.

Add the white wine, allow to reduce, then barely cover with the Sauce Béchamel. Cook until tender, then remove the artichoke bottoms and arrange in a serving dish.

Reduce the sauce and add the cream. Pass all the cooking ingredients firmly through a fine sieve and finish with the remaining butter. Pour this over the artichoke bottoms and sprinkle with the diced ham before serving.

SERVES 8

Quartiers d'Artichauts Dietrich

12 very small, tender artichokes
50 g (2 oz) onion, peeled and finely chopped
50 g (2 oz) butter
150 ml (¼ pint) thin Sauce Velouté, pages 9–10
150 ml (¼ pint) mushroom cooking liquor
Riz Pilaff, page 145
25 g (1 oz) raw white Piedmont truffle
50 ml (2 fl oz) double cream

Trim any tough or fibrous leaf ends from the artichokes, then cut them into quarters lengthways. Cook them with the onion in the butter for a few minutes, then add the Sauce Velouté and the *mushroom cooking liquor*. Simmer until tender.

Put the artichokes in the centre of a round serving dish, and surround with a border of Riz Pilaff containing shavings of raw white truffle. Keep warm. Reduce the cooking liquid to a few tablespoons, and finish with the cream. Pour this sauce over the artichokes and serve.

SERVES 4–6

Asperges au Gratin

20–30 sticks asparagus, trimmed and tied in bundles
salt
300 ml (½ pint) Sauce Mornay, page 13
75 g (3 oz) Parmesan, grated

Cook the asparagus in plenty of boiling salted water, keeping it fairly firm. Drain, and arrange the cooked asparagus in overlapping rows on a serving dish.

Coat the heads of each row with Sauce Mornay. Cover two-thirds of the unsauced stalks of the last row with a band of buttered greaseproof paper and coat the final uncovered third with sauce.

Sprinkle with the grated Parmesan and brown quickly under the grill. Remove the paper and serve immediately.

SERVES 4

Asperges à la Polonaise

20–30 sticks asparagus, trimmed and tied in bundles
salt
4 hard-boiled egg yolks
2 tablespoons chopped fresh parsley
25 g (1 oz) fine white breadcrumbs
125 g (4½ oz) butter

Cook the asparagus in plenty of boiling salted water. When cooked but still firm, drain and arrange in rows on an oval dish. Sprinkle the heads of each row with a mixture of chopped hard-boiled egg yolks and parsley. Keep warm.

Fry the breadcrumbs in the butter until both breadcrumbs and butter are golden brown, and coat the heads of asparagus with this just before serving.

SERVES 4–6

Pointes d'Asperges au Beurre

30–40 sticks asparagus, trimmed
salt
50 g (2 oz) butter

Cut off the asparagus tips about 5 cm (2 inches) from the point and tie in bundles. Cut the remaining tender parts into pieces the size of a pea. Wash all well and cook quickly in boiling salted water so as to keep both tips and cut tender parts very green.

As soon as they are cooked, drain well and place in a pan over a gentle heat to evaporate any remaining moisture. Remove from the heat, add the butter and toss gently to mix.

Place the small pieces of cut asparagus in a deep dish, snip the bundles and arrange the asparagus tips on top. *See photograph on page 141.*

SERVES 4

Aubergines à l'Egyptienne

4 aubergines
oil for deep frying
125 g (4½ oz) onion, peeled and chopped
3 tablespoons olive oil
salt
pepper
8 tomatoes, peeled and cut in thick slices
25 g (1 oz) butter
2 tablespoons chopped fresh parsley

Cut the aubergines in half lengthways. Cut round the edges, just inside the skins, and slash the centres, criss-cross fashion, to facilitate their cooking. Deep fry in hot oil (180°C, 350°F) then drain and scoop out the flesh. Fry the onions in 1 tablespoon of the oil. Season and fry the tomatoes, separately and gently, in another tablespoon of the oil and keep warm. Butter an ovenproof dish and arrange the aubergine skins in it. Chop the flesh of the aubergines and add the fried onion, then season to taste.

Fill the skins with this mixture, sprinkle with the remaining oil and cook in a moderate oven (180°C, 350°F, Gas Mark 4) for 30 minutes. When you remove them from the oven, place a few overlapping slices of fried tomato along each half aubergine and sprinkle with the chopped parsley.

SERVES 8

Aubergines à la Serbe

4 aubergines
oil for deep frying
150 g (5 oz) onion, peeled and chopped
50 g (2 oz) butter
250 g (9 oz) tomatoes, peeled, depipped and roughly chopped
100 g (4 oz) long-grain rice, dry weight
salt
150 g (5 oz) lamb, cooked and chopped
pepper
25 g (1 oz) dry white breadcrumbs

To garnish
300 ml (½ pint) Sauce Tomate, page 14
2 tablespoons chopped fresh parsley

Cut the aubergines in half lengthways. Cut round the edges, just inside the skins, and slash the centres, criss-cross fashion, to facilitate their cooking. Deep fry in hot oil (180°C, 350°F), then drain and scoop out the flesh.

Fry the onions gently in 40 g (1½ oz) butter until soft, add the tomato flesh and fry for a little longer. Cook the rice in lightly salted water.

Butter an ovenproof dish, using the remaining butter, and arrange the aubergine skins in it. Chop the flesh of the aubergines and add the fried onions, tomatoes, rice and lamb, then season to taste. Fill the aubergine skins with this mixture, sprinkle with the breadcrumbs and gratinate in a hot oven (220°C, 425°F, Gas Mark 7).

Just before serving, surround the stuffed aubergines with a *cordon* of Sauce Tomate and sprinkle with chopped parsley.

SERVES 8

Aubergines à la Napolitaine

4 small aubergines
salt
pepper
flour
oil for deep frying
2 tablespoons tomato purée
50 g (2 oz) Parmesan, grated
300 ml (½ pint) Sauce Tomate, page 14
1 tablespoon olive oil
1 tablespoon melted butter

Peel the aubergines and cut each one into 6 slices lengthways. Season, coat lightly with flour and deep fry in hot oil (180°C, 350°F).

Combine the tomato purée with half the Parmesan and spread the slices of aubergine with this. Re-form the aubergines to their original shape and arrange in an ovenproof gratin dish.

Coat with the Sauce Tomate, sprinkle with the remaining Parmesan, then sprinkle with the oil and melted butter, and gratinate in a hot oven (200°C, 425°F, Gas Mark 7).

SERVES 4

Aubergines Soufflées

2 large aubergines
oil for deep frying
150 ml (¼ pint) thick Sauce Béchamel, page 12
25 g (1 oz) Parmesan, grated
2 eggs, separated, and 1 egg white
25 g (1 oz) butter

Cut the aubergines in half. Cut round the edges, just inside the skins, and slash the centres, criss-cross fashion. Deep fry in hot oil (180°C, 350°F), then scoop out the flesh and chop finely.

Flavour the Sauce Béchamel with the grated Parmesan, thicken with the 2 egg yolks and add the chopped aubergine. Beat the 3 egg whites stiffly and fold into the mixture.

Arrange the skins on a buttered ovenproof dish and fill with this mixture. Cook in a moderate oven (190°C, 375°F, Gas Mark 5) for 10–15 minutes. Serve immediately.

SERVES 4

Broccoli à la Milanaise

450 g (1 lb) broccoli
salt
100 g (4 oz) butter
100 g (4 oz) grated cheese

Cook the broccoli in salted boiling water until tender but still firm. Drain well.

Butter an ovenproof gratin dish, using a quarter of the butter, and sprinkle with half the grated cheese. Place the broccoli on top and sprinkle this with the remaining grated cheese. Dot with another 25 g (1 oz) of the butter cut into small pieces and gratinate in a hot oven (220°C, 425°F, Gas Mark 7) or under the grill.

Cook the remaining butter until brown (or *à la noisette*) and coat the broccoli with this as soon as you remove it from the heat. Serve immediately.

SERVES 4–6

Carottes Glacées

450 g (1 lb) carrots
salt
25 g (1 oz) sugar
50 g (2 oz) butter

It is not necessary to blanch new carrots for this recipe: they can be scraped and left whole, or cut into 2 or 4 pieces according to size. Old carrots, on the other hand, should be peeled and trimmed to the shape of elongated olives and blanched before being cooked.

Place the prepared carrots in a pan with just enough water to cover. Add the salt, sugar and butter, and simmer gently without a lid until almost all the moisture has evaporated, leaving a syrupy reduction. Toss the carrots in this to make them glossy.

SERVES 4–6

Aubergines Soufflées

Carottes à la Crème

450 g (1 lb) carrots
salt
25 g (1 oz) sugar
50 g (2 oz) butter
150 ml ($\frac{1}{4}$ pint) double cream

P repare the carrots according to the recipe for Carottes Glacées, page 126, cutting and blanching if necessary. Place the prepared carrots in a pan with just enough water to cover. Add the salt, sugar and butter, and simmer gently until almost all the moisture has evaporated, leaving a syrupy reduction.

Heat the cream until boiling and add to the carrots. Allow to reduce to desired consistency and serve in a deep dish.

SERVES 4—6

Carottes Marianne

450 g (1 lb) new carrots, scrubbed and cut into coarse julienne
75 g (3 oz) butter
225 g (8 oz) tiny button mushrooms
1 tablespoon Glace de Viande, page 9

Beurre à la Maître d'Hôtel
50 g (2 oz) butter
1 tablespoon chopped fresh parsley
salt
pepper
a little lemon juice

C ook the *julienne* of carrots in 50 g (2 oz) of the butter, with the lid on the saucepan. Quickly sauté the mushrooms separately in the remaining butter and, when soft, add these to the carrots.

Prepare the Beurre à la Maître d'Hôtel by beating the butter until soft and smooth, adding all the other ingredients and mixing well together. Shake this into the prepared carrots and mushrooms just before serving, together with the meat glaze.

SERVES 4—6

Céleri Braisé

2 heads celery, scrubbed and trimmed to about 15 cm
(6 inches) in length
25 g (1 oz) butter
75 g (3 oz) thinly cut streaky bacon
1 onion, peeled and sliced
1 carrot, peeled and sliced
1 clove garlic, peeled and crushed
1 bay leaf
1 sprig thyme
salt
pepper
150 ml ($\frac{1}{4}$ pint) Fonds Blanc, page 9

B lanch the celery in boiling water for 10 minutes, then refresh and drain. Butter a flameproof braising pan and line with some of the bacon. Place the vegetables and herbs on top, cover with the celery, season lightly and place the remaining bacon on top. Cover and place on top of the stove to stew lightly for a few minutes. Barely cover with the stock, replace the lid and cook in a moderate oven (180°C, 350°F, Gas Mark 4) for about 50 minutes or until soft.

Remove the celery and drain. Remove any fat from the braising liquid, strain and reduce. (Discard the cooking vegetables and bacon.) Cut each head of celery in half, place in a serving dish and moisten with the reduced braising liquid.

SERVES 4—6

Purée de Céleri

750 g (1$\frac{1}{2}$ lb) white celery, cleaned and sliced
300 ml ($\frac{1}{2}$ pint) Fonds Blanc, page 9
250 g (9 oz) potatoes, peeled
75 g (3 oz) butter

B lanch the celery and drain. Cook in a covered pan in the white stock until tender. Boil the potatoes in lightly salted water, drain and mash.

Drain the celery as soon as it is cooked, reserving the cooking liquid. Pass the celery through a sieve together with a little of the cooking liquid, or process in an electric food processor, then sieve with a little of the cooking liquid.

Add the mashed potato, mix together and reheat. Finish with the butter, season to taste and serve in a deep dish.

SERVES 4—6

(from left to right, clockwise)
Purée d'Artichauts, Purée de Topinambours, Purée de Champignons

Purée de Céleri-rave

750 g (1½ lb) celeriac, peeled and sliced
salt
250 g (9 oz) potatoes
150 g (5 oz) butter
a little hot milk
white pepper

Cook the celeriac in lightly salted boiling water and drain well. Cook the potatoes in lightly salted boiling water, drain and mash. Pass the celeriac through a sieve and add the mashed potato.

Place the purée in a shallow pan and add 100 g (4 oz) of the butter. Allow to dry out quickly over a vigorous heat and bring to the desired consistency with a little hot milk. Finish with the remaining butter, season to taste and serve in a deep dish.

SERVES 6–8

Flan Grillé aux Champignons

450 g (1 lb) very tiny button mushrooms
2 tablespoons chopped onion
75 g (3 oz) butter
300 ml (½ pint) Sauce Béchamel, page 12
100 ml (3½ fl oz) double cream
salt
pepper
150 g (5 oz) Pâte à Foncer, page 26
1 egg, beaten

Fry the mushrooms and onion gently in 50 g (2 oz) of the butter until just golden brown, then add the Sauce Béchamel and cream and allow to cool. Season to taste.

Butter an 18-cm (7-inch) flan ring on a baking sheet, using the remaining butter, and line with the shortcrust pastry dough. Fill with the mushroom mixture, moisten the edges and cover with thin strips of pastry dough, made from trimmings, arranged trellis-fashion.

Brush the pastry trellis with the beaten egg and bake the flan in a hot oven (220°C, 425°F, Gas Mark 7) for about 25 minutes. Serve at once.

Small tartlets (*as shown in the photograph opposite*) can be prepared in the same way (reduce cooking time to 10 minutes) and make a particularly good garnish for tournedos.

SERVES 4–6

Champignons Farcis

12 large mushrooms
salt
pepper
2 tablespoons olive oil
12 tablespoons thick Sauce Duxelles, page 12
2–3 tablespoons white breadcrumbs
50 g (2 oz) melted butter

Remove the stalks from the mushrooms and use in the preparation of the Sauce Duxelles. Wash and dry the mushrooms well. Arrange them in a gratin dish, season and sprinkle with oil. Place in a moderate oven (180°C, 350°F, Gas Mark 4) for 5 minutes to extract some of their moisture.

Fill the cavities with the well-reduced Sauce Duxelles, stiffened if necessary with some of the white breadcrumbs.

Sprinkle the mushrooms with the remaining breadcrumbs and a few drops of melted butter. Gratinate in a hot oven (220°C, 425°F, Gas Mark 7).

SERVES 6

Purée de Champignons

1 kg (2 lb) mushrooms, coarsely chopped
150 g (5 oz) butter
100 ml (3½ fl oz) double cream
300 ml (½ pint) Sauce Béchamel, page 12
salt
pepper
grated nutmeg

Pass the mushrooms through a coarse sieve. Melt 50 g (2 oz) of the butter in a shallow pan, add the sieved mushroom and fry quickly until all the moisture has evaporated.

Add the cream to the Sauce Béchamel and reduce a little. Add this to the mushroom mixture, season with salt, pepper and a little nutmeg, and reduce further over a vigorous heat. Remove from the heat and finish with the remaining butter. Serve in a deep dish. *See photograph on page 129.*

SERVES 4–6

Flan Grillé aux Champignons

Cèpes à la Crème

2 tablespoons chopped onion
75 g (3 oz) butter
450 g (1 lb) ceps, sliced
300 ml ($\frac{1}{2}$ pint) double cream
salt
pepper

Fry the onion gently in a knob of butter without allowing it to brown. Stew the ceps gently in a covered pan in the remaining butter, add the fried onion and season.

When the ceps are cooked, drain and cover them with 200 ml (7 fl oz) of the cream, brought to boiling point. Allow to simmer gently until the cream has reduced to virtually nothing. At the last minute, stir in the remaining cream, check the seasoning and serve in a deep dish.

SERVES 6–8

Cèpes à la Provençale

450 g (1 lb) ceps
salt
pepper
4 tablespoons olive oil
2 tablespoons chopped onion
1 clove garlic, peeled and crushed
2 tablespoons white breadcrumbs
a few drops lemon juice
1 tablespoon chopped fresh parsley

Remove the stalks from the ceps and reserve them for later use. Slice the caps into fairly thick slices on the slant, season, and fry in hot oil until well-browned. Meanwhile, chop the reserved stalks finely.

When the slices of cep are almost ready, add the chopped reserved stalks, the onion, garlic and breadcrumbs to soak up any excess oil. Toss and cook gently for a few minutes.

Arrange in a deep dish and finish with a squeeze of lemon juice. Garnish with the chopped parsley.

SERVES 4—6

Morilles Farcies à la Forestière

1 kg (2 lb) large morels
50 g (2 oz) butter
50 g (2 oz) dry white breadcrumbs
2 tablespoons melted butter

For the stuffing
50 g (2 oz) butter
2 tablespoons olive oil
50 g (2 oz) onion, peeled and chopped
50 g (2 oz) shallot, peeled and chopped
salt
pepper
1 tablespoon chopped fresh parsley
50 ml (2 fl oz) dry white wine
100 ml (3$\frac{1}{2}$ fl oz) tomato-flavoured Sauce Demi-glace, page 10
1 clove garlic, peeled and crushed
25 g (1 oz) white breadcrumbs
100 g (4 oz) sausage meat

Wash the morels and cut off the stalks. Chop the stalks finely and reserve.

Prepare the stuffing by heating the butter and oil, and frying the onion and shallot gently for a few minutes. Add the reserved stalks and continue to cook gently until all the moisture has evaporated. Season with salt and pepper and add the parsley. Moisten with the wine and allow the liquid to reduce to virtually nothing. Add the Sauce Demi-glace, crushed garlic and white breadcrumbs. Allow to simmer gently until it acquires a firm consistency. Allow to cool completely then mix in the sausage meat.

Slit the morels through on one side and fill the openings with the prepared stuffing. Use a little of the butter to grease an ovenproof dish and place the stuffed morels in this, cut side down. Sprinkle with the breadcrumbs and melted butter and cook in a moderate oven (180°C, 350°F, Gas Mark 4) for 40 minutes. Serve straight from the dish.

SERVES 8

Cèpes à la Crème

Choux de Bruxelles à la Crème

450 g (1 lb) Brussels sprouts, trimmed
salt
50 g (2 oz) butter
150–200 ml (5–7 fl oz) double cream

Cook the sprouts in boiling salted water and drain them well without refreshing them. Heat in the butter for a few minutes to dry out any remaining moisture, and chop.

Stir in as much cream as they will absorb and serve.

SERVES 4–6

Soufflé de Chicorée

250 g (9 oz) curly endives
40 g (1½ oz) butter
40 g (1½ oz) flour
250 ml (8 fl oz) Fonds Blanc, page 9
salt
1 pinch sugar
3 eggs, separated
75 g (3 oz) Parmesan, grated

Blanch the endives in plenty of boiling water for 10 minutes and refresh. Squeeze out all the water, then chop.

Make a brown *roux* by mixing together 25 g (1 oz) of the butter and the flour in a heavy pan. Cook over a moderate heat, stirring continuously, until you obtain a golden brown colour. Gradually stir in the white stock, season with salt and a pinch of sugar, and cook for a few minutes. Add the endives, cover with a lid and braise in a moderate oven (180°C, 350°F, Gas Mark 4) for 1 hour until just cooked but still fairly stiff.

Pass the cooked endives through a sieve. Add the egg yolks and 50 g (2 oz) grated Parmesan. Beat the egg whites stiffly and fold these in.

Pour the soufflé mixture into a buttered 15-cm (6-inch) soufflé dish and sprinkle with the remaining Parmesan. Return to the same oven for 20–25 minutes. Serve immediately.

SERVES 4–6

Chicorée à la Crème

450 g (1 lb) curly endives
50 g (2 oz) flour
100 g (4 oz) butter
500 ml (18 fl oz) Fonds Blanc, page 9
salt
1 pinch sugar
150 ml (¼ pint) double cream

Blanch the endives in plenty of boiling water for 10 minutes. Then refresh, squeeze out all the water and chop.

Make a brown *roux* by mixing the flour with 40 g (1½ oz) of the butter in a heavy pan. Cook over a moderate heat, stirring continuously, until you obtain a golden brown colour. Gradually stir in the white stock, season with salt and a pinch of sugar and cook for a few minutes. Add the endives, cover with a lid and braise in a moderate oven (180°C, 350°F, Gas Mark 4) for 1½ hours.

When cooked, transfer the endives to a clean pan and stir in the cream and the remaining butter. Serve in a deep dish.

SERVES 6–8

Chou-fleur au Gratin

1 medium cauliflower, trimmed
salt
25 g (1 oz) butter
300 ml (½ pint) Sauce Mornay, page 13
50 g (2 oz) Gruyère, grated
25 g (1 oz) dry white breadcrumbs
2 tablespoons melted butter

Divide the cauliflower into florets and cook in boiling salted water. Drain well and heat in the butter to dry out any remaining moisture.

Arrange the florets upside-down in a closely-fitting round bowl to re-form into the original shape of the cauliflower and fill the centre with a few tablespoons of Sauce Mornay.

Coat the bottom of an ovenproof gratin dish with more Sauce Mornay and demould the cauliflower on top. Cover completely with the remaining sauce and sprinkle with a mixture of grated cheese and breadcrumbs. Finally, sprinkle with the melted butter and gratinate in a hot oven (220°C, 425°F, Gas Mark 7) or under the grill.

SERVES 4–6

Chou-fleur à la Polonaise

1 medium cauliflower, trimmed
salt
25 g (1 oz) butter
2 hard-boiled egg yolks
1 tablespoon chopped fresh parsley
125 g (4½ oz) butter
25 g (1 oz) fine white breadcrumbs

Divide the cauliflower into florets and cook in boiling salted water. Drain and place in a buttered dish. Sprinkle with a mixture of chopped hard-boiled egg yolk and chopped parsley. Keep warm.

Cook the butter until brown (or *à la noisette*), then quickly fry the breadcrumbs in it until golden brown. Pour over the cauliflower and serve immediately.

SERVES 4—6

Fritots de Chou-fleur

1 medium cauliflower
salt
pepper
3 tablespoons olive oil
2 tablespoons lemon juice
Pâte à Frire, page 26
oil for deep frying

To garnish
fried parsley
Sauce Tomate, page 14

Divide the cauliflower into florets and cook in boiling salted water for 8–10 minutes or until the cauliflower resists only slightly when pierced. Drain, season and marinate in the oil and lemon juice for 20 minutes.

Dip each floret in frying batter and deep fry in hot oil (180°C, 350°F) for about 4 minutes until golden brown. Drain well.

Arrange on a serviette on a dish and garnish with fried parsley. Serve accompanied by Sauce Tomate.

SERVES 4—6

Chou Marin à la Hollandaise

450 g (1 lb) young seakale shoots, trimmed of black parts
salt

To garnish
300 ml (½ pint) Sauce Hollandaise, page 13

Tie the seakale into bundles of 4—6 shoots and cook in the minimum of boiling salted water for about 20 minutes or until just tender.

Serve with Sauce Hollandaise.

SERVES 4—6

Chou Rouge à la Flamande

1 red cabbage, weighing about 1 kg (2 lb)
salt
pepper
grated nutmeg
2 tablespoons wine vinegar
25 g (1 oz) butter
4 apples, peeled, cored and sliced
1 tablespoon brown sugar

Cut the cabbage into quarters, then discard the outside leaves and core. Slice the rest of the cabbage into fine *julienne*. Season with salt, pepper and grated nutmeg, sprinkle with vinegar and place in a well-buttered ovenproof casserole.

Cover with a lid and cook in a moderate oven (180°C, 350°F, Gas Mark 4) for 1½ hours. Then add the apple and sugar and continue cooking for another 30 minutes or so, until tender.

Serve in a deep dish.

SERVES 4—6

Concombres Farcis

3–4 cucumbers
50 g (2 oz) butter

Chicken forcemeat
125 g (4½ oz) chicken flesh, chopped
50 g (2 oz) lean veal, chopped
75 g (3 oz) pork fat, chopped
1 pinch fine salt
1 pinch ground white pepper
1 pinch mixed spice
1 egg, beaten
2 tablespoons brandy

*F*irst prepare the forcemeat. Pound the meats and fat finely in a mortar or purée in a food processor. Season with the salt, pepper and mixed spice, and add the egg and brandy. Pass through a fine sieve.

Peel and cut the cucumbers into sections about 5 cm (2 inches) long. Blanch, drain and hollow out the centre of each piece, then set upright to form a round, tubular case. Place these side by side in a well-buttered, shallow flameproof casserole. Season lightly, dot with any remaining butter, cover and stew gently over a moderate heat for 7–8 minutes or until three-quarters cooked.

Fill these cucumber cases in a dome shape with the raw chicken forcemeat using a piping bag and tube, cover and place in a moderate oven (180°C, 350°F, Gas Mark 4) for 15 minutes or so to cook the forcemeat and to finish cooking the cucumbers.

SERVES 6–8

Courgettes à la Provençale

1 kg (2 lb) courgettes, sliced
salt
pepper
150 g (5 oz) butter
225 g (8 oz) long-grain rice, cooked weight, prepared as
Riz Pilaff, page 145
450 ml (¾ pint) Sauce Béchamel, page 12
50 g (2 oz) grated Parmesan
50 g (2 oz) breadcrumbs

*S*eason and cook the courgettes quickly in half the butter. Add the prepared Riz Pilaff and the Sauce Béchamel. Check the seasoning.

Place in an ovenproof gratin dish and sprinkle with a mixture of grated Parmesan and breadcrumbs. Melt the remaining butter, sprinkle this over the top and gratinate in a hot oven (220°C, 425°F, Gas Mark 7).

SERVES 8

Endives à l'Ardennaise

1 kg (2 lb) chicory (Belgian endive)
200 ml (7 fl oz) water
salt
pepper
100 g (4 oz) butter
125g (4½ oz) bacon, blanched and diced
100 g (4 oz) lean ham, chopped

*L*ay the heads of chicory in a flameproof pan. Add the cold water, season and add half the butter. Cover with buttered paper and a lid, bring to the boil and cook over a low heat for 15 minutes.

Then add the bacon and ham and cook for a further 15 minutes. Arrange the chicory in a serving dish with the bacon and ham and keep warm. Reduce the cooking liquid to about 65 ml (2½ fl oz), finish with the remaining butter and pour this over the chicory.

SERVES 4–6

Endives Mornay

1 kg (2 lb) chicory (Belgian endive)
200 ml (7 fl oz) water
juice of 1 lemon
100 g (4 oz) butter
600 ml (1 pint) Sauce Mornay, page 13
50 g (2 oz) grated cheese

Clean, wash and drain the heads of the chicory, then lay them in a wide saucepan. Add the water and lemon juice and half the butter. Cover with buttered paper and a lid, bring to the boil and cook over a low heat for 30–35 minutes.

Arrange the cooked endives on a layer of Sauce Mornay in an ovenproof gratin dish. Cover with more sauce and sprinkle with the grated cheese. Melt the remaining butter and sprinkle this over the cheese, then gratinate in a hot oven (220°C, 425°F, Gas Mark 7) or under the grill, until golden brown and bubbling.

SERVES 6–8

Epinards Mère Louisette

1 kg (2 lb) spinach
225 g (8 oz) butter
salt
pepper
75 g (3 oz) bread, crusts removed, cut in small dice
100 g (4 oz) lean boiled ham, diced small, warmed

Carefully wash, drain and dry the spinach, then chop roughly. Melt 150 g (5 oz) of the butter in a shallow pan, add the spinach, season and cook over a vigorous heat, stirring frequently. Meanwhile, fry the cubes of bread in the remaining butter until golden brown.

When the spinach is ready, mix the ham and croûtons into it. Place in a serving dish and serve immediately.

SERVES 4–6

Crêpes aux Epinards

450 g (1 lb) spinach
salt
75 g (3 oz) butter

Batter
125 g (4½ oz) flour
salt
pepper
grated nutmeg
1 egg
300 ml (½ pint) milk

Prepare the batter by sifting the flour into a bowl with a little salt, pepper and grated nutmeg. Add the egg and gradually whisk in the milk. Allow to stand in a cool place for 1 hour.

Meanwhile, cook the spinach in plenty of boiling salted water, refresh, drain and squeeze out all the moisture. Chop it roughly and add to the batter.

Cook as thickish pancakes in the butter in a small frying pan.

SERVES 4–6

Gombos Etuvés

450 g (1 lb) okra, trimmed
1 onion, peeled and sliced
25 g (1 oz) butter
100 g (4 oz) lean bacon, rinded and cut into large squares
salt
pepper

Blanch the okra lightly. Fry the onion gently in the butter and blanch the squares of bacon. Place all the ingredients in a heavy pan, moisten with a little water, season lightly and simmer gently, covered, for about 20 minutes.

To serve, arrange the pieces of bacon overlapping in a circle on a dish with the okra in the centre.

SERVES 4–6

Haricots Panachés

225 g (8 oz) fresh flageolet beans
salt
1 bouquet garni
1 carrot, peeled
1 onion, peeled
225 g (8 oz) French beans
pepper
50 g (2 oz) butter

*P*lace the flageolet beans in boiling salted water, bring back to the boil, add the bouquet garni, whole carrot and onion and simmer for approximately 30 minutes, until cooked but still firm to the bite.

Top, tail and string the French beans and cook in boiling salted water for about 12–15 minutes or until tender but still slightly crisp.

Drain both types of bean, season, toss in the butter and place in a serving dish.

SERVES 4–6

Haricots Blancs à la Bretonne

450 g (1 lb) haricot beans, soaked overnight
1 bouquet garni
1 carrot, peeled
1 onion, peeled
1 tablespoon chopped fresh parsley

Sauce Bretonne
25 g (1 oz) butter
50 g (2 oz) onion, peeled and chopped
120 ml (4 fl oz) dry white wine
175 ml (6 fl oz) Sauce Espagnole, page 10
175 ml (6 fl oz) Sauce Tomate, page 14
1 clove garlic, peeled and crushed
1 pinch chopped fresh parsley

*P*lace the beans in plenty of cold water, bring to the boil, add the bouquet garni, whole carrot and onion and simmer for about 1½ hours until cooked but still firm to the bite.

Meanwhile, prepare the Sauce Bretonne. Heat the butter in a pan, add the chopped onion and fry gently until golden brown. Add the white wine and reduce by half. Then add the Sauce Espagnole, the Sauce Tomate and the crushed garlic. Bring to the boil, simmer gently for 7–8 minutes and finish with the pinch of chopped parsley.

When the beans are cooked, drain, remove and discard the carrot and onion and mix with the Sauce Bretonne. Serve in a deep dish and sprinkle with the chopped parsley.

SERVES 8

Soufflé de Maïs au Paprika

4 cobs of corn, trimmed
1 onion, peeled and chopped
50 g (2 oz) butter
1 generous pinch paprika
2 tablespoons single cream
2 egg yolks
3 egg whites, stiffly beaten

*S*team or boil the cobs of corn for 5–8 minutes, or until a sample kernel can easily be removed from the cob. Drain the cobs and remove all of the kernels. (The yield should be approximately 350 g (12 oz).) Fry the onion gently in half the butter and add this to the corn. Sprinkle with the paprika. Pass through a sieve or purée in a food processor and then sieve. Place in a pan with 15 g (½ oz) butter and stir gently to dry the mixture out over a gentle heat.

Meanwhile, butter a 15 cm (6 in) diameter soufflé dish using the remaining butter. Mix in sufficient cream to the soufflé mixture to form a soft paste, add the egg yolks and fold in the stiffly beaten egg whites. Pour the mixture into the buttered soufflé mould and bake in a moderately hot oven (190°C, 375°F, Gas Mark 5) for 30–35 minutes, until well risen and browned and just firm to the touch. Serve immediately.

SERVES 4–6

Marrons Braisés et Glacés

450 g (1 lb) large chestnuts
600 ml (1 pint) Fonds Blanc, page 9

Make a shallow incision in the rounded side of the chestnuts and place on an ovenproof baking tray with a little water. Place in a hot oven (220°C, 425°F, Gas Mark 7) for 7–8 minutes, then remove both the outer shells and the inner skins, without breaking the chestnuts.

Arrange them in a single layer in a shallow ovenproof pan and barely cover with the stock. Cover with a lid and cook gently in a moderate oven (180°C, 350°F, Gas Mark 4).

When they are three-quarters cooked, after about 25–30 minutes, remove the chestnuts from the cooking liquid and reduce this to a light glaze. Roll the chestnuts in this to cover with a glossy coating and return to the oven to finish cooking.

SERVES 4–6

Purée de Marrons

450 g (1 lb) chestnuts
600 ml (1 pint) Fonds Blanc, page 9
1 stick celery
15 g ($\frac{1}{2}$ oz) sugar
100 g (4 oz) butter
a little hot milk

Make a shallow incision in the shells on the rounded side of the chestnuts and place on an ovenproof tray with a little water. Place in a hot oven (220°C, 425°F, Gas Mark 7) for 7–8 minutes, then remove both the outer shells and the inside skins without breaking the chestnuts.

Put the nuts in a pan, cover with the white stock and add the celery and sugar. Bring to the boil and allow to simmer gently for 35–40 minutes or until the nuts are soft.

Discard the celery, then drain the chestnuts and pass through a sieve. Return to the pan and stir in the butter over a hot stove. Add enough hot milk to give the purée the consistency of mashed potato. *See photograph on page 79.*

SERVES 4–6

Navets Farcis

6 large turnips, peeled to an even, regular shape
salt
450 g (1 lb) potatoes, peeled and quartered
175 g (6 oz) butter
pepper

Cut through the root ends of the turnips with a plain round pastry cutter rather smaller in diameter than the peeled turnips, cutting to about three-quarters of the way through each one. Blanch the turnips, then empty out their insides.

Cook the insides of the turnips in boiling salted water until just cooked. Cook the potatoes in another pan of boiling salted water until just cooked but still slightly firm.

Drain the cooked vegetables and dry them out in a moderate oven (180°C, 350°F, Gas Mark 4) for a few minutes, then pass them quickly through a sieve. Beat in half the butter and season.

Refill the turnips with this purée, smoothing it into a dome shape. Place the turnips in a shallow roasting tin, dot with the rest of the butter and return the turnips to the oven to complete their cooking. Baste frequently.

SERVES 6

Patates Douces Duchesse

1 kg (2$\frac{1}{4}$ lb) sweet potatoes, peeled
salt
75 g (3 oz) butter
pepper
grated nutmeg
3 egg yolks
1 whole egg

Cut the sweet potatoes into pieces and cook them quickly in salted boiling water, keeping them slightly firm. Drain and dry them out in a moderate oven (180°C, 350°F, Gas Mark 4) for a few minutes, then sieve. Place in the saucepan and add the butter. Season with salt, pepper and nutmeg and mix over a low heat. Remove and stir in the egg yolks.

Mould this mixture into flat cakes or pipe out rosettes with a piping bag and star tube on to a buttered baking tray. Beat the remaining egg and use this to brush the sweet potato shapes. Place in a hot oven (220°C, 425°F, Gas Mark 7) to brown for 7–8 minutes before serving.

SERVES 6–8

Pimentos pour garniture de viandes froides

500 g (1¼ lb) red peppers
1 large Spanish onion, peeled and chopped
100 ml (3½ fl oz) olive oil
300 ml (½ pint) white wine vinegar
salt
pepper
1 clove garlic, peeled and crushed
150 ml (5 fl oz) tomato purée
100 g (4 oz) sultanas

*S*lice the peppers in half, deseed them, then skin them by grilling them under a hot grill. Fry the chopped onion gently in the olive oil until golden brown, add the peppers and cook together for 15–20 minutes.

Add the vinegar and reduce by half. Season with salt and pepper, and add the garlic, tomato purée and sultanas. Cover with a lid and simmer gently for 1½ hours.

Serve cold, as an accompaniment to cold meats.

SERVES 6–8

Petits Pois à la Française

750 g (1½ lb) peas, freshly shelled
12 button onions
200 g (7 oz) butter, at room temperature
salt
1 pinch sugar
1 lettuce heart
2 sprigs parsley
2 sprigs chervil
3 tablespoons water

*T*ake a pan just a little larger than the total volume of all the ingredients and place in it the peas, button onions, 150g (5 oz) of the butter, salt, sugar, lettuce heart and herbs. Mix these ingredients together until they form a compact mass and keep in a cool place until required for cooking.

Then add the water, cover the pan tightly with a lid and place to cook over a gentle heat until the peas are tender.

When the peas are cooked, remove the herbs and lettuce heart, thicken the cooking liquid by adding the remaining butter away from the heat, and place in a deep dish. Cut the lettuce heart into quarters and arrange on top of the peas.

SERVES 6–8

Croquettes de Pommes de Terre

1 kg (2¼ lb) potatoes, peeled and cut into pieces
salt
100 g (4 oz) butter
pepper
grated nutmeg
4 egg yolks
flour
1 beaten egg
50 g (2 oz) breadcrumbs
oil for deep frying

*C*ook the potatoes quickly in salted water, keeping them slightly firm. Drain, dry out in a moderate oven (160°C, 325°F, Gas Mark 3) and pass through a sieve. Return to the pan and add the butter. Season with salt, pepper and grated nutmeg and mix well over the heat. Remove from the heat and stir in the egg yolks.

Divide the mixture into pieces, each weighing about 50 g (2 oz), and mould into a ball, cork or pear shape, using a little flour to stop the potato sticking. Dip into the beaten egg and breadcrumbs and deep fry in very hot oil (190°C, 375°F) until golden brown. Drain well and serve immediately.

SERVES 6

Pommes de Terre Soufflées

1 kg (2¼ lb) potatoes, peeled
oil for deep frying
salt

*C*ut the potatoes square at the sides and on the top and then cut into rectangular-shaped pieces 3 mm (⅛ inch) thick. Wash well and dry in a cloth.

Place in hot deep oil (180°C, 350°F) and turn up the heat immediately so as to bring the oil back to its original temperature as quickly as possible. Maintain this temperature until the potatoes are cooked, when they will float to the surface.

Drain the potatoes in a frying basket, then reimmerse immediately in fresh, very hot deep oil (190°C, 375°F). The sudden contact of the heat should cause the potatoes to puff up.

Remove, drain on a cloth, season lightly with salt and arrange on a serviette on a serving dish.

SERVES 4–6

(from left to right, clockwise)
Pointes d'Asperges au Beurre, Tomates Farcies à la Hussarde, Croquettes de Pommes de Terre

Pommes de Terre Anna

750 g (1½ lb) even-sized potatoes, peeled
20 g (¾ oz) butter, softened
salt
pepper
100 g (4 oz) butter, melted

Trim the potatoes to a neat cylindrical shape and cut them into thin slices on a vegetable slicer. Wash and dry well. Generously butter a Pommes Anna mould or a thick-bottomed ovenproof frying pan, approximately 20 cm (8 inches) in diameter, with softened butter then arrange a layer of overlapping slices of potato on the bottom. Season and sprinkle with melted butter. Arrange another layer, going in the opposite direction to the first, season and sprinkle with more melted butter.

Continue in this way until there are five or six layers and all the potato slices have been used – finish by coating well with butter. Cook in a hot oven (230°C, 450°F, Gas Mark 8) for 35–40 minutes, occasionally flattening the potatoes with a spatula to ensure they stick together. If necessary turn the pan around in the oven so that the top of the potatoes colours evenly.

Turn out onto a flat surface allowing any excess butter to drain away, then slide onto a serving dish.

SERVES 4–6

Soufflé de Pommes de Terre

500 g (1 lb 2 oz) potatoes, peeled and quartered
salt
100 g (4 oz) butter
50 ml (2 fl oz) double cream
6 eggs, separated, whites stiffly beaten

Cook the potatoes quickly in boiling salted water. When they are cooked, drain and dry them out in a moderate oven (180°C, 350°F, Gas Mark 4) for a few minutes, then pass through a sieve. Return to the pan, stir in 75 g (3 oz) of the butter, add the cream and the egg yolks then fold in the stiffly beaten egg whites.

Butter a 15-cm (6-inch) soufflé mould, using the remaining butter, and turn the mixture into this. Cook in a moderate oven (180°C, 350°F, Gas Mark 4) for 30–35 minutes until well risen and golden. Serve immediately.

SERVES 4–6

Gratin de Pommes de Terre à la Dauphinoise

1 kg (2¼ lb) waxy potatoes, peeled
salt
pepper
grated nutmeg
1 egg, beaten
750 ml (1¼ pints) boiled milk
175 g (6 oz) Gruyère, grated
1 clove garlic, peeled
75 g (3 oz) butter

Slice the potatoes thinly and place in a basin with the salt, pepper, nutmeg, egg, milk and 100 g (4 oz) of the grated cheese, and mix everything together.

Rub an ovenproof dish with the garlic and butter it liberally, using half the butter. Fill the dish with the potato mixture, sprinkle the remaining cheese on top, and dot with the remaining butter. Cook in a moderate oven (180°C, 350°F, Gas Mark 4) for 40–45 minutes.

SERVES 4–6

Pommes de Terre Normande

1 kg (2¼ lb) potatoes, peeled
100 g (4 oz) white of leek, chopped
50 g (2 oz) onion, peeled and chopped
50 g (2 oz) butter
1 tablespoon flour
750 ml (1¼ pints) boiling milk
salt
pepper
grated nutmeg
1 bouquet garni

Trim the potatoes to the shape and size of corks, then cut into slices.

Fry the leek and onion gently in the butter without allowing them to brown. Sprinkle with the flour, stir and add the boiling milk. Season with salt, pepper and nutmeg and add the prepared potatoes and bouquet garni.

Allow to simmer gently until the potatoes are tender, then turn out into a deep ovenproof dish, remove the bouquet garni and gratinate in a hot oven (220°C, 425°F, Gas Mark 7) or under the grill.

SERVES 4–6

Pommes de Terre Anna

Pommes de Terre Robert

1 kg (2¼ lb) potatoes
salt
pepper
6 egg yolks
1 tablespoon chopped chives
50 g (2 oz) clarified butter

*B*ake the potatoes and, when they are cooked, cut them in half and scoop out the insides. Discard the skins. Season the potatoes with salt and pepper and mash with a fork, adding the egg yolks and chives as you do so.

Heat the *clarified butter* in a thick-bottomed frying pan and spread the mashed potatoes in this in the form of a flat cake. Fry until well browned on the bottom, then turn and brown on the other side. Slide out on to a serving dish.

SERVES 4–6

Pommes de Terre Savoyarde

1 kg (2¼ lb) potatoes, peeled
salt
pepper
grated nutmeg
1 beaten egg
750 ml (1¼ pints) Fonds Blanc, page 9
175 g (6 oz) Gruyère, grated
1 clove garlic, peeled
75 g (3 oz) butter, softened

*S*lice the potatoes thinly and place in a basin with the salt, pepper, nutmeg, egg, stock and 100 g (4 oz) of the cheese, and mix everything together.

Rub an ovenproof dish liberally with the garlic and butter, using half the butter. Fill the dish with the potato mixture, sprinkle the remaining cheese on top and dot with the remaining butter.

Cook in a moderate oven (180°C, 350°F, Gas Mark 4) for 40–45 minutes.

SERVES 4–6

Quenelles de Pommes de Terre

1 kg (2¼ lb) potatoes, peeled and cut into pieces
salt
100 g (4 oz) butter
pepper
grated nutmeg
4 egg yolks
3 whole eggs
150 g (5 oz) flour
100 g (4 oz) grated cheese
50 g (2 oz) melted butter

*C*ook the potatoes quickly in boiling salted water, keeping them slightly firm. Drain, dry out well in a moderate oven (180°C, 350°F, Gas Mark 4) and pass through a sieve. Return to the saucepan and add half the butter. Season with salt, pepper and grated nutmeg and mix well over the heat. Remove from the heat and stir in the egg yolks, the whole eggs and the flour.

Divide this potato dough into 50 g (2 oz) pieces and shape like flat cakes, placing them on a floured, rimless saucepan lid. Lower them into boiling salted water and allow to poach gently for about 5–10 minutes. Meanwhile, butter an ovenproof gratin dish using about 15 g (½ oz) of butter, and sprinkle it with half the grated cheese.

Drain the quenelles well and arrange in the prepared dish. Sprinkle with the remaining cheese and the separate quantity of melted butter and gratinate quickly in a hot oven (220°C, 425°F, Gas Mark 7) or under the grill.

Heat the remaining butter until brown (or *à la noisette*) and coat the quenelles with this as soon as you remove them from the heat.

SERVES 6–8

Pommes de Terre Pailles

1 kg (2¼ lb) potatoes, peeled
oil for deep frying
salt

*C*ut the potatoes into long thin *julienne*, wash and dry well in a cloth. Deep fry for a few minutes in hot oil (180°C, 350°F), then drain in the frying basket. Just before serving, plunge them back into the hot oil and fry until very crisp.

Drain on a cloth and season with a little salt.

SERVES 6

Riz à la Grecque

50 g (2 oz) onion, peeled and chopped
100 g (4 oz) butter
250 g (9 oz) long-grain rice
600 ml (1 pint) Fonds Blanc, page 9
salt
pepper
25 g (1 oz) sausage meat
25 g (1 oz) lettuce, shredded
25 g (1 oz) red pepper
3 tablespoons Petits Pois à la Française, page 140

Fry the onion gently in a flameproof casserole in half the butter until golden in colour. Add the unwashed rice and stir over the heat until it takes on a milky appearance.

Add the Fonds Blanc, season lightly, bring to the boil then cover with a lid and cook in a moderate oven (180°C, 350°F, Gas Mark 4) for 18 minutes. Meanwhile, fry the sausage meat gently with the shredded lettuce. Grill the pepper under a hot grill, remove the skin and dice.

As soon as the rice is cooked, carefully fork in the remaining butter, cut into small pieces. Finally, a few minutes before serving, gently stir in the mixture of cooked sausage meat and lettuce, the diced red pepper and the peas, taking care not to break the grains of rice. Serve with meat or poultry.

SERVES 4—6

Riz Pilaff

50 g (2 oz) onion, peeled and chopped
100 g (4 oz) butter
250 g (9 oz) long-grain rice
600 ml (1 pint) Fonds Blanc, page 9
salt
pepper

Fry the onion gently in a flameproof casserole in half the butter until golden in colour. Add the unwashed rice and stir over the heat until it takes on a milky appearance.

Add the white stock, season lightly, bring to the boil, cover with a lid and cook in a moderate oven (180°C, 350°F, Gas Mark 4) for 18 minutes. As soon as it is cooked, carefully fork in the remaining butter, cut into small pieces.

Serve with fish, shellfish and poultry.

SERVES 4—6

Riz Portugaise

50 g (2 oz) onion, peeled and chopped
100 g (4 oz) butter
250 g (9 oz) long-grain rice
150 g (5 oz) tomatoes, peeled, depipped and roughly chopped
2 red peppers, peeled, deseeded and diced
600 ml (1 pint) Fonds Blanc, page 9

Fry the onion gently in half the butter until golden in colour. Add the unwashed rice and stir over the heat until it takes on a milky appearance.

Add the chopped tomato flesh and the diced red pepper, then add the stock. Season lightly, bring to the boil then cover with a lid and cook in a moderate oven (180°C, 350°F, Gas Mark 4) for 18 minutes. As soon as it is cooked, carefully fork in the remaining butter, cut into small pieces.

SERVES 4—6

Croquettes de Riz Safrané

50 g (2 oz) finely chopped onion
15 g ($\frac{1}{2}$ oz) butter
100 g ($3\frac{1}{2}$ oz) short-grain rice
300 ml ($\frac{1}{2}$ pint) Fonds Blanc de Volaille, page 9
pinch powdered saffron threads
1 tablespoon double cream
butter
flour
beaten egg
white breadcrumbs

Cook the onions gently in the butter to a golden colour. Add the unwashed rice and stir over the heat until it takes on a milky appearance.

Add the stock and the saffron, season with salt and pepper and bring to the boil. Cover with a lid and cook gently over a low heat without stirring for about 25 minutes or until the liquid has been almost completely absorbed. Remove the lid, mix in the cream and stir over the heat for a little longer so as to obtain a creamy, homogenous mixture. Tip onto a tray, butter the surface and allow to cool.

When cold, mould the rice into cork-shaped pieces then flour, dip in the beaten egg and then the breadcrumbs. Deep fry in very hot fat (190°C, 375°F). Drain and use as required.

SERVES 6—8

Salsifis au Gratin

450 g (1 lb) salsify, scraped, washed and placed in acidulated
water until ready to use
salt
juice of 1 lemon
150 ml ($\frac{1}{4}$ pint) thin Sauce Béchamel, page 12
2 tablespoons double cream
50 g (2 oz) Gruyère, grated
grated nutmeg
25 g (1 oz) dry white breadcrumbs
40 g (1$\frac{1}{2}$ oz) melted butter

Cook the salsify in boiling salted water to which the lemon juice has been added for about 15 minutes or until cooked but still firm to the bite. Drain and cut into 4–5 cm (1–2 inch) lengths; the thicker pieces can also be divided into 2 or 4 lengthways so that all the pieces are roughly the same size.

Place them in the thin Sauce Béchamel and cook for a little longer, both to complete the cooking and to reduce the sauce well. Add the cream, three-quarters of the grated cheese and the grated nutmeg.

Place in a deep ovenproof dish or *timbale*, sprinkle with the remaining cheese, the breadcrumbs and the melted butter. Gratinate in a hot oven (220°C, 425°F, Gas Mark 7).

SERVES 4–6

Tomates Sautées à la Provençale

6 large tomatoes
salt
pepper
3 tablespoons olive oil
2 tablespoons chopped fresh parsley
2 cloves garlic, peeled and crushed
2 tablespoons breadcrumbs

Cut the tomatoes in half and remove the pips. Season and place, cut side down, in hot oil in a flameproof casserole. When they are half-cooked, turn them over and sprinkle with the chopped parsley, crushed garlic, breadcrumbs and a few drops of olive oil.

Place in a moderate oven (160°C, 325°F, Gas Mark 3) for about 20 minutes to finish cooking. Arrange in a suitable dish and serve.

SERVES 6

Tomates Farcies à la Hussarde

4 large tomatoes
salt
pepper
3 tablespoons olive oil

Stuffing
75 g (3 oz) butter
3 eggs
50 g (2 oz) mushrooms, sliced
50 g (2 oz) lean boiled ham, diced
25 g (1 oz) breadcrumbs

Cut the tomatoes in half and remove the insides without damaging the tomatoes. Season the hollowed half tomatoes, place on an oiled baking sheet and sprinkle with a little oil. Cook in a moderately hot oven (190°C, 375°F, Gas Mark 5) for 5–6 minutes. Keep warm.

Heat half the butter in a pan and scramble the eggs with the mushrooms and ham (see remarks on the scrambling of eggs on page 30). Fry the breadcrumbs in the remaining butter. Fill the tomatoes with the scrambled eggs and sprinkle with the fried breadcrumbs. Arrange in a dish and serve immediately. *See photograph on page 141.*

SERVES 4

Tomates Farcies à la Portugaise

8 medium tomatoes
salt
pepper
3 tablespoons olive oil

Stuffing
225 g (8 oz) Riz Portugaise, page 145, warmed
2 tablespoons chopped fresh parsley

Cut a slice off each tomato at the stalk end and remove the insides without damaging the tomatoes. Season the tomatoes, place on an oiled baking sheet and sprinkle with a little more oil. Cook in a moderately hot oven (190°C, 375°F, Gas Mark 5) for 5–6 minutes.

Fill the tomatoes with warmed Riz Portugaise, piled in a dome shape, and sprinkle with chopped parsley.

SERVES 4

Tomates Farcies à la Carmélite

8 medium tomatoes
salt
pepper
3 tablespoons olive oil

Stuffing
4 hard-boiled eggs, chopped
300 ml (½ pint) Sauce Béchamel, page 12
50 g (2 oz) Gruyère, grated
a few drops olive oil

To garnish
Sauce Tomate, page 14

Cut a slice off each tomato at the stalk end, discard, then remove the insides without damaging the tomatoes. Season the tomatoes, place on an oiled baking sheet and sprinkle with a little more oil. Cook in a moderately hot oven (190°C, 375°F, Gas Mark 5) for 5–6 minutes.

Mix the chopped hard-boiled eggs with the Sauce Béchamel and fill the tomatoes with this mixture. Sprinkle with the grated cheese and a few drops of oil, then gratinate under the grill. Arrange in a serving dish and surround with a *cordon* of Sauce Tomate.

SERVES 4

Tomates Farcies à la Provençale

6 large tomatoes
2 tablespoons olive oil

Stuffing
2 tablespoons chopped onion
3 tablespoons olive oil
4 tomatoes, peeled, depipped and roughly chopped
1 pinch chopped fresh parsley
1 clove garlic, peeled and crushed
salt
pepper
4 tablespoons breadcrumbs, soaked in stock and passed through a sieve
2 anchovies, passed through a sieve
3 tablespoons fatty gravy
2 tablespoons dry white breadcrumbs
50 g (2 oz) Gruyère, grated

Cut the tomatoes in half, remove the pips and place, cut side down, in a frying pan containing a little very hot oil. Fry them lightly, then turn over to cook the outsides. Arrange in an ovenproof dish.

To make the stuffing, fry the onion gently in 1 tablespoon oil until light brown. Add the tomato flesh, parsley and garlic, then season lightly. Cover and cook gently for 10 minutes. Finish by adding the prepared breadcrumbs, the prepared anchovies and a little fatty gravy. Stuff the tomatoes with this mixture.

Sprinkle the stuffed tomatoes with the dry white breadcrumbs mixed with the grated cheese, and the remaining 2 tablespoons oil. Gratinate under the grill.

These tomatoes may be served hot or cold.

SERVES 6

Purée de Topinambours

750 g (1½ lb) Jerusalem artichokes, peeled, sliced and placed in acidulated water until ready to use
150 g (5 oz) butter
250 g (9 oz) potatoes, peeled
salt
4 tablespoons boiling milk
pepper

Cook the Jerusalem artichokes very gently in half the butter. Meanwhile, cook the potatoes in boiling salted water, drain and mash.

When the artichokes are soft, drain and pass through a sieve, then mix the resulting purée, over the heat, with the remaining butter. Add enough mashed potato to give a good consistency and finish with a few tablespoons of boiling milk.

Season to taste and serve in a suitable dish. *See photograph on page 129.*

SERVES 4–6

147

SALADS

Salade Aïda

1 curly endive
150 g (5 oz) tomatoes, peeled and sliced
150 g (5 oz) tender raw artichoke bottoms, sliced
150 g (5 oz) green peppers, skinned and thinly sliced
3–4 hard-boiled eggs, yolks and whites separated

Dressing
6 tablespoons olive oil
2 tablespoons wine vinegar
2 teaspoons made French mustard
salt
pepper

*P*lace the curly endive in a large salad bowl and arrange the sliced tomatoes, artichoke bottoms, green peppers and sliced hard-boiled egg whites on top.

Make the dressing by mixing together all the ingredients. Pour over the top of the salad and toss gently.

Sprinkle with the finely sieved hard-boiled egg yolks.

SERVES 6–8

Salade Alice

8 large red apples
juice of 2 lemons
250 g (9 oz) redcurrants
250 g (9 oz) fresh almonds, shredded, or walnuts, broken
200 ml (7 fl oz) single cream
salt
2 lettuce hearts, quartered

*C*ut off a slice at the stalk end of each apple, rub with lemon juice and reserve for use as lids. Empty the centres of the apples by scooping out small balls of apple the size of a pea, using a spoon cutter. Leave a thin layer of apple next to the skin and discard the cores. Place the balls of apple in a basin and sprinkle with more lemon juice. Rub the insides of the apples with lemon juice, too, to prevent discoloration.

Mix the apple balls with the redcurrants and the finely shredded almonds or pieces of walnut. Just before serving, mix these with some lightly salted cream, acidulated with the remainder of the lemon juice.

Fill the apples with this mixture and replace the lids. Arrange in a circle on a bed of crushed ice and place a quartered heart of lettuce between each apple.

SERVES 8

Salade Aïda

Salade à l'Andalouse

225 g (8 oz) long-grain rice, dry weight
salt
1 small clove garlic, peeled and crushed
1 small onion, peeled and chopped
1 tablespoon chopped fresh parsley
450 g (1 lb) tomatoes, peeled and quartered
225 g (8 oz) sweet peppers, cut into julienne

Dressing
6 tablespoons olive oil
2 tablespoons wine vinegar
salt
pepper

Boil the rice in lightly salted water, cool under running water and drain well. Add the garlic, onion and chopped parsley to the rice, and mix well. Combine the rice mixture with the quartered tomatoes and the *julienne* of sweet peppers.

To make the dressing, combine all the ingredients while stirring briskly. Pour the dressing over the salad and toss gently but thoroughly.

SERVES 8

Salade Aurore

3 eating apples, peeled, cored and sliced
18 fresh green walnuts, skinned and halved
1 lettuce

Dressing
6 tablespoons double cream
1 tablespoon tomato purée
1 teaspoon made English mustard
juice of 2 lemons
salt
1 pinch sugar

Arrange the sliced apples and walnuts in a salad bowl and surround with lettuce leaves. Make the dressing by mixing together all the ingredients and pour over the top. *See photograph on page 93.*

SERVES 4—6

Salade Beaucaire

2 sticks celery, cut into julienne
350 g (12 oz) raw celeriac, peeled and cut into julienne
2 hearts chicory (Belgian endive), cut into julienne
3 tablespoons olive oil
1 tablespoon wine vinegar
1 teaspoon made French mustard
100 g (4 oz) lean boiled ham, cut into julienne
1 cooking apple, peeled, cored and cut into julienne
100 g (4 oz) button mushrooms, cut into julienne
6 tablespoons Sauce Mayonnaise, page 13
2 tablespoons chopped fresh parsley, chervil and tarragon, mixed
150 g (5 oz) cooked beetroot, peeled and sliced
150 g (5 oz) cooked potatoes, peeled and sliced

Place the *julienne* of celery, celeriac and chicory in a bowl. Mix together the oil, vinegar and mustard, pour on to the salad ingredients, toss and leave for 1 hour.

Then add the julienne of ham, apple and mushrooms and the mayonnaise, and toss everything together. Arrange in a salad bowl and sprinkle with the chopped herbs.

Surround the salad with a border of alternate slices of beetroot and potato.

SERVES 4—6

Salade Belle de Nuit

20 crayfish, prepared as for Ecrevisses à la Nage, page 60
175 g (6 oz) black truffle, sliced

Dressing
3 tablespoons olive oil
1 tablespoon wine vinegar
salt
freshly milled black pepper

Remove the tails from the crayfish when cold and arrange, alternating with the sliced truffle, in a serving dish. Combine all the dressing ingredients, seasoning well with the milled pepper, then pour carefully over the salad.

SERVES 6—8

Salade Brésilienne

225 g (8 oz) long-grain rice, dry weight
salt
1 small pineapple, peeled and diced

Dressing
6 tablespoons single cream
2 tablespoons lemon juice
salt
pepper

Cook the rice in salted boiling water, cool under cold running water, drain and allow to cool. Mix with the diced fresh pineapple.

Combine all the dressing ingredients, pour over the salad and toss well.

SERVES 8

Salade Créole

6 small ripe melons
salt
1 pinch ground ginger
350 g (12 oz) boiled rice, cooked weight, well drained
6 tablespoons double cream
2 tablespoons lemon juice

Slice off the stem ends of the melons and reserve for later use. Scoop out the melon seeds and discard. Carefully scoop out the flesh with a spoon and cut into large dice. Season with salt and ginger, add the rice and mix together.

At the last moment, add the cream and lemon juice and check the seasoning. Refill the hollowed melons with this mixture and replace the reserved tops as lids.

Serve on a bed of finely crushed ice.

SERVES 6

Salade Cressonière

1 kg (2 lb) potatoes, peeled
salt
300 ml ($\frac{1}{2}$ pint) dry white wine
1 bunch watercress
3 hard-boiled eggs, chopped
1 tablespoon chopped fresh parsley

Dressing
6 tablespoons olive oil
2 tablespoons wine vinegar
salt
pepper

Boil the potatoes in salted water and cut into thin slices while still warm. Place in a basin and mix thoroughly with the wine, which the potatoes will absorb.

When you are ready to serve, add the watercress to the potatoes. Mix all the dressing ingredients together, pour over the salad and toss gently.

Arrange the salad in a dome shape and sprinkle with chopped hard-boiled egg mixed with chopped parsley.

SERVES 8

Salade Danicheff

250 g (9 oz) asparagus tips, lightly boiled and thinly sliced
250 g (9 oz) celeriac, peeled, lightly boiled and thinly sliced
250 g (9 oz) potatoes, peeled, lightly boiled and thinly sliced
250 g (9 oz) tender raw artichoke hearts, sliced
250 g (9 oz) raw mushrooms, sliced

To garnish
16 crayfish tails, cooked
4 hard-boiled eggs, quartered
25 g (1 oz) truffle, sliced

Dressing
thin Sauce Mayonnaise, page 13

Arrange all the salad ingredients in *bouquets* on a serving dish and garnish with the cooked crayfish tails, quartered hard-boiled eggs and slices of truffle.

Dress with thin Sauce Mayonnaise.

SERVES 8

Salade à la Flamande

2 medium onions
4 heads chicory (Belgian endive), thinly sliced
350 g (12 oz) potatoes, cooked and cut into julienne
100 g (4 oz) salt herring fillet, soaked, drained and diced

Dressing
6 tablespoons olive oil
2 tablespoons wine vinegar
salt
pepper
1 tablespoon chopped fresh parsley
1 tablespoon chopped fresh chervil

*B*ake the onions in the oven in their skins, then allow to cool, peel and chop finely. Mix this chopped onion with the sliced endive, the *julienne* of potatoes and the diced herring fillet which has been previously soaked to remove excess salt and drained well. Place all these ingredients in a salad bowl.

Mix together the dressing ingredients, pour over the salad and toss gently.

SERVES 6–8

Salade aux Fruits à la Japonaise

1 small pineapple, peeled and cut as required (see below)
juice of 1 lemon
225 g (8 oz) tomatoes, skinned, depipped and cut as required (see below)
1 pinch sugar
3 oranges, peeled and cut as required (see below)
6 lettuce hearts or 3 hearts cos lettuce, halved

Dressing
150 ml ($\frac{1}{4}$ pint) whipping cream
a few drops lemon juice
1 pinch salt

*I*f this salad is to be served on hearts of ordinary lettuce, the pineapple, tomato and orange should be cut into small squares; if on half hearts of cos lettuce, they should be cut into thin slices.

Sprinkle the pineapple with most of the lemon juice. Season the tomato with the sugar, very little salt and a few drops of lemon juice. Do not season the oranges.

Keep the fruit very cold until required, then arrange them on the hearts of lettuce or the half hearts of cos lettuce.

Acidulate the cream with the lemon juice and season with a pinch of salt. Sprinkle the fruit with a little of this dressing and serve the rest separately.

SERVES 6

Salade des Gobelins

225 g (8 oz) celeriac, peeled and cooked but still firm
225 g (8 oz) potatoes, peeled and cooked but still firm
4 tender raw artichoke bottoms, sliced
150 g (5 oz) mushrooms, sliced
150 g (5 oz) truffles, sliced
100 g (4 oz) asparagus tips, cooked

Dressing
150 ml ($\frac{1}{4}$ pint) Sauce Mayonnaise, page 13,
flavoured with 1 teaspoon lemon juice and
1 tablespoon chopped fresh tarragon

*C*oarsely grate the celeriac and the potatoes. Place in a salad bowl with all the other salad ingredients. Dress with mayonnaise, flavoured with lemon juice and tarragon, and toss all together gently.

SERVES 6

Salade Hollandaise

350 g (12 oz) boiled long-grain rice, well drained
150 g (5 oz) cooking apple, peeled, cored and diced
150 g (5 oz) smoked herring fillet, diced

Dressing
6 tablespoons olive oil
2 tablespoons white wine vinegar
2 teaspoons made French mustard
salt
pepper

*C*ombine all the salad ingredients in a salad bowl. Make the dressing by mixing together all the ingredients, pour over the salad and toss lightly.

SERVES 6–8

Salade aux Fruits à la Japonaise

Salade Irma

1 large or 2 small cucumbers, peeled, deseeded and diced
225 g (8 oz) French beans, cut in diamond shapes and cooked
225 g (8 oz) asparagus tips, cooked
225 g (8 oz) cauliflower florets, cooked
1 lettuce heart, finely shredded
1 bunch watercress, shredded

Dressing
150 ml ($\frac{1}{4}$ pint) Sauce Mayonnaise, page 13
4 tablespoons double cream
1 tablespoon mixed chopped fresh tarragon and chervil

To garnish
4–6 nasturtium flowers
6 radishes, thinly sliced

Mix together the cucumber, beans, asparagus tips and cauliflower florets. Combine the dressing ingredients, pour over the salad and toss. Arrange in a deep salad bowl.

Cover with the finely shredded lettuce heart and shredded watercress. Garnish with choice nasturtium flowers and thin slices of radish.

SERVES 4–6

Salade Italienne

225 g (8 oz) long-grain rice, dry weight
450 g (1 lb) fresh peas, shelled
350 g (12 oz) carrots, peeled
300 ml ($\frac{1}{2}$ pint) Fonds Blanc, page 9

Dressing
6 tablespoons olive oil
2 tablespoons wine vinegar
salt
pepper

Cook the rice in lightly salted boiling water, cool under running water and drain well. Cook the peas in lightly salted boiling water, drain and cool. Cut the carrot into dice, cook in the stock, drain and cool.

Combine all the salad ingredients and those for the dressing. Pour the dressing over the salad and toss lightly.

SERVES 8

Salade de Légumes

175 g (6 oz) small balls of carrot, cut with a spoon cutter
175 g (6 oz) small balls of turnip, cut with a spoon cutter
175 g (6 oz) potato, peeled
175 g (6 oz) French beans, cut into diamond shapes
175 g (6 oz) peas, shelled
175 g (6 oz) asparagus tips
175 g (6 oz) cauliflower
salt

Dressing
6 tablespoons olive oil
2 tablespoons wine vinegar
salt
pepper
1 tablespoon chopped fresh parsley
1 tablespoon chopped fresh chervil

Cook all the vegetables separately in lightly salted boiling water until cooked but still firm. Do not refresh after cooking but drain well and allow to cool naturally. Dice the potato and divide the cauliflower into florets.

Arrange the first six vegetables in *bouquets* on a dish, paying particular attention to colour contrast. Put a mound of cauliflower florets in the centre.

Combine all the dressing ingredients and pour over each bouquet of vegetables.

SERVES 8

Salade Lorette

2 sticks celery, cut into julienne
100 g (4 oz) corn salad (lamb's lettuce)
225 g (8 oz) cooked beetroot, peeled and cut into julienne

Dressing
3 tablespoons olive oil
1 tablespoon wine vinegar
salt
pepper

Combine all the salad ingredients and those for the dressing. Pour the dressing over the salad and toss. Arrange in a dome shape in a salad bowl.

SERVES 4–6

Salade Irma

Salade Montfermeil

225 g (8 oz) salsify, peeled
4 hard-boiled eggs, separated into yolks and whites
225 g (8 oz) artichoke bottoms, cooked and thinly sliced
225 g (8 oz) potatoes, cooked and thinly sliced
2 tablespoons chopped fresh fines herbes: parsley, chives, chervil
and tarragon

Dressing
6 tablespoons olive oil
2 tablespoons wine vinegar
salt
pepper

*B*oil the salsify and slice into small *bâtons* while still warm. Cut the hard-boiled egg whites into *julienne*. Mix the salsify with the artichoke bottoms, potatoes and hard-boiled egg whites. Make the dressing by mixing all the ingredients together. Pour over the salad and toss gently.

Arrange the salad in a dome shape in a salad bowl and cover completely with the sieved hard-boiled egg yolks. Sprinkle with the fresh *fines herbes*.

SERVES 6

Salade Niçoise

225 g (8 oz) French beans, cooked and diced
225 g (8 oz) potatoes, peeled, boiled and diced
225 g (8 oz) small tomatoes, peeled, quartered and depipped
50 g (2 oz) capers
75 g (3 oz) black olives, stoned
50 g (2 oz) anchovy fillets

Dressing
6 tablespoons olive oil
2 tablespoons wine vinegar
salt
pepper

*M*ix together the diced French beans, diced potatoes and prepared tomatoes in a salad bowl. Combine the dressing ingredients, pour over the salad and toss gently. Arrange in a dome shape in a salad bowl.

Decorate with the capers, olives and anchovy fillets.

SERVES 6

Salade d'Oranges

3 ripe oranges, peeled

Dressing
a few drops Kirsch

*C*ut the oranges in half vertically, remove the seeds and cut the flesh into thin, evenly sized pieces. Sprinkle with a little Kirsch.

SERVES 6 AS ACCOMPANIMENT TO RICH ROAST MEATS

Salade Orientale

225 g (8 oz) small tomatoes, skinned, halved and depipped
4 cloves garlic, peeled and crushed
2 tablespoons olive oil
1 large red pepper
1 large green pepper
225 g (8 oz) French beans
225 g (8 oz) long-grain rice, dry weight
salt

Dressing
6 tablespoons olive oil
2 tablespoons wine vinegar
salt
pepper
50 g (2 oz) anchovy fillets, diced

*F*ry the tomato halves very gently with the crushed garlic in the olive oil. Grill the peppers, remove their skins, deseed and dice. Boil the French beans and slice into small *bâtons*. Boil the rice in salted water until cooked and drain well.

Mix all these ingredients together. Combine all the dressing ingredients, pour over the salad while still warm and allow to cool. Arrange in a dome shape in a salad bowl.

SERVES 8

Salade Russe

100 g (4 oz) carrots, peeled, boiled and diced
100 g (4 oz) turnips, peeled, boiled and diced
100 g (4 oz) potatoes, peeled, boiled and diced
100 g (4 oz) truffles, diced
100 g (4 oz) French beans, boiled and diced
100 g (4 oz) mushrooms, diced and cooked with a little lemon
juice and butter
100 g (4 oz) salt ox tongue or lean boiled ham, diced
100 g (4 oz) lobster, cooked and diced
100 g (4 oz) gherkins, diced
100 g (4 oz) smoked sausage, diced
100 g (4 oz) anchovy fillets, diced
100 g (4 oz) peas, boiled
100 g (4 oz) capers

Dressing
300 ml ($\frac{1}{2}$ pint) Sauce Mayonnaise, page 13

To garnish
100 g (4 oz) beetroot, cooked, peeled and sliced
50 g (2 oz) caviare

*M*ix together all the salad ingredients and combine with the mayonnaise. Arrange in a salad bowl, and garnish with the beetroot and caviare.

SERVES 6–8

Salade Tourangelle

225 g (8 oz) French beans, cooked and cut into diamond shapes
225 g (8 oz) flageolet beans, cooked
225 g (8 oz) waxy potatoes, cooked and cut into thick julienne

Dressing
100 ml (3$\frac{1}{2}$ fl oz) Sauce Mayonnaise, page 13
2 tablespoons single cream
1 tablespoon chopped fresh tarragon

*C*ombine all the ingredients for the salad and all those for the dressing. Pour the dressing over the salad vegetables and toss gently.

SERVES 6

Salade Trédern

24 crayfish (see below)
24 oysters, shucked
a few drops lemon juice
3 tablespoons asparagus tips
50 g (2 oz) truffles, very thinly sliced
2 tablespoons double cream

Dressing
150 ml ($\frac{1}{4}$ pint) Sauce Mayonnaise, page 13

*P*repare and cook the crayfish according to the recipe for Ecrevisses à la Nage, page 60. Drain and shell, reserving the shells for later use. Poach the oysters with the lemon juice and their own juices and remove their beards. Boil the asparagus until just tender. Place all these ingredients, while still lukewarm, in a bowl and add the sliced truffles.

Pound the crayfish shells finely with the cream and pass through a fine sieve. Add the pink, crayfish-flavoured cream to the mayonnaise and dress the salad.

SERVES 4–6

Salade Waldorf

350 g (12 oz) dessert apples, peeled and diced
350 g (12 oz) celeriac, peeled and diced
225 g (8 oz) fresh walnuts, peeled and halved

Dressing
150 ml ($\frac{1}{4}$ pint) thin Sauce Mayonnaise, page 13

*P*lace all the salad ingredients in a salad bowl, dress with the mayonnaise and toss gently.

SERVES 6–8

DESSERTS & ICES

Crème à l'Anglaise

200 g (7 oz) caster sugar
6 egg yolks
½ teaspoon arrowroot
600 ml (1 pint) boiling milk

Place the sugar, egg yolks and arrowroot in a basin and whisk until the mixture thickens and forms a slowly dissolving ribbon when the whisk is lifted out of the bowl.

Add the boiling milk, a little at a time, place over the heat and stir with a wooden spoon until the yolks thicken the mixture and it sticks to the back of the spoon. Do not allow the custard to come to the boil, as this will cause it to separate.

As soon as it is cooked, pass the custard through a fine strainer and keep it warm in a *bain-marie*. When required as a sauce this egg custard may be flavoured as desired with, for example, vanilla, orange or lemon zest infused in the milk, or with 50 ml (2 fl oz) of a liqueur, added at the last moment. When flavoured, the Crème à l'Anglaise takes the name of the flavouring. For example, if flavoured with rum, the Crème à l'Anglaise becomes Sauce au Rhum, and so on.

MAKES 600 ML (1 PINT)

Crème Frangipane

750 ml (1¼ pints) milk
1 vanilla pod
100 g (4 oz) sugar
100 g (4 oz) flour
2 eggs
4 egg yolks
salt
75 g (3 oz) butter
25 g (1 oz) macaroons, crushed

Bring the milk to the boil and infuse with the vanilla for 30 minutes. Place the sugar, flour, eggs, egg yolks and salt in a pan and stir with a wooden spoon. Slowly stir in the hot milk and bring to the boil, stirring continuously. Allow to boil for 2 minutes, then transfer to a basin.

Add 50 g (2 oz) of the butter and the crushed macaroons and stir. Smooth the surface with the remaining butter on the point of a knife to prevent a skin from forming.

MAKES 750 ML (1¼ PINTS)

Crème Chantilly

1 litre (1¾ pints) double cream
125 g (4½ oz) caster sugar
1 teaspoon vanilla essence

Whisk the cream until it becomes stiff enough to stand in peaks on the whisk. Add the sugar and vanilla essence: mix well. This cream should be prepared at the last moment.

MAKES 1 LITRE (1¾ PINTS)

Sirop

450 g (1 lb) sugar
600 ml (1 pint) water

Place the sugar and water in a pan, bring to the boil and skim. Allow to cool and use as required.

This syrup may be flavoured where necessary by the addition of an appropriate essence such as vanilla, or it may be flavoured by infusing with vanilla pod, orange or lemon zest and so on.

MAKES APPROXIMATELY 1 LITRE ($1\frac{3}{4}$ PINTS)

Sauce au Chocolat

225 g (8 oz) plain chocolate
300 ml ($\frac{1}{2}$ pint) cold water
1 tablespoon vanilla sugar
3 tablespoons double cream
1 knob butter

Put the chocolate in the cold water, then heat very gently until it is fully dissolved. Add the vanilla sugar and simmer gently for 25 minutes. Finish with the cream and butter.

MAKES 300 ML ($\frac{1}{2}$ PINT)

Pâte à Foncer Fine

250 g (9 oz) plain flour, sifted
1 pinch salt
25 g (1 oz) caster sugar
1 egg, beaten
150 g (5 oz) butter, softened
25 ml (1 fl oz) water

Make a well in the flour and place the salt, sugar, egg, butter and water in the centre. Mix the flour gradually into the other ingredients until it is incorporated and forms a paste. Roll the paste into a ball, then push small pieces away from the ball with the heel of the hand, thus assuring the complete blending of all the ingredients. Do this twice.

Form into a ball then wrap in a cloth and place in the refrigerator, preferably for a few hours, before use.

MAKES APPROXIMATELY 500 G ($1\frac{1}{4}$ LB)

Biscuits à la Cuiller

8 eggs
275 g (10 oz) caster sugar
1 tablespoon orange flower water
185 g ($6\frac{1}{2}$ oz) flour, sifted
butter

Separate the eggs and beat the whites stiffly. Whisk 250 g (9 oz) of the sugar and the egg yolks in a basin until thick and pale. Add the orange flower water, fold in half the stiffly beaten egg whites, then rain in the flour followed by the rest of the whites, folding and cutting all the ingredients together with a spoon so as to keep the mixture light.

Place the mixture in a piping bag with a plain 1 cm ($\frac{1}{2}$ inch) diameter tube and pipe in 9 cm ($3\frac{1}{2}$ inch) lengths on to sheets of thick, buttered paper. Sprinkle all over with the remaining caster sugar, then shake off the surplus by holding the paper at both ends and agitating it slightly.

Spray a few fine drops of water over the biscuits to help them become pearly, then bake in a moderate oven (170°C, 335°F, Gas Marks 3 and 4) for 12–15 minutes, or until lightly browned.

MAKES APPROXIMATELY 40 BISCUITS

Abricots Bourdaloue

450 g (1 lb) apricots, halved and stoned
150 ml ($\frac{1}{4}$ pint) vanilla-flavoured Sirop, above left
1 large cooked flan case made with Pâte à Foncer Fine, left
300 ml ($\frac{1}{2}$ pint) Crème Frangipane, page 158
100 g (4 oz) macaroons, crushed
2 tablespoons melted butter

Poach the halved apricots in the vanilla-flavoured syrup and allow to cool thoroughly.

Cover the bottom of the cooked flan case with a layer of frangipane cream containing half the crushed macaroons. Arrange the apricot halves on top of this and cover with more frangipane cream.

Sprinkle the surface with the remaining crushed macaroons and the melted butter and glaze quickly in a hot oven or under the grill.

SERVES 6–8

Abricots Meringués

450 g (1 lb) apricots, halved and stoned
150 ml (¼ pint) vanilla-flavoured Sirop, page 159
100 g (4 oz) short grain rice, dry weight, prepared as Riz pour
Entremets, page 176
icing sugar

Meringue
4 egg whites
225 g (8 oz) fine caster sugar

To garnish
redcurrant jam
apricot jam

*P*oach the halved apricots in the vanilla-flavoured syrup and allow to cool thoroughly. Place a layer of the prepared rice on a dish and arrange the halves of poached apricot on top.

Make the meringue by whisking the egg whites stiffly and sprinkling in the caster sugar, mixing lightly with a spoon so that the egg whites do not lose their lightness.

Cover the apricots with meringue, piled in a dome shape, and decorate with more meringue, using a piping bag and tube.

Dredge with icing sugar and place in a warm oven (160°C, 325°F, Gas Mark 3) for approximately 45 minutes to cook and colour the meringue.

On removing the dish from the oven, decorate the meringue by piping redcurrant and apricot jam on it using fine plain tubes.

SERVES 6

Ananas à la Royale

1 large pineapple, with leaves
fresh fruit salad (see below)
6–8 large strawberries, halved
Kirsch
4 peaches, peeled and halved
300 ml (½ pint) vanilla-flavoured Sirop, page 159

*C*ut the top off the pineapple leaving its leaves intact, and put this to one side for use later. Scoop out the inside of the pineapple, leaving a case about 1 cm (½ inch) thick.

Make a fresh fruit salad using fruit of your choice, but including the inside of the pineapple. Macerate both the fruit salad and the halved strawberries in Kirsch for at least 30 minutes. Meanwhile, poach the peaches in the vanilla syrup until just tender and allow to cool.

Fill the pineapple case with the fruit salad and place the filled pineapple in the middle of a large glass bowl. Surround the base of the pineapple with the poached peaches and decorate the peaches with the strawberries. Replace the top of the pineapple before serving.

SERVES 8

Beignets d'Ananas Favorite

1 pineapple
75 g (3 oz) sugar
3 tablespoons Kirsch
2 tablespoons pistachios, shelled, skinned and chopped
600 ml (1 pint) thick Crème Frangipane, page 158, almost cold
oil for deep frying
icing sugar

Light frying batter
100 g (4 oz) flour, sifted
1 tablespoon melted butter
1 pinch salt
1 pinch sugar
1 egg
50 ml (2 fl oz) beer

*F*irst, prepare a light frying batter. Mix all the ingredients together with a little lukewarm water, using a spoon. Do not overmix and leave in a warm place for an hour.

Meanwhile, cut the pineapple into round slices, 8 mm (⅜ inch) thick. Cut each slice in half and remove both the outer skin and the outer core. Sprinkle with the sugar and Kirsch and allow to macerate for 30 minutes.

Add the pistachios to the thick, almost cold frangipane cream. Dry the pieces of pineapple and dip into the prepared frangipane cream. Place the coated slices of pineapple on a tray and allow to become quite cold.

Stir the light frying batter. Remove the pineapple slices from the tray and dip carefully into this batter. Deep fry in hot oil (180°C, 350°F), drain and dredge liberally with icing sugar. Glaze quickly in a hot oven (220°C, 425°F, Gas Mark 7) or under the grill.

Arrange the pineapple slices slightly overlapping each other on a folded serviette on a suitable dish.

SERVES 6–8

Bavarois aux Fraises

Bananes Flambées

6 bananas, peeled and cut in half lengthways
100 g (4 oz) caster sugar
flour
1 egg, beaten
50 g (2 oz) clarified butter
2 tablespoons Kirsch, warmed

Sprinkle the bananas with 75 g (3 oz) of the caster sugar. Dip in the flour, then in the beaten egg, and then in the flour again. Fry in *clarified butter*.

Arrange the fried bananas side by side on an oval dish and sprinkle with the remaining sugar. Pour over the warmed Kirsch and set it alight just as you bring it to the table.

SERVES 6

Bananes en Salade

6 bananas
25 g (1 oz) orange zest, cut into very fine julienne
50 ml (2 fl oz) Sirop, page 159
75 g (3 oz) sugar
2 tablespoons Kirsch

Choose bananas that are just ripe but still fairly firm. Blanch the *julienne* of orange zest, cook it in the sugar syrup for a few minutes and drain.

Peel the bananas and cut into round slices. Place these on a dish, sprinkle with the sugar and orange zest, and allow to macerate for 15 minutes.

Arrange the slices of banana and the zest in a serving bowl, sprinkle with Kirsch and toss lightly, taking care not to break the slices.

SERVES 6

Cerises Dubarry

250 g (9 oz) Pâte à Foncer Fine, page 159
25 g (1 oz) caster sugar
450 g (1 lb) cherries, stoned
450 ml ($\frac{3}{4}$ pint) Crème Chantilly, page 158
75 g (3 oz) macaroons, crushed

Line a 20-cm (8-inch) flan ring on a baking sheet with shortcrust pastry dough and prick the bottom to prevent it from rising during cooking. Sprinkle it with the caster sugar, then fill it with the stoned cherries, packing them tightly.

Bake in a moderately hot oven (200°C, 400°F, Gas Mark 6) for 20 minutes. Then reduce the temperature to 180°C, 350°F, Gas Mark 4, for another 15 minutes or until the pastry edges have baked to a golden brown.

Allow to cool. When the tart is completely cold, cover the cherries with most of the Crème Chantilly mixed with half the crushed macaroons. Smooth the top and sides of the cream and coat with the remaining crushed macaroons. Finish by piping rosettes of Crème Chantilly around the tart to decorate.

SERVES 6

Cerises Jubilée

450 g (1 lb) large cherries, stoned
300 ml ($\frac{1}{2}$ pint) Sirop, page 159
$\frac{1}{2}$ tablespoon arrowroot
2 tablespoons Kirsch, warmed

Poach the cherries in sugar syrup, then remove and place them in 4 deep individual serving dishes. Reduce the syrup and thicken with the arrowroot, diluted in a little water.

Coat the cherries with the thickened syrup, pour $\frac{1}{2}$ tablespoon warmed Kirsch into each dish and set it alight just as you bring them to the table.

SERVES 4

Pêches Cardinal

Cerises au Claret

450 g (1 lb) cherries
450 ml (¾ pint) claret
75 g (3 oz) caster sugar
1 cinnamon stick
2 tablespoons redcurrant jelly

To serve
Biscuits à la Cuiller, page 159

Remove the cherry stalks and place the cherries in a flameproof *timbale*. Cover with the claret and add the sugar and cinnamon stick. Cover with a lid and poach over a low heat for 15 minutes.

Allow the cherries to cool in the red wine syrup, then drain this off and reduce by a third. Add the redcurrant jelly to thicken it and sweeten it slightly.

Pour the syrup back over the cherries and serve very cold, accompanied by Biscuits à la Cuiller.

SERVES 4–6

Figues à la Carlton

9 fresh figs
450 g (1 lb) raspberries
caster sugar to taste
600 ml (1 pint) Crème Chantilly, page 158

Peel the figs, cut them in half and place in the refrigerator. Prepare a raspberry purée by passing the raspberries through a sieve and adding caster sugar to taste.

Stir the Crème Chantilly into the raspberry purée and pour over the figs to cover completely.

SERVES 6

Fraises Romanoff

50 ml (2 fl oz) orange juice
3 tablespoons Curaçao
450 g (1 lb) strawberries
300 ml (½ pint) Crème Chantilly, page 158

Pour the orange juice and Curaçao over the strawberries and leave to macerate in the refrigerator for at least 30 minutes. Arrange the macerated strawberries, orange juice and liqueur in a chilled dish and cover the fruit with most of the Crème Chantilly. Decorate with the remaining Crème Chantilly, using a piping bag and tube.

SERVES 4

Fraises Fémina

450 g (1 lb) strawberries
50 g (2 oz) caster sugar
50 ml (2 fl oz) Grand Marnier
500 ml (18 fl oz) Glace à l'Orange, page 186

Sprinkle the strawberries with the caster sugar, then mix with the Grand Marnier and leave to macerate in the refrigerator for at least 1 hour.

Drain the strawberries and mix the liquid from the maceration into the orange ice. When you are ready to serve, cover the bottom of a chilled glass bowl with a layer of the Grand Marnier-flavoured orange ice and arrange the strawberries neatly on top.

SERVES 4–6

Bavarois aux Fraises

400 g (14 oz) strawberries, cleaned and hulled
250 g (9 oz) granulated sugar
200 ml (7 fl oz) water
20 g (¾ oz) leaf gelatine, soaked and drained
juice of 1 lemon
350 ml (12 fl oz) double cream, lightly whipped
almond oil

To serve
Crème Chantilly, page 158

Figues à la Carlton

Pass the strawberries through a fine sieve to give approximately 350 ml (12 fl oz) purée, free of pips.

Place the sugar and water in a pan, heat gently until the sugar has dissolved then bring to the boil, skim and simmer for 5 minutes. Remove from the heat, add the soaked and drained *leaf gelatine*, stir to melt thoroughly, then cool but not so much as to set.

Add this syrup to the fruit purée together with the lemon juice and mix thoroughly. Fold in the lightly whipped cream when the mixture becomes more viscous but just before it starts setting.

Pour into a 1.2 litre (2 pint) lightly oiled jelly mould, cover with a round of greaseproof paper and leave to set in the refrigerator for at least 2 hours. When required for serving, the mould should be plunged quickly into warm water, dried and turned out onto a serving dish. Decorate with a little Crème Chantilly. *See photograph on page 161.*

SERVES 6–8

Mont Blanc aux Marrons

450 g (1 lb) chestnuts
500 ml (18 fl oz) milk
50 g (2 oz) sugar
1 vanilla pod
300 ml (½ pint) Crème Chantilly, page 158

To shell the chestnuts, make a shallow incision in the round side of the shell and place on an ovenproof tray with a little water. Place in a hot oven (220°C, 425°F, Gas Mark 7) for 7–8 minutes, then remove both the outer shells and the inner skins without breaking the chestnuts.

Heat the milk, sweeten with the sugar and infuse with the vanilla pod. Simmer the chestnuts gently in the flavoured milk for 35–40 minutes.

When they are cooked, drain well and pass through a coarse sieve into a ring mould and refrigerate. Demould before serving and fill the centre with Crème Chantilly, forming it into a rugged, irregular shape.

SERVES 4–6

Melon à l'Orientale

4 small ripe melons
icing sugar to taste
450 g (1 lb) wild strawberries
4 tablespoons Kirsch
softened butter

To serve
wafer biscuits

Cut a round incision in the top of each melon. Remove this 'lid' and reserve. Discard the seeds and filament, scoop out the flesh and cut into cubes. Sprinkle the inside of each melon with icing sugar and fill with alternate layers of strawberries and diced melon, sprinkling each layer with sugar.

Pour a tablespoonful of Kirsch into each melon, close with the reserved lid and seal the join with softened butter. Refrigerate for 2 hours. Serve accompanied by wafer biscuits.

SERVES 4

Oranges en Surprise

6 large oranges
500 ml (18 fl oz) Glace à l'Orange, page 186
6 sprigs of lemon geranium or mint

Meringue
150 g (5 oz) fine caster sugar
3 egg whites

Cut off the top quarters of the oranges and reserve. Remove the flesh, place the skins in the freezer to set firm, then fill with orange ice. Replace in the freezer.

To prepare the meringue, place the caster sugar and egg whites in a bowl and mix together. Place in a *bain-marie* over a gentle heat and whisk continuously until the mixture is thick enough to hold its shape between the wires of the whisk. Remove from the heat and whisk until cold.

Take the filled oranges from the freezer and, using a piping bag and star tube, cover the ices with meringue. Place in a very hot oven (240°C, 475°F, Gas Mark 9) for just 2–3 minutes so that the heat colours the meringue but does not melt the ice. On removing the oranges from the oven, replace the reserved 'lids' and decorate with lemon geranium or mint.

SERVES 6

Oranges en Surprise

Pêches Impératrice

4 peaches, peeled, halved and stoned
300 ml ($\frac{1}{2}$ pint) vanilla-flavoured Sirop, page 159
225 g (8 oz) short-grain rice, dry weight, prepared as Riz pour
Entremets, page 176
1 tablespoon Kirsch
1 tablespoon Maraschino
50 g (2 oz) macaroons, crushed

Sauce à l'Abricot
100 g (4 oz) very ripe or lightly stewed apricots, stoned
150 ml ($\frac{1}{4}$ pint) Sirop, page 159
1–2 tablespoons Kirsch

Poach the peaches in the vanilla-flavoured syrup and allow to cool thoroughly. Flavour the prepared rice with Kirsch and Maraschino and cover the bottom of an ovenproof serving dish with it. Arrange the poached halves of peach on the rice and cover them with another layer of rice.

Prepare the apricot sauce by passing the apricots through a fine sieve or puréeing them in a food processor and diluting with a little sugar syrup. Bring to the boil, skimming carefully, and simmer. The sauce is ready when it coats the back of a spoon. Flavour to taste with a little Kirsch.

Spread a layer of apricot sauce over the rice and sprinkle with the crushed macaroons. Place in a moderate oven (160°C, 325°F, Gas Mark 3) for 10–12 minutes. Do not allow the surface to brown.

SERVES 8

Pêches Cardinal

6 peaches, peeled, halved and stoned
300 ml ($\frac{1}{2}$ pint) vanilla-flavoured Sirop, page 159
225 g (8 oz) raspberries
caster sugar to taste
1 tablespoon Kirsch
500 ml (18 fl oz) Glace à la Vanille, page 184
100 g (4 oz) fresh almonds, skinned and cut into fine strips

Poach the peaches in the vanilla-flavoured syrup and allow to cool thoroughly. Meanwhile, prepare the raspberry purée by passing the raspberries through a sieve and flavouring to taste with the caster sugar and Kirsch.

Arrange the peaches in a serving dish on a bed of vanilla ice cream and coat with raspberry purée. Sprinkle the surface with the fine strips of skinned fresh almonds. *See photograph on page 163.*

SERVES 6

Poires Hélène

4 large pears, peeled and cored from the bottom
600 ml (1 pint) vanilla-flavoured Sirop, page 159
300 ml ($\frac{1}{2}$ pint) Sauce au Chocolat, page 159
500 ml (18 fl oz) Glace à la Vanille, page 184
50 g (2 oz) crystallized violets

Poach the pears in the vanilla-flavoured syrup and allow to cool thoroughly. Meanwhile, prepare the chocolate sauce. Keep warm.

Arrange the pears on a bed of vanilla ice cream and sprinkle with crystallized violets. Serve with the hot chocolate sauce.

SERVES 4

Poires Condé

450 g (1 lb) small pears, peeled and cored from the bottom
300 ml ($\frac{1}{2}$ pint) vanilla-flavoured Sirop, page 159
100 g (4 oz) crystallized fruits, diced
2 tablespoons Kirsch
100 g (4 oz) short-grain rice, dry weight, prepared as Riz pour
Entremets, page 176
$\frac{1}{2}$ tablespoon arrowroot

Poach the pears in the syrup and drain, reserving the syrup. Soak the crystallized fruits in half the Kirsch and add most of these to the prepared rice, reserving a few for decoration. Arrange a border of this rice round a serving dish and arrange the poached pears in the centre. Decorate with the reserved crystallized fruits.

Reduce the reserved pear syrup, thicken with a little arrowroot and flavour with the remaining Kirsch. Pour this over the top of the pears.

SERVES 6–8

Poires Condé

Poires Pralinées

4 large pears, peeled, halved and cored
600 ml (1 pint) vanilla-flavoured Sirop, page 159
300 ml ($\frac{1}{2}$ pint) Crème Frangipane, page 158
100 ml ($3\frac{1}{2}$ fl oz) double cream
150 ml ($\frac{1}{4}$ pint) Crème Chantilly, page 158
300 ml ($\frac{1}{2}$ pint) Sauce au Chocolat, page 159

Almond Praline
225 g (8 oz) sugar
225 g (8 oz) almonds

Poach the pears in the vanilla-flavoured sugar syrup and allow to cool thoroughly. Meanwhile, prepare the almond praline. Melt the sugar very slowly with a small quantity of cold water and cook to a light caramel colour. Mix in the almonds, pour onto an oiled marble slab and allow to cool thoroughly. Crush coarsely in a mortar.

Arrange the pears in a dish and coat with Crème Frangipane, softened by the addition of the cream. Place a nicely moulded tablespoon of Crème Chantilly between each pear half, and sprinkle the whole with the coarsely crushed almond praline.

Serve accompanied by hot or cold chocolate sauce.

SERVES 4

Douillons Normande

4 large desert apples, peeled
300 g (11 oz) Pâte à Foncer Fine, page 159
50 g (2 oz) caster sugar
1 beaten egg
butter

Remove the core of the apples using an apple corer. Place each apple on a square piece of shortcrust pastry dough, fill the centres of the apples with sugar and fold the pastry over to enclose the apples. Place a fancy round of the same pastry on top and brush with beaten egg. Score with the point of a knife and seal the edges.

Grease a baking sheet, place the apples on this and place in a hot oven (220°C, 425°F, Gas Mark 7) for 5 minutes to set and lightly colour the pastry, then lower the temperature to 180°C, 350°F, Gas Mark 4, and continue cooking the apples for a further 25–30 minutes.

SERVES 4

Charlotte de Pommes

50 g (2 oz) butter
1 loaf white bread
75 g (3 oz) melted butter
12 large Pippin apples, peeled, cored and sliced
2 tablespoons caster sugar
grated rind of $\frac{1}{2}$ lemon
1 pinch ground cinnamon
3 tablespoons good apricot jam

Sauce à l'Abricot
100 g (4 oz) very ripe or lightly stewed apricots
150 ml ($\frac{1}{4}$ pint) Sirop, page 159
1–2 tablespoons Kirsch

Butter a 1-litre ($1\frac{3}{4}$-pint) charlotte mould, using 25 g (1 oz) of the butter. Cut the bread into slices about 5 mm ($\frac{1}{4}$ inch) thick and brush with the melted butter; reserve a thin round piece of bread and more melted butter for the top of the mould (see below). Line the bottom and sides of the mould with slightly overlapping slices of bread.

Meanwhile, gently fry the slices of apple in a shallow pan with the remaining butter, the caster sugar, lemon rind and ground cinnamon. When the apples are cooked and reduced to a very thick purée, add the apricot jam.

Place this mixture in the prepared mould, bringing it just above the top of the mould so as to allow for shrinkage. Cover with the reserved piece of bread, dipped in melted butter, and cook in a moderately hot oven (200°C, 400°F, Gas Mark 6) for 35–40 minutes.

Prepare the apricot sauce by passing the apricots through a fine sieve or puréeing them in a food processor and diluting with a little sugar syrup. Bring to the boil, skimming carefully, and simmer. The sauce is ready when it coats the back of a spoon. Flavour to taste with a little Kirsch.

Remove the cooked charlotte from the oven, turn it upside down on a serving dish, and allow it to rest for a few minutes before removing the mould. Serve with the apricot sauce.

SERVES 8

Charlotte de Pommes

Crème Villageoise aux Pommes

150 g (5 oz) boudoir biscuits
1 tablespoon Kirsch
1 tablespoon Maraschino
750 g (1½ lb) apples, peeled, cored and sliced
215 g (7½ oz) caster sugar
4 egg yolks
8 whole eggs
1 litre (1¾ pints) hot milk

Sprinkle the biscuits with the Kirsch and Maraschino. Stew the apples with 30 g (1 oz) of the sugar and a little water to a thick purée. Arrange the biscuits in a deep ovenproof dish in layers, alternating with layers of apple purée.

Mix the remaining caster sugar with the egg yolks, eggs and hot milk. Pour this mixture over the biscuits and apple purée, and cook in a *bain-marie* in a moderate oven (180°C, 350°F, Gas Mark 4) for about 35 minutes or until set.

SERVES 8

Pommes Châtelaine

6 medium dessert apples, peeled
75 g (3 oz) caster sugar
100 g (4 oz) butter, softened
75 g (3 oz) glacé cherries, diced
6 tablespoons apricot purée, prepared as for Pommes au Beurre,
above right
300 ml (½ pint) thin Crème Frangipane, page 158
75 g (3 oz) macaroons, finely crushed
2 tablespoons melted butter

Core the apples, using an apple corer. Arrange them in an ovenproof dish and fill the centres with a mixture of caster sugar and softened butter, using all the sugar and 75 g (3 oz) of the butter. Pour a little water round them and bake in a moderate oven (180°C, 350°F, Gas Mark 4) for about 1 hour or until the apples are soft.

Use the remaining butter to grease an ovenproof dish and arrange the cooked apples on it. Mix the glacé cherries with the apricot purée and fill the apple centres with this mixture.

Cover with thin frangipane cream and sprinkle with the finely crushed macaroons and melted butter. Glaze quickly under a hot grill.

SERVES 6

Pommes au Beurre

6 medium dessert apples, peeled
3 tablespoons lemon juice
150 g (5 oz) butter
6 tablespoons vanilla-flavoured Sirop, page 159
3 brioches, cut into rounds
icing sugar
100 g (4 oz) caster sugar
1 tablespoon brandy
100 g (4 oz) poached apricot flesh, passed
through a fine sieve to purée

Core the apples, using an apple corer, and place in boiling water, containing a little lemon juice, for 2 minutes. Butter a shallow ovenproof dish, using 25 g (1 oz) of the butter, and arrange the apples in it. Add the vanilla-flavoured syrup, cover with a lid and bake in a moderate oven (180°C, 350°F, Gas Mark 4) for 1 hour or until the apples are soft.

Dredge the slices of brioche with icing sugar and brown slightly under the grill. When the apples are cooked, arrange each apple on a slice of brioche. Reserve the cooking syrup.

Mix together the remaining butter with an equal quantity of caster sugar, flavour with brandy and fill the centre of each apple with this brandy butter.

Lightly thicken the vanilla-flavoured cooking syrup with the apricot purée and pour this over the apples.

SERVES 6

Crème Moulée au Caramel

600 ml (1 pint) milk
200 g (7 oz) sugar
1 vanilla pod
4 egg yolks
3 whole eggs

Bring the milk to the boil and dissolve half of the sugar in it. Add the vanilla pod and allow to infuse for 20 minutes, then remove the pod.

Meanwhile, cook the remaining sugar with a little water to a light caramel colour. Line the bottom and sides of a 1-litre (1¾-pint) charlotte or other suitable mould with this caramel.

Beat the egg yolks and whole eggs together in a bowl then pour in the milk little by little, whisking well as you do so. Pass through a fine strainer and allow to rest for a few minutes. Then

Pommes au Beurre

remove any froth which has formed on the surface. Pour into the prepared mould.

Cover the mixture and cook in a *bain-marie* in a moderate oven (160°C, 325°F, Gas Mark 3) for 40—45 minutes, or until set. The water in the bain-marie must not be allowed to boil at any time during the cooking. (If this is allowed to happen, the high temperature will cause the air mixed in with the mixture to expand and form a mass of tiny bubbles; when the cream has cooled it will consequently be riddled with little holes which will spoil its appearance.)

As soon as the cream is cooked, remove it from the bain-marie and allow to become completely cold over at least 2—3 hours, to ensure an adequate set for demoulding. To demould the cream, turn the mould over carefully on to a serving dish and leave for a few minutes before removing.

SERVES 4—6

Omelette Célestine

5 eggs
50 g (2 oz) butter
2 tablespoons apple purée, prepared as for Charlotte de Pommes,
page 170
3 tablespoons apricot jam
icing sugar

Beat 2 of the eggs until the whites and yolks are thoroughly blended. Heat half the butter in an omelette pan until it begins to brown. Pour in the beaten eggs, shake the pan and stir briskly with a fork to ensure even cooking. (See the instructions for omelette-making on page 36). Spread the centre of the omelette with the apple purée and fold as usual.

Make a second, slightly larger omelette using the other 3 eggs, and spread its centre with the apricot jam.

Now place the first, folded omelette on top of the second larger one and fold the larger omelette over the smaller. Dredge with icing sugar and glaze for a few minutes in a hot oven (220°C, 425°F, Gas Mark 7).

SERVES 2 OR 3

Crêpes Suzette

125 g (4½ oz) flour, sifted
50 g (2 oz) caster sugar, including 1 tablespoon vanilla sugar
1 pinch fine salt
3 eggs
300 ml (½ pint) milk
butter

To flavour
100 g (4 oz) butter, softened
100 g (4 oz) caster sugar
3 tablespoons Curaçao
a few drops tangerine or orange juice

Place the flour, sugar and salt in a basin. Gradually add the eggs and milk, whisking well to form a smooth batter. Prepare the flavouring by mixing the softened butter with the sugar and adding the Curaçao and tangerine or orange juice.

Pour a little pancake batter into a hot pan containing a little butter. Cook to a light brown colour then toss the pancake to cook the other side.

Spread the pancakes with the flavoured butter, fold into four, and arrange, overlapping, on a hot dish for serving.

SERVES 4—6

Crêpes du Couvent

125 g (4½ oz) flour, sifted
50 g (2 oz) caster sugar, including 1 tablespoon vanilla sugar
1 pinch fine salt
3 eggs
300 ml (½ pint) milk
butter
4 medium pears, peeled and finely diced

Place the flour, sugar and salt in a basin. Gradually add the eggs and milk, whisking well to form a smooth batter. Pour a little pancake batter into a hot pan containing a little butter. Sprinkle with a little diced pear and cover with more of the pancake mixture. Toss to cook on both sides, arrange on a serviette and serve very hot.

SERVES 4—6

Crêpes Suzette

Omelette Norvégienne

25 g (1 oz) butter
flour
Glace à l'Orange, page 186, or other cream or fruit ice

Genoise paste
225 g (8 oz) caster sugar
6 eggs
grated rind of $\frac{1}{2}$ orange
175 g (6 oz) flour, sifted
90 g (3$\frac{1}{2}$ oz) melted butter
butter
flour

Meringue
6 egg whites
350 g (12 oz) fine caster sugar

To prepare the genoise paste, mix the sugar and eggs in a bowl and place over a gentle heat in a *bain-marie* so that the mixture becomes slightly warm. Whisk until it thickens and forms a ribbon when you lift the whisk from the bowl. Remove from the heat and continue to whisk until it is cold. Now add the orange rind, fold in the flour and add the melted butter in a thin stream. Spread on a buttered and floured baking tin measuring 30 cm by 15 cm (12 inches by 6 inches) and bake in a moderately hot oven 190°C, 375°F, Gas Mark 5) for 20–25 minutes or until golden brown and firm to the touch. Allow to cool, then cut out an oval shape of genoise to fit neatly on the serving dish (see below).

To make the meringue, whisk the egg whites stiffly and sprinkle in the caster sugar, mixing lightly with a spoon so that the egg whites do not lose their lightness.

Place the oval-shaped base of genoise on an ovenproof oval serving dish. Place an oval pyramid of ice-cream on top of the genoise, and cover with a layer of meringue. Smooth over with a palette knife so as to give an even coating of meringue about 2 cm ($\frac{3}{4}$ inch) thick.

Decorate quickly with some more meringue, using a piping bag and tube, and place in a very hot oven (240°C, 475°F, Gas Mark 9) for 2–3 minutes so that the meringue cooks and browns rapidly but the heat does not penetrate to the ice-cream inside. Serve immediately.

SERVES 8

Pouding au Pain à la Française

1 litre (1$\frac{3}{4}$ pints) milk
1 vanilla pod
250 g (9 oz) sugar
350 g (12 oz) fine white breadcrumbs
6 egg yolks
4 whole eggs
4 egg whites, stiffly beaten
butter

To serve
Crème à l'Anglaise, page 158

Bring the milk to the boil with the vanilla pod and sugar. Soak 300 g (11 oz) of the breadcrumbs in it and pass through a sieve. Stir in the egg yolks and whole eggs, and then fold in the stiffly beaten egg whites.

Butter a deep 2-litre (3-pint) border mould and sprinkle with the remaining breadcrumbs. Pour the mixture into the prepared mould and cook in a *bain-marie* in a moderate oven (180°C, 350°F, Gas Mark 4) for about 45–50 minutes. Allow to settle for a few minutes before demoulding onto a serving dish.

Serve accompanied by Crème à l'Anglaise.

SERVES 8–10

Riz pour Entremets

225 g (8 oz) short-grain rice
750 ml (1$\frac{1}{4}$ pints) milk
125 g (4$\frac{1}{2}$ oz) sugar
1 pinch salt
1 vanilla pod
40 g (1$\frac{1}{2}$ oz) butter
6 egg yolks

Wash the rice and bring to the boil. Drain, wash again in warm water, and drain again. Bring the milk to the boil with the sugar, salt, vanilla pod and butter. Strain and add the rice. Put in a flameproof casserole, bring back to the boil, cover with a lid and cook gently in a moderate oven (180°C, 350°F, Gas Mark 4) for 25–30 minutes without stirring.

When the rice is cooked, remove from the oven and add the egg yolks, mixing them in quickly and carefully with a fork so as not to break up the grains of rice which should remain whole.

SERVES 6–8

Omelette Norvégienne

Riz à l'Impératrice

225 g (8 oz) short-grain rice, dry weight, prepared as
Riz pour Entremets, page 176
3 tablespoons redcurrant jelly, warmed
500 ml (18 fl oz) Crème à l'Anglaise, page 158
15 g ($\frac{1}{2}$ oz) leaf gelatine, soaked
100 g (4 oz) crystallized fruit, finely diced
4 tablespoons apricot purée, prepared as for Pommes au Beurre,
page 172
500 ml (18 fl oz) double cream, whipped

Make the Riz pour Entremets; cool. Meanwhile, prepare a large ring mould by coating the bottom with the warmed redcurrant jelly; set in the refrigerator. Prepare the Crème à l'Anglaise and, when almost cooked, add the drained *leaf gelatine*. Stir until cool but not set.

Stir the crystallized fruit and apricot purée into the rice. Add the Crème à l'Anglaise and the whipped cream. Pour the mixture into the mould and place to set in the refrigerator. Demould just before serving.

SERVES 8–10

Pouding Saxon

150 g (5 oz) butter
150 g (5 oz) caster sugar
150 g (5 oz) flour, sifted
300 ml ($\frac{1}{2}$ pint) boiling milk
5 egg yolks
5 egg whites, stiffly beaten

To serve
Crème à l'Anglaise, page 158

Stir 125 g ($4\frac{1}{2}$ oz) of the butter over a gentle heat until soft and smooth. Mix in the caster sugar and flour, then add the boiling milk. Bring to the boil, stirring continuously, and continue to stir until the paste leaves the spoon cleanly.

Take off the heat, carefully mix in the yolks, one at a time, and then gently fold in the beaten whites. Butter 8 or 10 individual ovenproof moulds, using the rest of the butter. Divide the mixture between the moulds and cook in a *bain-marie* in a moderately hot oven (200°C, 400°F, Gas Mark 6) for 15–20 minutes. Serve accompanied by Crème à l'Anglaise.

SERVES 8–10

Pouding au Riz

6 egg whites, stiffly beaten
225 g (8 oz) short-grain rice, dry weight, prepared as
Riz pour Entremets, page 176
25 g (1 oz) butter
flour

To serve
Crème à l'Anglaise, page 158

Fold the stiffly beaten egg whites into the prepared rice. Butter a suitable ovenproof mould and sprinkle with flour. Pour in the rice and cook in a *bain-marie* in a moderately hot oven (190°C, 375°F, Gas Mark 5) for 25 minutes or until set and firm to the touch. Allow to rest for 7–8 minutes, then demould on to a dish. Serve accompanied by Crème à l'Anglaise.

SERVES 6–8

Oeufs à la Neige

600 ml (1 pint) milk
1 vanilla pod
200 g (7 oz) granulated sugar
6 egg yolks
$\frac{1}{2}$ teaspoon arrowroot

Meringue
6 egg whites
350 g (12 oz) fine caster sugar

First prepare the meringue by whisking the egg whites stiffly and sprinkling in the caster sugar. Mix lightly with a spoon. Meanwhile, bring the milk to the boil, infuse with the vanilla pod and sweeten with the sugar. Mould the meringue into egg shapes, using two spoons, and drop into the simmering milk. Turn them over when half-cooked, so they poach evenly. When firm, remove from the pan, drain, and strain the milk.

Make a Crème à l'Anglaise by whisking the egg yolks and arrowroot together in a bowl and adding the hot, strained milk, a little at a time. Place over the heat and stir with a wooden spoon until the yolks thicken the mixture slightly. Do not allow the custard to boil as this will cause it to separate. Cool.

Arrange the cooked meringues in a bowl and coat with the cold custard. Serve very cold.

SERVES 6–8

Riz à l'Impératrice

Ile Flottante

1 Biscuit de Savoie (see below)
50 ml (2 fl oz) Kirsch
50 ml (2 fl oz) Maraschino
125 g (4½ oz) apricot jam, slightly thinned with lemon juice
50 g (2 oz) currants, soaked in Kirsch to swell, then
drained and dried
50 g (2 oz) flaked almonds
600 ml (1 pint) Crème Chantilly, page 158
25 g (1 oz) pistachio nuts, finely shredded

To serve
600 ml (1 pint) Crème à l'Anglaise page 158

Cut a dry Biscuit de Savoie horizontally into slices approximately 1 cm (½ inch) thick. Sprinkle each slice with the Kirsch and Maraschino, spread with apricot jam and sprinkle with half the soaked currants and the flaked almonds.

Reconstitute the Biscuit de Savoie, placing the slices on top of one another, and coat the whole neatly with Crème Chantilly. Sprinkle the cream with the finely shredded pistachio nuts, then with the remaining currants. Place in a deep glass dish and surround with the Crème à l'Anglaise.

SERVES 8

Biscuit de Savoie

7 eggs
250 g (9 oz) caster sugar
1 tablespoon vanilla sugar
75 g (3 oz) flour and 75 g (3 oz) cornflour, sifted together
25 g (1 oz) butter
cornflour for dredging

Separate the eggs and beat the egg whites stiffly. Whisk the sugar and egg yolks together until the mixture becomes thick and pale. Add the vanilla sugar, the sifted flour and cornflour mixture, then fold in the stiffly beaten egg whites.

Butter a deep round cake tin 15 cm (6 inches) in diameter and dredge with cornflour. Pour the sponge paste into this, filling it no more than two-thirds full. Bake in a moderate oven (180°C, 350°F, Gas Mark 4) for about 30 minutes, then lower the temperature to 160°C, 325°F, Gas Mark 3, for a further 30 minutes, until the sponge is cooked and dry.

MAKES APPROXIMATELY 750 G (1¾ lb) SPONGE

Pouding Malakoff

600 ml (1 pint) Crème à l'Anglaise, page 158
15 g (½ oz) leaf gelatine, soaked
300 ml (½ pint) double cream
100 g (4 oz) boudoir biscuits
1 tablespoon Kirsch
100 g (4 oz) purée of apples and pears, prepared as for
Charlotte de Pommes, page 170
almond oil
100 g (4 oz) currants and sultanas, mixed and soaked
50 g (2 oz) fresh almonds, skinned and cut into strips
25 g (1 oz) preserved orange peel, diced

Sabayon
100 g (4 oz) caster sugar
2 egg yolks
100 ml (3½ fl oz) dry white wine
1 tablespoon Kirsch

Prepare the Crème à l'Anglaise and, when it is almost cooked, add the *leaf gelatine*. Pass through a fine strainer into a bowl and stir continuously until cool but not set. Add the double cream.

Sprinkle the boudoir biscuits with the Kirsch and spread each one with the apple and pear purée.

Lightly oil a 1.5-litre (2½-pint) charlotte mould with almond oil and pour in a 1-cm (½-inch) layer of the Crème à l'Anglaise. On top of this, place a layer of the prepared boudoir biscuits. Sprinkle with the currants and sultanas, almonds and orange peel. Cover with another layer of Crème à l'Anglaise, another layer of boudoir biscuits, and so on until the mould is full. Place in the refrigerator and allow to set.

Meanwhile, prepare a Kirsch-flavoured sabayon. Place the sugar and egg yolks in a basin and whisk until the mixture thickens and forms a ribbon when the whisk is lifted from the bowl. Mix in the dry white wine, then place the basin in a pan of very hot water over a gentle heat, and whisk until the mixture becomes thick and frothy. Flavour to taste with the Kirsch and allow to cool.

Demould just before serving and coat with the Kirsch-flavoured sabayon.

SERVES 8

Subrics de Semoule

500 ml (18 fl oz) milk
100 g (4 oz) sugar
1 vanilla pod
125 g (4½ oz) semolina
75 g (3 oz) butter
6 egg yolks
50 g (2 oz) clarified butter

To decorate
firm redcurrant or quince jelly

*P*lace the milk, sugar and vanilla pod in a saucepan, bring to the boil and infuse for a few minutes. Remove the vanilla pod and transfer the milk to an ovenproof dish. Rain in the semolina and mix well. Add 50 g (2 oz) of the butter and a few grains of salt and stir well. Cover with a lid and cook in a moderate oven (180°C, 350°F, Gas Mark 4) for 25 minutes.

Remove the dish from the oven, then stir the egg yolks into the mixture and spread the mixture out in a layer about 2 cm (¾ inch) thick on a buttered tray. Coat the surface with the remaining butter to prevent a skin forming and allow to cool.

Cut the mixture into circles about 6 cm (2½ inches) in diameter. Heat the *clarified butter* in a frying pan and fry the subrics (or semolina cakes) until golden. Arrange on a dish and place a spoonful of jelly on the centre of each subric.

MAKES 6–8

Soufflé aux Violettes

100 ml (3½ fl oz) milk
1 vanilla pod
50 g (2 oz) sugar
1 tablespoon flour
50 g (2 oz) crystallized violets
25 g (1 oz) butter
2 egg yolks
3 egg whites, stiffly beaten
icing sugar

*B*ring most of the milk to the boil, reserving just a little cold milk for later, and infuse with the vanilla pod for 30 minutes. Remove the pod. Then add 40 g (1½ oz) of the sugar and stir until dissolved. Mix the flour with the reserved cold milk and add to the mixture. Stir over the heat for 2 minutes.

Crush half the crystallized violets and add to the mixture. Take off the heat and add half the butter and both egg yolks. Fold in the stiffly beaten egg whites.

Use the remaining butter and sugar to line a 15-cm (6-inch) soufflé mould and pour the soufflé mixture into this. Arrange a circle of whole crystallized violets on top.

Cook in a moderately hot oven (200°C, 400°F, Gas Mark 6) for 25–30 minutes until well risen and just firm to the touch.

About 2 minutes before removing the soufflé from the oven, dredge the surface with the icing sugar (this will caramelize and form a glaze). Serve immediately.

SERVES 4

Soufflé aux Avelines

100 ml (3½ fl oz) milk
50 g (2 oz) sugar
1 tablespoon flour, sifted
25 g (1 oz) butter
2 egg yolks
3 egg whites, stiffly beaten
icing sugar

Hazelnut Praline
25 g (1 oz) sugar
25 g (1 oz) hazelnuts
almond oil

*F*irst make the hazelnut praline: melt the sugar slowly with a little water and cook to a light caramel colour. Mix in the hazelnuts, pour on to an oiled marble slab or tray and allow to become cold. Crush in a mortar or with a rolling pin.

Bring most of the milk to the boil, reserving just a little cold milk for later, and infuse with the hazelnut praline. Then add 40 g (1½ oz) of the sugar and stir until dissolved. Mix the flour with the reserved cold milk and add to the mixture. Stir over the heat for 2 minutes.

Remove from the heat, mix in half the butter and both egg yolks. Fold in the stiffly beaten egg whites.

Use the remaining butter and sugar to line a 15-cm (6-inch) soufflé mould and pour the soufflé mixture into this. Cook in a moderately hot oven (200°C, 400°F, Gas Mark 6) for 25–30 minutes until well risen and just firm to the touch.

About 2 minutes before removing the soufflé from the oven, dredge the surface with icing sugar (this will caramelize and form a glaze). Serve immediately.

SERVES 4

Soufflé au Chocolat

100 ml (3½ fl oz) milk
1 vanilla pod
50 g (2 oz) chocolate
50 g (2 oz) sugar
1 tablespoon flour
25 g (1 oz) butter
2 egg yolks
3 egg whites, stiffly beaten
icing sugar

*B*ring most of the milk to the boil, reserving just a little cold milk for later, and infuse with the vanilla pod for 30 minutes. Then dissolve the chocolate in the hot milk and add 40 g (1½ oz) of the sugar. Mix the flour with the reserved cold milk and add this to the pan. Stir over the heat for 2 minutes. Take off the heat and add half the butter and both egg yolks. Fold in the stiffly beaten egg whites.

Use the remaining butter and sugar to line a 15-cm (6-inch) soufflé mould and pour the soufflé mixture into this. Cook in a moderately hot oven (200°C, 400°F, Gas Mark 6) for 35–40 minutes until well risen and just firm to the touch.

About 2 minutes before removing the soufflé from the oven, dredge the surface with icing sugar (this will caramelize and form a glaze). Serve immediately.

SERVES 4

Meringues Germaine

4 small Gervais cream cheeses
150 ml (¼ pint) thick double cream
3 tablespoons caster sugar
225 g (8 oz) strawberries
red food colouring (optional)
a few drops vanilla essence or Kirsch
8 dry meringue shells

*M*ash the cream cheeses in a bowl with a wooden spoon and add the cream and sugar. Make a strawberry purée by passing the strawberries through a sieve, and add this purée to the cream cheese mixture. (If the colour is not sufficiently pink, you may add a few drops of red colouring.)

Flavour to taste with the vanilla essence or Kirsch as desired, and sandwich between meringue shells.

SERVES 4

Biscuit Monte-Carlo

12 egg whites
650 g (1 lb 6 oz) caster sugar
600 ml (1 pint) Crème Chantilly, page 158
50 g (2 oz) plain chocolate, grated
75 g (3 oz) plain chocolate, melted
25 g (1 oz) crystallized violets

*C*over several slightly moistened baking trays with sheets of greaseproof paper. Position 5 15-cm (6-inch) flan rings on these baking trays.

Whisk the egg whites until stiff and sprinkle in the caster sugar, mixing lightly with a spoon so that the egg whites do not lose their stiffness.

Half-fill each flan ring with the meringue and bake in a very cool oven (110°C, 225°F, Gas Mark ¼) for 7–8 hours until the meringue is completely dry.

Sandwich the rounds of meringue on top of one another with Crème Chantilly, sprinkling each layer with grated chocolate. Glaze the top layer of meringue with melted chocolate and decorate the sides with more Crème Chantilly using a piping tube. Pipe small rosettes of Crème Chantilly on top of the Biscuit Monte-Carlo, and place a crystallized violet on top of each rosette.

SERVES 8

Glace aux Asperges

175 g (6 oz) green asparagus tips
1 litre (1¾ pints) milk
300 g (11 oz) caster sugar
10 egg yolks

*B*lanch the asparagus tips for 2 minutes and drain. Pound quickly while adding a few tablespoons of the milk. Bring the remaining milk to the boil and put the asparagus mixture into the boiling milk to infuse for 20 minutes or so.

Stir the caster sugar and egg yolks together in a basin until the mixture becomes thick and white. Gradually mix in the boiling milk and asparagus mixture, place over a gentle heat and cook until the mixture coats the back of the spoon. Stir continuously and do not allow to boil, or the mixture will curdle.

Pass through a strainer into a basin and stir occasionally until cold. Pour into a sorbetière or ice-cream maker and freeze.

MAKES 1 LITRE (1¾ PINTS)

Meringues Germaine

Glace aux Avelines

100 g (4 oz) hazelnuts
1 litre (1¾ pints) milk
300 g (11 oz) caster sugar
10 egg yolks

*L*ightly toast the hazelnuts then pound finely, adding a few tablespoons of the milk. Stir the resulting mixture into the remaining milk and heat to boiling point. Allow to infuse for 20 minutes or so.

Stir the caster sugar and egg yolks together in a basin until the mixture becomes thick and white. Gradually mix in the boiling milk and hazelnut mixture, place over a gentle heat and cook until the mixture coats the back of the spoon. Stir continuously and do not allow to boil, or the mixture will curdle.

Pass the mixture through a strainer into a basin and stir occasionally until cold. Pour into a sorbetière or ice-cream maker and freeze.

MAKES 1 LITRE (1¾ PINTS)

Glace à la Vanille

1 litre (1¾ pints) milk
1 vanilla pod
300 g (11 oz) caster sugar
10 egg yolks

*B*ring the milk to the boil, add the vanilla pod and allow to infuse for 20 minutes. Remove the vanilla pod.

Stir the caster sugar and egg yolks together in a basin until the mixture becomes thick and white. Gradually add the boiling milk, place over a gentle heat and cook until the mixture coats the back of the spoon. Stir continuously and do not allow to boil, or the mixture will curdle.

Pass through a strainer into a basin and stir occasionally until cold. Pour into a sorbetière or ice-cream maker and freeze.

MAKES 1 LITRE (1¾ PINTS)

Coupe Adelina Patti

500 ml (18 fl oz) Glace à la Vanille, opposite
24 brandied cherries
50 g (2 oz) caster sugar
300 ml (½ pint) Crème Chantilly, page 158

*P*lace the vanilla ice cream in 4 coupe glasses or bowls. Drain the brandied cherries, roll in caster sugar and arrange in a circle on top of each coupe. Decorate each glass with a generous whirl of Crème Chantilly.

SERVES 4

Coupe Hélène

500 ml (18 fl oz) Glace à la Vanille, opposite
50 g (2 oz) crystallized violets
300 ml (½ pint) Crème Chantilly, page 158
40 g (1½ oz) plain chocolate, grated

*P*lace the vanilla ice cream in 4 coupe glasses or bowls. Decorate with a circle of crystallized violets, place a dome of Crème Chantilly in the centre, and decorate the cream with grated chocolate.

SERVES 4

Coupe Germaine

50 g (2 oz) glacé cherries
2 tablespoons Kirsch
500 g (18 fl oz) Glace à la Vanille, opposite
100 g (4 oz) marrons glacés
300 ml (½ pint) Crème Chantilly, page 158

*M*acerate the glacé cherries in the Kirsch for at least half an hour. Place the vanilla ice cream in 4 coupe glasses or bowls and arrange the macerated glacé cherries in a group on top of each coupe.

Pass the candied chestnuts through a coarse sieve, which will produce a purée that looks rather like vermicelli, and place this on top of the glacé cherries. Surround with a decorative border of Crème Chantilly.

SERVES 4

Coupe Hélène (left), Coupe Adelina Patti (right)

Coupe Gressac

500 ml (18 fl oz) Glace à la Vanille, page 184
12 small macaroons
3 tablespoons Kirsch
2 peaches, poached, peeled, halved and stoned
75 g (3 oz) fine sweet redcurrants
300 ml (½ pint) Crème Chantilly, page 158

Place the vanilla ice-cream in 4 coupe glasses or bowls. Soak the macaroons in the Kirsch and arrange these on top. Cut the peaches in half and fill the centres with redcurrants. Arrange these on top of the macaroons and decorate with a border of Crème Chantilly.

SERVES 4

GLACES AUX FRUITS

The basis of these ices is a syrup, made of sugar and water, to which some fruit purée or juice is then added.

The following recipes for fruit ices give excellent results as they stand but if thought desirable the density of the final cold mixture can be checked on a *saccharometer* and adjusted before freezing. If too dense add cold water, if too light add a little syrup made from 6 parts of sugar to 5 parts of water.

Glace à l'Orange

5–6 medium oranges, to give 450 ml (16 fl oz) juice
450 g (1 lb) sugar
375 ml (14 fl oz) water
juice of 1 lemon

Remove the zest from the oranges and reserve. Place the sugar and water in a pan, bring to the boil, skim and boil gently for 2 minutes. Add the orange zest, reboil then allow to cool. Squeeze the oranges to give 450 ml (16 fl oz) juice.

When cold add the juice from the oranges and the lemon to the syrup. Pass through a fine strainer then pour into a sorbetière or ice-cream maker. (The density of the cold mixture before freezing should be 20°–22° Baumé, measured on a *saccharometer*.)

MAKES APPROXIMATELY 1 LITRE (1¾ PINTS)

Glace à la Groseille

450 g (1 lb) sugar
375 ml (14 fl oz) water
1 kg (2 lb) ripe redcurrants, to give 450 ml (16 fl oz) juice
lemon juice, if necessary

Place the sugar and water in a pan, bring to the boil while stirring, skim and boil gently for 2 minutes. Remove from the heat and allow to cool.

Meanwhile, wash and crush the redcurrants then pass through a fine strainer to give 450 ml (16 fl oz) juice. Add to the cold syrup. Add a little lemon juice if thought necessary, then pass again carefully through a very fine strainer. Pour into a sorbetière or ice-cream maker and freeze. (The density of the cold mixture before freezing should be 19°–21° Baumé, measured on a *saccharometer*.)

MAKES APPROXIMATELY 1 LITRE (1¾ PINTS)

Glace à l'Ananas

450 g (1 lb) sugar
375 ml (14 fl oz) water
1 medium size, ripe pineapple, to give 500 ml (18 fl oz) pulp
juice of 2 lemons
2 tablespoons Kirsch

Place the sugar and water in a pan, bring to the boil while stirring, skim and boil gently for 2 minutes then allow to cool. Meanwhile, carefully remove the outer skin of the pineapple, cut in half and discard the fibrous central core.

Grate or finely crush the pineapple flesh to give 500 ml (18 fl oz) pulp and add to the cold syrup together with the lemon juice and Kirsch. Allow to macerate for 2 hours. Pass through a fine strainer then pour into a sorbetière or ice-cream maker and freeze. (The density of the cold mixture before freezing should be 18°–20° Baumé, measured on a *saccharometer*.)

MAKES APPROXIMATELY 1 LITRE (1¾ PINTS)

Bombe Formosa

500 ml (18 fl oz) Glace à la Vanille, page 184
125 g (4½ oz) caster sugar
100 ml (3½ fl oz) water
4 egg yolks
225 g (8 oz) strawberries, puréed
100 g (4 oz) small crystallized strawberries or
225 g (8 oz) fresh strawberries
300 ml (½ pint) double cream, whipped
caster sugar

Thoroughly chill a 1-litre (1¾-pint) bombe mould, then line with vanilla ice cream and replace in the freezer.

Meanwhile, place the sugar and water in a pan, heat to dissolve and allow to cool. Whisk this cool syrup together with the egg yolks in the top of a double saucepan or *bain-marie* over a low heat until the mixture becomes thick and white.

Remove from the heat and continue whisking until cold. Add the puréed strawberries and crystallized strawberries, if used (see below), and fold in half of the whipped cream.

Fill the centre of the prepared mould with the strawberry bombe mixture and, cover, first with a circle of greaseproof paper and then with the lid. Freeze for at least 2 hours.

Demould the bombe onto a chilled, round dish and decorate with the remaining whipped cream, lightly sweetened with caster sugar. If preferred, you may omit the crystallized strawberries in the bombe mixture and place fresh ones around the bombe.

SERVES 6–8

Bombe Frou-Frou

500 ml (18 fl oz) Glace à la Vanille, page 184
75 g (3 oz) crystallized fruits, cut in small dice
2 tablespoons rum
125 g (4½ oz) caster sugar
100 ml (3½ fl oz) water
4 egg yolks
300 ml (½ pint) double cream, whipped
caster sugar
vanilla essence

Thoroughly chill a 1-litre (1¾-pint) bombe mould, then line with vanilla ice cream and replace in the freezer to set well. Macerate the crystallized fruits in the rum.

Meanwhile, place the sugar and water in a pan, heat to dissolve and allow to cool. Whisk this cool syrup together with the egg yolks in the top of a double saucepan or *bain-marie* over a low heat until the mixture becomes thick and white.

Remove from the heat and continue whisking until cold. Add the crystallized fruits and rum and fold in half the whipped cream.

Fill the centre of the prepared mould with the bombe mixture and cover, first with a circle of greaseproof paper and then with the lid. Freeze for at least 2 hours.

Demould the bombe onto a chilled, round dish and decorate with the remaining whipped cream, lightly sweetened with caster sugar and flavoured with vanilla essence.

SERVES 6–8

Bombe Hilda

500 ml (18 fl oz) Glace aux Avelines, page 184
125 g (4½ oz) caster sugar
100 ml (3½ fl oz) water
4 egg yolks
2 tablespoons Chartreuse
300 ml (½ pint) double cream, whipped
caster sugar

Hazelnut Praline
175 g (6 oz) caster sugar
175 g (6 oz) skinned hazelnuts

First make the hazelnut praline: melt the sugar slowly with a little water and cook to a light caramel colour. Mix in the hazelnuts, pour onto an oiled marble slab and allow to become cold. Crush in a mortar then pass through a fine sieve.

Thoroughly chill a 1-litre (1¾-pint) bombe mould, then line with the hazelnut ice cream and replace in the freezer to set well.

Meanwhile, place the sugar and water in a pan, heat to dissolve and allow to cool. Whisk this cool syrup together with the egg yolks in the top of a double saucepan or *bain-marie* over a low heat until the mixture becomes thick and white. Remove from the heat and continue whisking until cold. Add the Chartreuse and praline and fold in half the whipped cream.

Fill the centre of the prepared mould with the bombe mixture and cover, first with a circle of greaseproof paper and then with the lid. Freeze for at least 2 hours.

Demould the bombe onto a chilled, round dish and decorate with the remaining whipped cream, lightly sweetened with caster sugar.

SERVES 6–8

GLOSSARY

bain-marie a container of hot water in which food items, placed in a utensil, can be either kept hot or gently cooked, without reaching too high a temperature.

bâtons foods such as carrot or turnip cut into neat small sticks, the size determined by the requirements of the dish. For vegetable garnishes or salads a suitable size would be approximately 2 cm ($\frac{3}{4}$ inch) in length and 4 mm ($\frac{1}{8}$ inch) square in diameter.

beurre manié a quick form of thickening made of one part of flour and two parts of soft butter mixed to a smooth paste. Mostly used in the final thickening of certain fish sauces, it should be added in small pieces towards the end of the cooking time and the sauce whisked well. It should be re-boiled but not over-cooked.

biscotte a dry plain rusk; it is cut from a specially prepared and baked bread which is then baked again until crisp and dry. There are many commercially available varieties. Those which are close textured and rather biscuit-like are the least suitable for garnishing.

bouquets items of garnish arranged in neat piles or bunches around the prepared food.

brunoise vegetables cut into thin slices, then into strips, then cut across to give neat regular dice approximately 2 mm ($\frac{1}{16}$ inch) square.

clarified butter used for frying items (such as bread) under circumstances in which ordinary butter would burn and spoil the finished flavour. Place the required amount of butter in a deep narrow pan and stand in a container of hot water to melt and settle for half an hour or so. Carefully remove any scum from the top then carefully strain off the clear butter fat without disturbing the sediment at the bottom.

cocotte cooking utensils made in ovenproof earthenware, porcelain or metal and, more often than not, with a fitting lid. They can be oval or round, shallow or deep in shape and food is usually cooked and served directly from them. The egg cocotte is a small ovenproof porcelain dish for cooking eggs in; it often has a handle.

cordon a small amount of gravy or sauce poured in a thinnish line around the food on a serving dish.

fluted or grooved lemon, carrot, etc. cut incised grooves from top to bottom and at regular intervals round the item then cut into slices of the thickness required. A special cutter for this purpose is available from specialist kitchen equipment suppliers.

julienne items of food cut into regular strips about 4 cm ($1\frac{1}{2}$ inches) in length by 1–2 mm ($\frac{1}{16}$ inch) thick.

to lard cut salt pork fat or speck into even strips 8 cm (3 inches) long and 3 mm ($\frac{1}{8}$ inch) square in diameter and keep in some ice cold water. Thread a strip into the end of a small larding needle and pull into the item of food (along the grain, if meat) so as to leave the two ends showing. Repeat at regular intervals along and around the item of food.

This process is used on meat, poultry, game and fish. Sometimes items such as tongue, truffle, carrot etc. are used for larding, instead of pork fat.

larding bacon the salt-cured, thick layer of back fat from pork. Obtainable from supermarkets and delicatessens as 'speck'.

lardons slices of de-rinded streaky bacon approximately 6 mm ($\frac{1}{4}$ inch) thick, then cut from top to bottom at the same thickness to give bâtons (q.v.). Blanch in boiling water and fry as required. Their size may be smaller or larger according to the needs of the dish in preparation.

leaf gelatine highly refined gelatine produced in thin, transparent, almost colourless sheets, approximately 3 g ($\frac{1}{10}$ oz) each, giving 7–9 sheets per 25 g (1 oz).

liaison a thickening or binding agent designed to give body and consistency to flavoured liquids or to form an homogenous mixture. They include the starches such as arrowroot and cornflour, beurre manié (q.v.), the roux (q.v.), egg yolks and egg yolks and cream. The last is used for thickening soups and sauces in the proportion of 2 egg yolks to 100 ml ($3\frac{1}{2}$ fl oz) cream, mixed together and added to the liquid in preparation. Whenever egg yolks are used in a liaison without flour or a flour-based sauce, the liquid must be re-heated to thicken but not boiled or separation will take place.

macédoine a mixture of various raw or cooked vegetables or fruit, usually cut in dice. For a macédoine of vegetables cut equal amounts of carrots and turnips into 7 mm ($\frac{1}{3}$ inch) dice and mix, when cooked, with equal amounts of cooked peas and beans. A macédoine of fruit is a mixed fruit salad in which the fruits can be either diced or sliced.

matignon very small dice or very thin slices of carrot, celery, onion and raw ham or unsmoked bacon cooked in a little butter with thyme and bay leaf, then deglazed with a little white wine. Used for flavouring and as a part of the dish in preparation.

mirepoix roughly chopped or sliced carrot, celery, onion and unsmoked bacon together with thyme and bay leaf. Used as a flavouring for soups, stews, in braising, etc.

mushroom cooking liquor finely chop 450 g (1 lb) white mushrooms, place in a pan with the juice of a quarter lemon, 25 g (1 oz) butter, a pinch of salt and 50 ml (2 fl oz) water. Cover, heat slowly and simmer for a few minutes only. Squeeze firmly through muslin or a fine strainer to extract the liquid.

à la noisette this term is applied to the cooking of butter to a nut brown colour. Place the required amount of soft butter in a hot pan and heat quickly while shaking the pan until it just begins to turn brown. It should be made and used as required, at the last minute.

pain d'épice a type of spiced bread made with flour and honey, flavoured with spices and aerated with yeast. Sometimes diced fruit peel is added.

panada a fairly stiff mixture of breadcrumbs, flour, rice, etc. cooked in milk or water and added to a forcemeat of fish, meat or poultry to help bind or extend it.

en papillote this refers to the cooking of items of food in a paper bag. Cut a sufficiently large heart shape from a sheet of greaseproof paper. Brush well with oil, place the prepared food on one side, fold over and seal the edges of the paper well. Place on a lightly oiled dish then in a moderate oven to cook. This will result in the paper colouring and swelling with the trapped steam from the cooking. It is customary to serve the item thus prepared still in its paper enclosure.

paupiette for fish this is a lightly flattened fillet spread with a suitable forcemeat and rolled up for cooking. Its shape can be secured by wrapping round with a band of buttered paper and tying with twine. For meat this is a flattened rectangle of meat spread with forcemeat, rolled and tied with twine.

paysanne vegetables such as carrot or turnip cut into small thin square or round slices approximately 1.5 cm ($\frac{1}{2}$ inch) across.

poêlé a method of cooking somewhat akin to pot roasting. It is very suitable for good quality, tender items of meat, poultry and game. The seasoned food is placed in a suitable deep pan or oven-proof casserole on a bed of roughly chopped or sliced vegetables and herbs, coated with sufficient butter for basting, then covered with a tight fitting lid. The cooking takes place in the oven; take care to baste frequently and remove the lid during the final stages so as to colour the item of food.

repère this is a stiff paste made from flour and water, used as a band to seal the join of a cooking utensil and its lid when cooking an item of food in the oven. It helps to prevent loss of moisture and flavour. Useful proportions for sealing a 1.5-litre ($2\frac{1}{2}$-pint) oval terrine or casserole are 250 g (9 oz) flour and 100 ml ($3\frac{1}{2}$ fl oz) water mixed to a smooth paste. The repère is discarded before serving.

roux a combination of flour and fat cooked together and used as a thickening agent for soups, sauces etc.

For white roux, six parts of flour and five parts of clarified butter are cooked together slowly with frequent stirring to a sandy texture. As this roux is used mainly for white sauces take care not to colour it.

For brown roux, the same ingredients and method as white roux are used but the mixture is cooked slowly to an even light brown colour. Do not over-colour as this will impart a bitter taste to the finished dish or sauce.

In either case the roux should be allowed to cool before liquid is added to it. This will prevent the thickened liquid from becoming elastic in texture.

saccharometer this is an instrument for measuring the density of a syrup at 20°C (68°F). The most commonly used type is calibrated in degrees B (Baumé), after the name of the inventor.

salpicon cooked foodstuffs or fruit cut in small regular dice, usually added to a sauce, forcemeat or other mixture and of a size in keeping with its requirements e.g. if needed for croquettes of chicken, approximately 3 mm ($\frac{1}{8}$ inch) square.

timbale this word has a number of definitions:

a) any type of deep pastry case or forcemeat case which is filled with a prepared and sauced food,

b) deep round silver, earthenware or porcelain dishes used for the service of well-sauced dishes,

c) moulded items of food either small or large, e.g. small dariole moulds of poached vegetable purées for garnishing.

INDEX

DATE DUE	RETURNED